W9-BNV-466

SHANGHAI
REFUGE

SHANGHAI

REFUGE

A Memoir of the

World War II Jewish Ghetto

Ernest G. Heppner

University of Nebraska Press   Lincoln & London

Library of Congress Cataloging-in-Publication Data
Heppner, Ernest G., 1921–
Shanghai refuge : a memoir of the World War II Jewish ghetto /
Ernest G. Heppner.
p.   cm.
Includes bibliographical references and index.
ISBN 0-8032-2368-4(cl)
1. Heppner, Ernest G., 1921–   . 2. Refugees, Jewish—China—Shanghai—
Biography.   3. Jews, German—China—Shanghai—Biography.   4. Jews—
Germany—Biography.   5. Shanghai (China)—Biography.   6. Germany—
Biography.   I. Title.
DS135.C5H464   1994
951'.1304'092—dc20
[B]   93-20038 CIP
Frontispiece: Refugees selling their belongings on Kungping Road.
(From the author's collection)

This book is dedicated to
THE MEMORY
of my father Isidor and my sister Else,
who were unable to find a safe haven and
were sent to the death camps, never to be
heard from again,
and to
the more than two thousand Jewish refugees
who died in Shanghai between 1938 and 1948,
among them Illo's mother
and my sister-in-law Alice's parents,
THE FUTURE:
David, Benjamin, and Miriam,
for whom it was written,
and Illo, who shares my past,
my present, and
my future

Contents

Illustrations

Preface

n May 1986 the Jewish Community Relations Council of my hometown of Indianapolis asked me to give a talk on the Shanghai Jewish community. The occasion was Yom Ha-Shoah, the day of remembrance, established to assure that present and future generations would never forget one of the most fearsome episodes in mankind's history.

Temple Beth-El Zedeck was the site for the commemoration, and it was filled almost to capacity. The rabbis and cantors of the five congregations in Indianapolis participated in the service, and a concentration camp survivor wrote and performed an original candle-lighting service. Six children of Holocaust survivors came forward; each lit a candle and made appropriate remarks. Their six candles represented the six million Jews murdered by the Nazis during the Holocaust. Six million is an awesome number. It may be possible to imagine it in terms of money or purchasing power or insects, but how does one conceptualize the magnitude of six million human lives that are lost?

Imagine a timepiece—huge—with large numbers,
and the clock ticks off the minutes, one after another,
for six long years:
—and every minute—for sixty minutes an hour—
—for twenty-four hours a day—for seven days a week—
—for fifty-two weeks a year—for six long years—
during every one of those three million, one hundred forty-four thousand, nine hundred sixty minutes, two Jews were murdered for that awful total of more than six million, two hundred thousand.[1]

That was the second time I had told the Shanghai story in Indianapolis, and once again I was struck by the audience's lack of knowledge about this chapter of recent history. When I made this presentation the first time in January 1976 at Indianapolis Hebrew Congregation, it was obvious that the local Jewish community had limited knowledge about the Holocaust and none at all about the Shanghai ghetto.

In preparing for that first talk I found invaluable help in my friend Kurt Redlich. A native Viennese, he was a concentration camp survivor, a lawyer, and a gentleman. He had been an influential member of the Shanghai *Jüdische Gemeinde*, (Jewish Communal Association) and one of the judges of its arbitration court. When my wife and I married in the ghetto, we asked him to perform the civil ceremony. We met the Redlichs again in 1954 when we moved to Indianapolis, as he and his wife had also done, and we became close friends. He had a keen mind and was a storehouse of historical information. He freely shared his encyclopedic knowledge of the Shanghai Jewish community not only with me but also with historian David Kranzler, who was the first to document the history of the Jewish European refugee community in Shanghai, China, in his doctoral dissertation. Without Kranzler's gracious permission to cite from his comprehensive work, it would have been extremely difficult for me to confirm some of the events I described.

After the second talk I found myself haunted by the faces of my father and sister. They did not leave me as I lay awake at night while long forgotten memories of my boyhood came back to me. I cannot forget the expression on my sister Else's face, or my father's, when I left them that dreary day in March of 1939 to start my long journey to Shanghai. I had said *Auf Wiedersehen*, see you again, fearing in my heart that I would never see them again.

Every year, around the ninth of November, the anniversary of the November Pogrom, which has come to be known by the euphemism "Crystal Night," the events of those horrifying days and nights come back to haunt me. Yet when sometime in the 1950s I applied for restitution from the German government, I found it difficult to fill out the forms and answer the questions. I could not remember the name of schools I had attended or my last address before emigration in 1939. I was forced to ask my older brother Heinz for assistance. Heinz, who lives with his wife and family in London, England, had kept detailed records of that time and was able to furnish me with all the necessary answers. The psychiatrist to whom I went for advice did not seem at all surprised. "These were extremely traumatic experiences and you simply blocked them from your memory," he explained.

The invitation to speak on my Shanghai experiences at Beth-El Zedeck in 1986 caused my memory loss to crumble. Afterward, memories of the events fell into place, slowly, like a jigsaw puzzle, piece by piece. It was like waking up after an operation; it all began to come together, clearly—the places and the people. It seemed as if events rolled backward into the past from that fateful November day in 1938, all of it centered on the burning synagogue in Breslau. My memories flashed by in reverse order until I imagined being pushed in my perambulator by my nanny.

Once these events had come back into my mind, I worried that they might disappear again. How could I hold on to those painful yet precious memories, now that they had reappeared almost miraculously? I slept less and rose earlier than usual until I found myself arriving at my office before six o'clock in the morning. I would sit at my desk, staring out the window at the dark lake. I started dictating, describing what had come back from my subconscious mind. A week and a stack of micro tapes later I felt more at peace with myself.

During that time, it occurred to me that no fully documented factual account by a survivor of the Shanghai ghetto period had been published in the United States. I was deeply concerned that this important segment of Jewish history would be forgotten. It needed to be preserved for the sake of the more than 2,000 victims of that period and those Jews who not only survived but maintained their dignity, self-respect, and decency while living in semi-starvation in the slums of the ghetto.

I realized that writing this story would be an immense task. Too many years had passed, memories had faded, friends who had kept notes and could verify facts were scattered all over the globe. But Kurt Pollack of Los Angeles for several years published the *Hongkew Chronicle* as a volunteer. This publication became a major resource for the exchange of information and for finding friends who, after leaving China, had become widely separated. All of them— including Hans Gumpert, Fritz Huber, Kurt Maimann, Esther Marcus, Les "Seppl" Salter, Peter Witting, and many others—offered their help and material and recalled specific incidents of interest. Kurt Redlich had passed away; however, before his death he had given me two boxes filled with material pertaining to the Shanghai Jewish community, as well as copies of his voluminous correspondence with Kranzler and with Charles Jordan, the postwar representative of the American Jewish Joint Distribution Committee (JDC), the agency responsible for aiding overseas Jews in distress. Until she passed away, a very valuable resource for the living conditions of the refugees was my mother. She had been a caseworker for one of the Shanghai refugee relief committees and then, until May 1942, had worked for Laura L. Margolis, the JDC's Shanghai representative.

Lacking a formal education, I had never learned the methodology of historical research, nor was I aware of the immense resources available. I am indeed most grateful to the archivists and librarians without whose cooperation I would not have been able to find the sources necessary to document my story. I thank Judy McGeath of the interlibrary loan department of the Indianapolis Public Library for her efforts in locating and making available to me microfilm of journals and newspapers, including Shanghai newspapers. I met with Denise Bernard Gluck, director of archives for the JDC, and her assistant Regina Chimberg, as well as Diane Speelmann of the Leo Baeck Institute, who introduced me to the fascinating world of historical research. On my first visit to the JDC archives, I learned from Denise Gluck that Laura Margolis, whom I had never met personally in Shanghai, was living in nearby New Jersey. I went to see her, and she shared with me many of her impressions and experiences. Since then, we have become good friends and remain in frequent contact. I am indebted also to Susan Pettiss, former resettlement officer with the U.S. office of the International Refugee Organization (IRO), for freely sharing her photographs and notes regarding the "bonded" trains and permitting me to cite from her material. Without the assistance and cooperation of Marilla B. Guptil, chief of the Archives Unit of the United Nations, I would not have found the powerful photographs taken by Arthur Rothstein after our liberation.

Several of the refugees had kept journals, one of which, Hans Jacoby's *Tagebuch* (diary), I found at the Baeck Institute. It provided me with a great deal of insight and a different perspective on events that I knew about only from hearsay. Horst P. Eisfelder of Carnegie, Australia, had kept meticulous notes for his memoir "Chinese Exile" and volunteered to read portions of my manuscript. Through regular correspondence he checked and verified events to assure accuracy. Colonel (ret.) Harry W. Atkinson, my former boss at the Joint U.S. Military Advisory Group (JUSMAG) in Nanjing, spared no effort to research the Air University Library of the U.S. Air Force Historical Research Center, to furnish me with long-forgotten details, and to check the chapter about JUSMAG for accuracy.

I thank all my friends who for the past four years voiced their constant interest in the progress of my work. I am especially indebted to my good friends Audrey Grossman, Thomas D. Mantel, Edwin Gordon, and Lee Lewellen, who read various stages of the manuscript, for their suggestions, advice, and continual encouragement. A special bear hug goes to Rochelle Cohen for giving so freely of her time, re-reading the edited manuscript and making valuable suggestions. To Stephanie Goss Caffera I extend not only my love and affection but also my admiration for her very analytical and critical review of this work.

And finally, I must express my thanks and appreciation to the historian Carolyn Blackwell, who assisted me with my research and whose comprehensive knowledge of Germany in the 1930s and the history of the Holocaust was of inestimable value.

In reflecting on the Shanghai experience it occurred to me that no single account could accurately depict the lives of all the Jews of Shanghai. Most refugees lived and worked in the Japanese-occupied district of Hongkew and had little contact with other foreigners in the International Settlement or the French Concession, or with the Chinese. Refugees who lived in one of the camps barely managed to exist; others led lives that varied from very primitive to comfortable. For the few who had financial resources, the degree of comfort, prior to the establishment of the ghetto, was quite high. Each person's experience, therefore, was unique. Many did not have the opportunities that had come my way.

To preserve their privacy, the names of two persons have been changed at their request. In a few other instances I was unable to recollect specific names and was forced to use partial substitutions.

This book is a factual account of my life in Germany and China and my experiences as a "greenhorn" in the United States. It describes some of the events which at that time affected not only the Jewish refugees but society as a whole. We were the pawns of international politics and intrigue and had little, if any, control over our destinies. What follows are my recollections of this period of history; they illustrate the diversity of Jewish life and faith under extreme duress and life-threatening circumstances. They reaffirm the high value that Judaism places on human life and the necessity for world Jewry to assume responsibility for our brethren wherever and whoever they may be.

To the reader who would like to study the Jewish community of Shanghai in greater detail, I suggest David H. Kranzler, *Japanese, Nazis, and Jews*, the only authoritative history of the Shanghai Jewish refugee community of 1938–45.

*   *   *

Additional Note on the Sources

On the sources for the accounts in this book, a few merit particular note. The bulk of the material is of course drawn from my personal experience, but I should stress also that among the refugees was my mother, Hilda Heppner, whose work exposed her on a daily basis to the needs and problems of the refugees. In time, she became the buffer between the refugees and the aid committee; her knowledge of the organizations charged with helping the refugees was direct and ongoing. I learned much from our discussions of the problems facing the refugees and what was being done to help them.

Additional and important sources for the account are Felix Gruenberger's article "The Jewish Refugees in Shanghai," which appeared in *Jewish Social Studies*. Gruenberger's article, which was completed in 1948, confirms that "in the very beginning, there were some productive loans [to refugees], but this practice was soon discontinued. The refugees were made entirely dependent on the committee. They received their support in kind instead of cash and were forced to accept underpaid work on threat of having this support withdrawn" (p. 333).

Finally, I am indebted to Professor Kranzler, whose Ph.D. dissertation (Yeshiva University, 1971) contains the prophetic November 1938 letter of Paul Komor, executive director of the International Committee for the Organization of European Immigrants in China, to local businessman B. S. Barbash on the difficulties Komor was having in raising funds (p. 441):

"May I say that I am quite in agreement with your views and appreciate your efforts to raise funds. It is to be feared that local Jewry, like in other parts of the world, will only realize the actual situation when they get to feel, on their own persons and those of their families, the things which the Emigrants arriving here have experienced. But then, here as elsewhere, it will be too late.

"For my part, I have long since realized the impossibility of financial efforts so far made meeting the needs of the actual situation and I have already intimated to my committee my desire to resign. I am not made of the stuff that can turn away the needy and helpless, a thing which I have to do almost daily. Possibly, some of the gentlemen with steel-concrete constitutions can take my place."

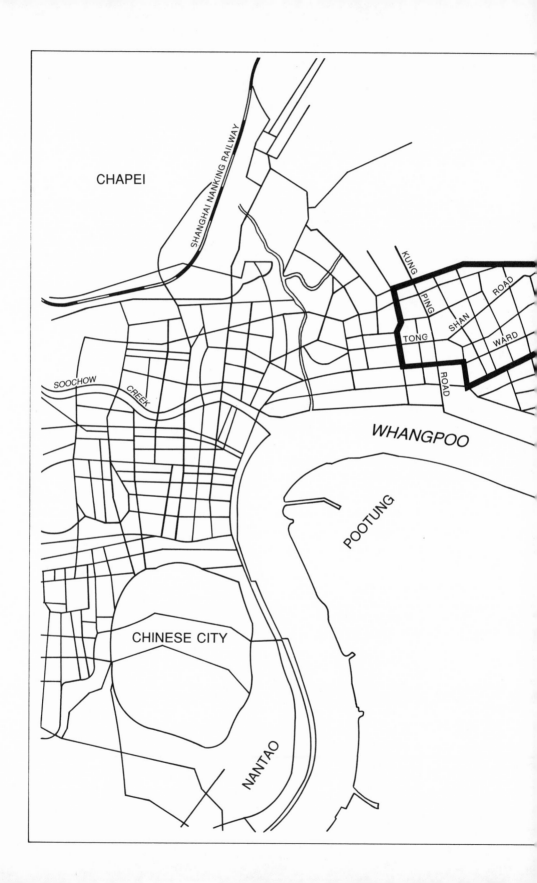

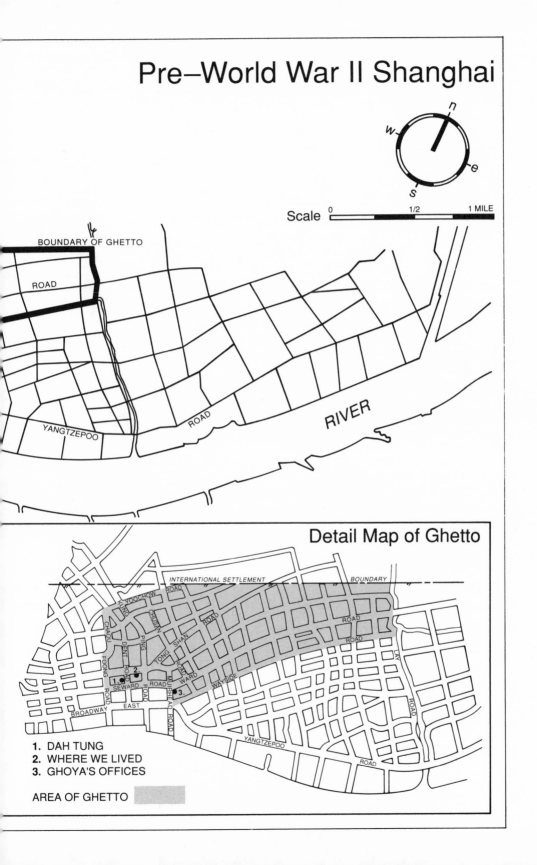

Pre–World War II Shanghai

Scale 0   1/2   1 MILE

BOUNDARY OF GHETTO

ROAD

YANGTZEPOO ROAD

RIVER

Detail Map of Ghetto

INTERNATIONAL SETTLEMENT BOUNDARY

ROAD

ROAD

YOOCHOW ROAD

CHUSAN ROAD

TONG SHAN ROAD

WARD ROAD

WAYSIDE

DENT ROAD

PING ROAD

SEWARD ROAD

MUIRHEAD ROAD

CHAOU FOONG ROAD

BROADWAY EAST

YANGTZEPOO ROAD

LAY ROAD

1. DAH TUNG
2. WHERE WE LIVED
3. GHOYA'S OFFICES

AREA OF GHETTO

GERMANY

The 1930s

1

Under the Nazi Boot

The majority of Jews in Weimar Germany were thoroughly assimilated, and most were a part of the broad middle class. Jews attended the synagogue or temple of their choice and enjoyed all the cultural amenities for which Germany was famous. The Jewish community felt secure. Then, in 1933, the Weimar Republic failed, and Germany became a totalitarian state.

After World War I, Germany had suffered rampant inflation, massive unemployment, and severe economic dislocation. During the 1920s the National Socialist German Workers Party (NSDAP, the Nazis) used this opportunity to transfer the sense of helplessness felt by the majority of Germans into anger against Jews. Religious anti-Semitism, which had existed since the early years of the Christian church, became a useful tool for political anti-Semites. From the beginning, Hitler's racist ideology was included in the Nazi program that laid down the aggressive policy toward Jews.[1]

My father, Isidor Heppner, was born in 1878 in Lissa, in the province of Posen. Like his father, he became a *Bäckermeister*, a master baker. A quiet and unassuming man, he operated the small matzoth bakery he had inherited from his father, Marcus. In 1919, after Germany lost World War I, Posen became Poznan; it belonged to that section of disputed land which Germany had to give up to Poland. That year Isidor's first wife died during an influenza epidemic, leaving him with a fourteen-year-old girl and a twelve-year-old boy.

My father was among the many Germans who left Poznan and migrated back to the Fatherland. There he settled in Breslau, where he built an automated matzoth factory. He searched for a wife and mother for his children, Else and Heinz. When he visited friends in Berlin, they introduced him to a beautiful young woman from the Cologne area, Hilda Liffmann, and he fell in love with her. After a brief courtship they became engaged. In July 1920 they were married by Rabbi Leo Baeck, the son of Rabbi Samuel Baeck, who had also lived in Lissa and had been a friend of the family. At that time Leo Baeck was a *liberal* rabbi in Berlin who would become one of the most respected individuals in German Jewry. Not only was he an outstanding scholar and philosopher and religious leader, but he led the Berlin Jewish community in the struggle against the Nazis.[2] In 1943 Rabbi Baeck was deported to the *Theresienstadt*, the Terezin ghetto. When the camp was liberated by the Allies in May 1945, Rabbi Baeck voluntarily remained until late June, when the German Jewish survivors had left or he had received assurance that those remaining would receive proper care.

My birth certificate shows that Ernst Günther Emanuel Heppner was born on August 4, 1921, in the Jewish hospital of Breslau, the second son of the factory owner (*Fabrikbesitzer*) Isidor Heppner. In Germany a child was categorized at birth by his father's occupation; consequently, that category remained with me throughout my life in Germany. When my sister Else, who was sixteen years older, heard that my parents had given me the name Ernst, she cried bitterly, insisting that my father had promised her that she could name the new baby. My father, a mild-mannered, good-natured man, went back to the city administration office and added the name Günther to my birth certificate.

My family belonged to the well-established middle class, and we lived on the second floor of a large apartment building in the city of Breslau, province of Silesia. (After World War II a section of Silesia was deeded to Poland, and today Breslau is called Wroclaw.) During the fall and winter my father operated our matzoth factory; during the summer months my mother and my sister Else managed the family's resort hotel in Altheide, a spa some sixty-five miles southeast of Breslau, near the Czechoslovakian border. The hotel catered to heart patients, serving only strictly kosher food. On the staff was a person trained to slaughter the chickens and an occasional ox in accordance with Jewish religious law. We also employed our own cantor to chant the ancient liturgy and to lead the guests in Sabbath services. As a boy, I spent the summers in Altheide, occupying a room with a balcony on the top floor. From my room I could look out at the lush meadows and hills that surrounded the hotel and gave it its name, Bellevue.

After I was enrolled in school in Breslau, I occasionally went to Altheide in the winter as well, and I liked nothing better than to go for a ride in a horse-drawn sleigh or, better yet, to be allowed to drive it. During the summers I explored the meadows that stretched out behind Bellevue all the way to the highway leading to the nearest town, Glatz. I collected insects and loved to show off my collection of butterflies, beetles, locusts, and katydids. I got into trouble on more than one occasion when I left the door to the chicken coop open; it took the help hours to find the chickens and get them back into the coop. The preferred Friday evening meal was chicken, but occasionally carp, farmed in local ponds, was served. On special occasions there was goose, baked to a golden crispness and served with sweet-and-sour red cabbage.

In the rear of the hotel, under the dining room, was the laundry in which the hotel's linens were washed in huge cauldrons and then hung outside on lines to dry. Electric irons were not yet in use, so the sheets were pushed and pulled through a mangle, a wooden contraption about fifteen feet long that looked something like a conveyor belt. One person would turn the huge crank and a second would push the edges of the linen between the first rollers, while a third, standing at the other end, would pull the linens as they appeared between another set of rollers. It was heavy work, and the laundresses frequently rotated their positions. At regular intervals all rugs would be taken down to the laundry area, hung over the laundry lines and beaten with a beater made of cane. Near the dining room, on a shelf in the hallway, stood the radio (I think it was a Blaupunkt or a Mende) with four movable wire spools, two on either side, which acted as antennas and assisted in bringing in remote cities. The radio included a loudspeaker—a novelty—which made it unnecessary to move a "cat's whisker" over a piece of quartz in order to hear the music on earphones.

During the summers there were frequent thunderstorms, usually at night. Often, lightning hit the lightning arresters on our roof. Since Altheide, like most other small resort villages, had no professional fire fighters, whenever there was a fire, a siren summoned volunteers. No matter how quickly the men were able to get to the fire station, however, it took a while to harness the horses that pulled the pumpers and the other carriages. But what a beautiful sight it was when the horses, equipment, and men, with bells clanging wildly, raced down the village street to fight a fire started by lightning.

Because of the possibility of fire, a gong was rung to awaken the hotel guests whenever severe storms threatened. Slowly, drowsily, the guests would gather in the dining room, clad in their robes, to wait for the storm to subside. I did not like to sit with the grownups. Unless my governess came to get me, I stayed in my room. I loved to watch the storm's progress and was fascinated by the spectacular lightning flashes across the sky and over the hills. One evening, during a particularly heavy thunderstorm, lightning apparently hit the arresters and for some inexplicable reason, instead of following the ground wire down into the earth, jumped to my balcony. One of those rare, luminous lightning balls raced several times around my room, momentarily hanging suspended in the air until, with a sharp explosive sound, it disappeared back out the balcony door, leaving behind a crying and frightened boy.

My mother was the thirteenth of fifteen children, and she frequently went away on pleasure trips and to visit her many relatives and friends. I was reared chiefly by my sister. Else, at the age of four, had fallen ill in the synagogue while attending services. The diagnosis was poliomyelitis, and after her recovery she was able to walk only with the aid of two heavy leg braces and two canes. She needed help walking up or down the stairs and getting in or out of her wheelchair. When she had to go on long trips, it took two people to get her into a horse-drawn carriage or, when she was in Breslau, onto a streetcar. I loved my sister very much and helped her in every way I could. She was an excellent pianist, and nothing could make me leave the room when she was playing Liszt's Second Rhapsody. She often would play after dinner, with guests in attendance. My favorite musical pieces were songs by Franz Schubert and Johann Loewe's ballads, and I would sing them in my thin, clear soprano voice as my sister accompanied me.

Every August, elaborate preparations were made to celebrate my birthday. A party provided fun and games for the children of the hotel's guests. On my fifth birthday I rebelled. I did not care much for the boys and girls staying at Bellevue and wanted to invite one of my regular playmates, a little girl who was the daughter of one of the workers at a livery service. My request was met with utter disbelief and consternation by my nanny and my mother. This simply was not done, I was told in no uncertain terms. Although I was only five years old, I had heard enough talk about money to know the difference between rich and poor, and it was made clear to me that stable help ranked much lower than even kitchen help. But I was not to be swayed. I could not understand why I was not permitted to invite Lisa to my birthday party when I played with her on other days. By the time the tables were set, the party favors arranged, and everything ready, I was nowhere to be seen. Gretchen, my nanny, knew all my hiding places and finally found me in the gazebo, hidden from view by a grove of hazelnut bushes. Gretchen knew better than to try to change my mind when I had a certain look on my face.

My mother, however, was not concerned about pleasing me on my birthday. In typical German fashion she was concerned only about "what other people would say." German children were disciplined; they were not supposed to have opinions. She was furious, but with the guests waiting and the party ready to begin, she had no option but to dispatch a bellboy to Lisa's home and wait for the child to get dressed and be brought back. Lisa arrived within the hour in her heavily starched best Sunday dress, timid and shy at her first invitation to such an affair. We all had fun, and after cake and hot chocolate we played all the games children at that age love to play. And I made sure that Lisa got just as many party favors as the children of the guests before she went on her way home.

I started kindergarten in Breslau, but since my mother ran the hotel, I attended first grade in the one-room schoolhouse in Altheide. The first day of school was a big event, and it was customary to give the child a *Schultüte*, a large, decorated cardboard cone filled with candies. But because my mother was concerned that the village families were too poor to give their children such an expensive gift, and also to avoid any cause for anti-Semitism, she refused to get me one. I loved sweets and was bitterly disappointed—especially when, after all, most of the other children came to school carrying the prized candy-filled cones.

I was the only Jewish child in the school, and I learned quickly that I was different from the other children. I was privileged, while most of the other children walked, to ride my bike along the highway to school. The following year, when I attended grade school in Breslau, I was relieved to find another Jewish boy in my class.

Religion was a mandatory subject at school, and at regular intervals a rabbi came to teach the Jewish children. German school records contained the religion and profession of the children's fathers, and whenever the teacher called the roll, he would mockingly inquire what kind of factory my father owned. Before long all the pupils in my school knew that my family manufactured matzoth. I was subjected to harassment and beatings by other boys for being a "Christ killer" and repeatedly heard the accusation that my family used the blood of Christian children to make the matzoth. I learned very early to live with crude anti-Semitism. For me, being beaten and spat at and cursed became part of growing up as a Jew. When I fought back and bloodied other boys' noses, I was reported to the principal, and my "rowdy behavior" was noted in my report cards. Fortunately, I was a whiz on my bike. When the other boys lay in wait for me at some corner, I did one of my trick "wheelies" and sped away. (On more than one occasion when I was older, my father was called to the police station to get me released after I was stopped for "recklessness" on a bike, speeding and hanging on to the back of trucks.)

I always had been a loner, and except for one other Jewish student, whose name I cannot recall, I had no close friends and felt miserable in school. Fortunately, my mother recognized my need to associate with other boys away from school and enrolled me in a Jewish *Pfadfinder* (pathfinders) youth group, *Das Schwarze Fähnlein* the Black Pennant, which resembled the Boy Scouts. The leaders were of college age, and the group's philosophy was oriented toward spartan ideals. We had paramilitary training and regularly practiced survival tactics.

I was about nine years old when I won my parents' permission to go to a Black Pennant summer camp. The knapsacks we used were the fur-covered, regulation German army type called *Tornister*, each equipped with a mess kit and one square tarpaulin. To make a six-man tent, several such tarpaulins were laboriously buttoned together. The itinerary called for our group to hike or hitchhike from Breslau in a northerly direction, following the Oder River, until we reached the Baltic Sea. There we waited until we found a boat to take us to Königsberg, by-passing Gdanzk (the former German city of Danzig), located in the so-called "Polish Corridor." We hiked south to the Mazurian lakes until we found a previously selected island. To cross the water we used a ferry, a wooden raft large enough to hold a few head of cattle. A wire had been strung from the mainland across the water, and we pulled ourselves and the ferry over to the island. The heavily wooded island was divided by a ridge, which separated two camps housing boys from different regions of Germany and provided a natural border for our war games.

Camp life was very primitive, and the training was tough. We were not supposed to start the campfire with matches but had to emulate our idols, the American Indians, and use a hard and a soft wooden stick. Once started, the fire was maintained around the clock by guards for the length of our stay. We cooked our meals on the campfire, and every night we sat around it singing idealistic Cossack or Nordic songs. The food usually consisted of bean soup, various types of sausages, potatoes with corned beef, or rice with prunes (typical of real camp food, the rice was slightly burned).

Unlike American Boy Scouts, who wear scarves as part of their uniform, new members of the Black Pennant were required to earn their scarves. I badly wanted to earn mine and worked hard for it. The tests resembled some of those by which the Boy Scouts earn badges, but there were differences. More emphasis was put on survival skills. For instance, after several days of training and preparation I was led into a wooded area after dark and told to find my way back to camp in the shortest possible time. It was a beautiful starlit night, and although the campfire had been allowed to burn down to cinders, I did not have much trouble finding my way. I loved to play practical jokes, and this occasion was no exception. When I reached the perimeter of the camp I was able to sneak into my tent, unseen by the leaders and the two guards. The other boys were already fast asleep, but the leaders stayed up waiting for me to return. I was discovered at the next change of the guard, sleeping soundly.

I avoided swimming in the lake. I did not want any of my friends to know that I had never learned how to swim. Although my mother had sent me to the local indoor pool to take swimming lessons, I had played hooky to avoid the cold water. One day, however, I could not avoid participating in a war game that pitted the crews of two boats against each other. I was sitting in the bow when another boy pushed an oar into my chest and pitched me backward into the water, which was said to be 100 feet deep. The boys were too occupied with their fighting to notice my calls and my desperate struggle to stay afloat. I was choking and thrashing around in the water when my hand grabbed something soft. It was a short piece of rope dangling from the boat. I managed to hold on until I caught my breath. Then I pulled myself closer to the bow of the boat, but as soon as I had reached it, the rotted rope broke. By that time the fighting teams had separated far enough for one of my buddies to notice my plight and extend an oar. Exhausted, I needed help to climb back into the boat. When my weakness was ridiculed by the others, I explained that I had been hit on my head by an oar and that when I fell overboard, I had swallowed too much water. That's how I learned to swim.

War games were fun and exciting. "We" were the Germans, "they" were the enemy, and it never occurred to me to ask who were the "enemy" we were fighting.

Later, we also camped in winter, which was not as comfortable. The tents had no floors, and wind and snow penetrated the seams where the tarpaulins were buttoned together. Amazingly, we rarely suffered more than minor frostbite, but I hated the treatment for frostbitten toes, which consisted of bathing one's feet alternately in warm water and snow. Perhaps raising boys in this spartan fashion was excessively harsh. I have lost contact with all my camping friends and have no way of knowing whether any survived the Holocaust or how they may have benefited from this type of training. But I know it instilled in me a sense of discipline; it strengthened and helped me not only to survive the streets of Shanghai but to engage in some hazardous activities as well.

One weekend as we were hiking along the Oder River, we heard calls for help from three boys who were stranded on an ice floe, which was slowly moving down the river. Hans, our group leader, used this opportunity to demonstrate the practical use of a lasso. We had learned to throw a boomerang and a lasso with mixed success, and now we watched as Hans tried to reach the boys with his rope. It took several attempts, but finally the lasso reached them. The boys first held on to the rope but were almost pulled off the slippery ice floe. They then looped the rope around the edge of the ice, and very slowly we were able to pull the floe to shore.

I was not yet ten years old when I finished four years of elementary school. At this juncture, most children were enrolled by their parents in vocational or technical high schools. A college prep school for boys was called a gymnasium; girls attended a lyceum. In the gymnasium, students started training for the university entrance exams, the *Abitur*, while those on the vocational-technical track started apprenticeships. I was not asked, but it was understood that I would pursue an academic career. Studying Latin did not appeal to me at all; I considered it a waste of time, but my protests did not stop my mother from enrolling me in the gymnasium. Math interested me, but I made little progress because all too often my questions were left unanswered by unsympathetic teachers.

I was brought up in the very conservative—almost orthodox—branch of Judaism and as a young boy took the observance of Jewish traditions very seriously. Woe to the maid or cook who accidentally put a dairy kitchen utensil into a meat drawer, since tradition required strict separation of meat and milk products. After my Bar Mitzvah however, like many of my friends, I began to question the relevance of the orthodox restrictions. I was disturbed particularly by the greed of one of the rabbis whose stamp of approval, "Under the supervision of Rabbi ——," appeared on all my family's letterheads and product packages and was essential to the business.

The discussion around our dinner table sometimes focused on the actions of some of these rabbis, which appeared to come close to a shakedown. I was impressed by one particular instance that had my father worried and upset for several seasons. In the factory a huge rectangular storage tank held the water that was to be mixed with flour. It had been especially manufactured of galvanized metal, welded to form an almost seamless unit. Once in a while one of the supervising rabbis would closely examine the edges of the water tank, claiming that it was conceivable for nonkosher food particles to lodge in a microscopic recess of the tank's welded seams. Invariably a cash donation into the outstretched hand would settle the matter, at least until the next time it was brought up. Observing dietary laws in the factory as well as in the hotel, and trying to satisfy the demands of some of these rabbis, was most frustrating to my parents.

The lack of unanimity among the rabbis also made my friends and me wonder. It was obvious to us from their endless hair-splitting arguments about how to rule on some questionable point of tradition that the rabbis did not get their wisdom from the Almighty. It seemed to us that they were attempting to interpret what their learned predecessors, who had lived ages ago in a different world, had decided among themselves. *Halachah*, the observance of Jewish laws, was one of the hottest topics among Jewish teenagers. My friends and I discussed the observance of Jewish traditions for hours on end. We questioned whether the old traditions were a viable option for modern Jews who no longer lived in a *shtetl*, a ghetto in Eastern Europe. Should we continue to follow blindly in the footsteps of our parents or grandparents and obey some obscure rabbi who, living centuries ago, decided what would be in the best interest of his flock? Would it benefit my friends and me if we did so? If indeed some of the traditions had originated centuries ago for aesthetic or health reasons, were they still valid today? Would we be better Jews for observing the old customs, denying ourselves all that nature provided?

On one of our trips my mother and I discussed the many dilemmas we faced when traveling. When my mother took me to dinner in a nonkosher restaurant for the first time, she explained that, living in a Christian world, it was often impossible to find a restaurant serving kosher food. I knew she was right, yet I was upset and got into a heated argument with her. Finally, I realized that there was no alternative, and I rationalized that not observing the laws away from home would not hurt me or, for that matter, anyone else—and the food seemed to taste better than at home.

Many Jews in Central Europe had come to the conclusion that the external symbols of Jewishness and the maintenance of the traditional laws were inconsequential. In the 1930s, being a Jew meant living life under difficult circumstances; we did not need to be reminded of our Jewish heritage. My family did observe all the laws, however, and the tradition forbidding work on the Sabbath. I considered it a nuisance that my activities were severely curtailed and that I could not ride my bike or use electricity on the Sabbath.

I was inquisitive by nature, but when my teachers ignored me and would not respond to my many questions, I stopped studying. Once my physical education teacher, who was also my home room teacher, asked the class to make an unusual formation during calisthenics. When I wondered aloud what this might lead to, the teacher boxed my ears so hard that my hearing was temporarily impaired. To make matters worse, my mother arranged for this teacher to tutor me, so twice a week I was forced to visit his home and do my homework there. More than once my parents were called in to meet with the principal, who informed them that I was very talented but lazy and a troublemaker.

Until 1933 many people wore their party's insignia in their lapels. I had done the same, wearing the lapel pin with the arrows of the Social Democrats. It almost got me into a fight with a group of older boys from the Hitler Youth. When I saw the bloody street fights between the Brownshirts and the Communists, I decided that I should not ask for still more trouble. I noticed more and more men on the streets wearing brown shirts with the popular black riding boots (I owned a pair of such boots myself), and as time progressed more and more men wore the round pin with the swastika in their lapels. Worst of all, teachers now openly wore the Nazi emblem.

I was not yet twelve years old when Hitler managed to become chancellor of Germany in January 1933. Who could foretell that the National Socialist German Workers Party would soon be able to dominate Germany totally and aim for the conquest of Europe and, eventually, the rest of the world? The Nazis moved quickly to consolidate their power and in March established the first concentration camp at Dachau, near Munich. On April 25, 1933, one of the first of the anti-Jewish laws was proclaimed: in order to solve the problem of Germany's overcrowded school system, the immediate implementation of a quota system for non-Aryan students (those who had one or more Jewish grandparents) was established.

This beginning of the isolation of the Jewish population hit schoolchildren the hardest.[3] Every school day the anti-Semitic pressure became more noticeable as teachers joined pupils in verbal and, in some cases, physical attacks on Jewish children. Nazi propaganda was introduced into every facet of the teaching material and curriculum. Especially obnoxious to me were the teachings about the "science" of race, and the continuous references to "foreign elements" and racially inferior pupils. It became difficult if not impossible for Christian pupils to have contact with their former Jewish friends. For the next two school years I was an outcast. I was no longer permitted to participate in any class excursions or my gymnastic activities, and I was told that I was no longer wanted on the soccer team where I had played left center. Fortunately, my favorite sport, slalom and long-distance ski racing, was something I did with a Jewish sports club, so I was able to continue this activity for a little while longer.[4] As I became more and more uninterested in school, I became more involved in scouting activities.

When schools were required to have morning assemblies, I became even more rebellious and my situation as a Jew more precarious. Every morning before classes started, rain or shine, we assembled in the school yard. Standing at attention one morning, I pretended that my right arm hurt and that I was unable to raise it to salute the swastika flag while the "Horst Wessel" song, anthem of the Brownshirts, was played. Not saluting was punished in a variety of ways. The most common form of punishment in our schools consisted of being forced to hold your right forearm stretched out horizontally and being hit repeatedly on the fingers with a bamboo rod. You were not allowed to withdraw your hand; if you did, you received additional strokes from the teacher or the principal. For me as well as other boys, it was a matter of pride not to move a muscle or to show any pain. A more humiliating but less painful punishment was bending over and getting hit on your backside.

About one month after my fourteenth birthday, on September 15, 1935, additional racial policies were implemented at Nuremberg. Contact between Jews and non-Jews was severely restricted. Jewish doctors and lawyers were no longer permitted to have non-Jews as patients and clients. Most public places such as parks and theaters were put off limits to Jews. We were no longer permitted to have non-Jewish household help. My life, like that of all Jews, changed dramatically. My parents were forced to sell Bellevue, the resort hotel, for a nominal amount to non-Jews. Since my father's matzoth business was seasonal, the loss of the resort was a severe economic blow.

Finally, I was expelled from school, not because of my behavior or lack of academic performance, but school principals had been encouraged at their discretion to expel Jewish students. I was elated at my new freedom from the daily provocations, especially since I was no longer forced to participate in saluting the swastika and singing Nazi songs.

Every year before Christmas, German theaters presented children's operas, and my parents had taken me to see them. But I had never had the opportunity to see a classic opera: *Juden verboten* said the sign at the entrance. I knew every aria and every word of Bizet's *Carmen* and was determined to see this opera just once, regardless of the authorities. I chained my bike to a lamppost behind the Breslauer Stadt theater. If there happened to be an identification check, I was prepared to make a run for it. But no one even looked at the boy sitting alone in a seat near a fire exit, and despite being somewhat tense, I enjoyed the performance tremendously.

My family regularly discussed how long the Nazi government would last. We hoped that the German people would "come to their senses" sooner or later, but I could not agree that in the long run there would be little to worry about; I had experienced my share of anti-Semitism, and I simply wanted to get away. Many German Jews regarded Polish Jews as socially and economically inferior and reasoned that anti-Semitism was directed primarily toward the immigrants, the Polish Jews. German Jews had fought and died for Germany in World War I, and my father, like many other Jewish men, was a decorated veteran. "German veterans and their families have nothing to fear, nothing will happen to them" was a repeated belief and cause for hope. Yet almost imperceptibly the jaws of the vise started to close tighter and tighter. Doubts crept into the conversation at the dinner table, and the question of emigration was raised more often.

Reliable news of possible places to which we could emigrate was hard to come by. Because some countries gave visas to people with specific professions and skills, the Jewish organizations advised German Jews to learn any manual trade or take a "quickie course" in order to acquire a skill that might be useful in a foreign country. "When you go to a new country you have to know a trade," we were told. With this in mind, my mother learned how to use a sewing machine and make neckties. When she practiced, I looked over her shoulder and thought it was great fun; I even made some ties for myself. I took two related courses, locksmithing and welding, both of which I enjoyed thoroughly. (I already had learned typing, but I could not imagine ever using that skill to make a living.)

Because I proved to be very skillful with my hands, my mother took me to see an old family friend for an apprenticeship. Herr Michelsohn, a Jew, was the owner of Göls & Co., an industrial machinery corporation. The company occupied a large yard and several warehouses filled with an assembly of new and used steam boilers and engines, pumps, and lots of pipes of all kinds. Most of this machinery was to be cleaned and overhauled for resale. Eager to learn something useful, I signed on as a "volunteer," a term used in Germany for an apprentice receiving only token pay. (Like all employees, I had a few German marks withheld from my nominal pay for *Sozialversicherung*, the German equivalent of American Social Security. Never in my wildest dreams could I have anticipated the future benefits. Fifty years later, living in the United States, I would become eligible for pension benefits under German law and receive a monthly check because I had once been employed by a German firm, even for a short while.) Several of the employees were non-Jews, including the yard master, Artur, who had been a trusted employee for many years. One morning Artur arrived wearing black boots and brown shirt of the SA (*Sturm-abteilung* or stormtrooper) uniform, but no one dared to comment. Despite his appearance, Artur maintained a correct, businesslike relationship with the Jewish employees.

At Göls I was given every opportunity to practice the locksmithing and welding skills I had acquired in the preparatory courses taken for use "abroad." I also learned how to operate the crane that lifted and moved the heavy machinery around the yard and how to clean and repair steam boilers and engines.

One hot summer day I was asked by the foreman to get the cart that held the acetylene welding equipment and to cut up the thick-walled pipes of a scrap steam boiler. I had left my overalls at home, so I wrapped a gunnysack around my waist and fastened it with baling wire. With the help of another apprentice, whose task was to turn the pipes slowly as cutting progressed, I started cutting the heavy pipes. It was hot as I worked, and I suddenly smelled something burning. Both my assistant and I wore dark welding goggles and did not notice that sparks had ignited the ragged edge of the burlap bag hanging around my waist. Before I knew what was happening, the oily fabric burst into flames, engulfing me from head to toe. No one had warned me not to wear burlap bags when using the cutting torch, but I had been well trained in what to do in case of fire. Instinctively, I shut off the torch, hit the ground, and rolled to extinguish the flames, while the other apprentice slapped at me with his bare hands until the fire was extinguished. Herr Michelsohn's secretary telephoned my home, asking for someone to bring me some replacement clothing. I got off with a few blisters and singed eyelashes, eyebrows, and hair, but I had developed a healthy respect for fire.

After a while I became restless; I was not used to the discipline of regular work. The *Schwarze Fähnlein* no longer met, and I had very few friends left. I felt repressed and would have liked to go skiing but knew of no one with whom I could go. "Why don't you go to the Steins?" my mother suggested. The Steins, who owned a resort hotel in Spindlermühle, were related to my father's first wife, and they owed our family some money. "I'll call them and see to it that they give you a nice room," my mother said with finality. I had skied before at Spindlermühle, a Czechoslovak resort close to the German border. The slopes were excellent and the powder plentiful. Located near the Schneekoppe (Snowcap), the highest peak in the Riesengebirge or Giant Mountains, Spindlermühle claimed one of the highest ski jumps in Europe and a bobsled track. My mother phoned Herr Michelsohn to say that I would take a vacation for a week or so.

My sister packed a small bag for me, and I packed my old favorite *Tornister* and took the train across the mountains to Czechoslovakia. The Steins were not very happy to see me, because I had come during the busy season, and they resented the loss of income for my room. So they ignored me and, though they provided room and board, did not give me the spending money arranged for by my mother. Almost all the guests were German, and their complaints about the poor quality of the Czech cigarettes gave me an idea. Since I did not have enough spending money to buy candy, I offered to buy them German cigarettes at a mountain lodge I knew of on the German side of the border, provided I could get some chocolate bars for my efforts. I knew the surrounding border area quite well, so on the next cloudy, snowy day I set out after lunch, skiing to a hilly, wooded spot that I hoped was out of sight of both the German and Czech border guards. I watched for a while but saw no movement. Finally I fastened my goggles and checked again to be sure that my ski bindings were tight. My poles dug deep into the powder as I propelled myself forward. As fast as I could, I schussed down the steep slope and across the border with enough momentum to carry me to a ravine that led uphill, almost to the edge of a stand of pine trees above the lodge. Only a few skis stood next to the entrance. It had been a short, easy run, but I was breathing hard from the excitement. After I removed my skis, I went into the lodge's coffee shop and ordered my favorite raspberry soda. I relaxed and waited till it became darker. Finally, I bought the supply of cigarettes and stacked them tightly in my backpack.

Just as I had hoped, snow began to fall heavily. The first crossing had been easy, but the return proved more difficult. I had scouted the area carefully, but it looked different from the German side. I skied to the spot I had selected previously and saw that it was in a clear line of sight of the German guard shack. Although the situation was not good, I had no choice but to return to the point of my previous border crossing. My problem was that the return would be slow because it was mostly uphill. I picked a slope that would lead me along the stand of pines and help shield me from the guards. Since the snow was deep, I was not concerned about tripping over roots or fallen branches. Dusk had fallen and my navy blue ski suit made me almost invisible. The schuss down the ravine was shorter than I had estimated and I didn't gain enough speed. Fortunately, I had decided to wax my skis not for downhill speed but for climbing. The backpack was not heavy, but still I made slow progress in the deep powder as I worked my way uphill along the pines.

I was already on Czech soil, and was nearing the crest from which I had started when I heard a shot ring out. The impact pitched me forward into the snow, but strangely I felt no pain. The ski bindings still held, and only my ankle hurt from my strange position. Stunned by my sudden fall and partially buried in the soft snow, I rolled over on my side. I rubbed my back against the backpack, but I still felt no pain. There was no sound. The air was still and snow continued to fall. I raised my head, but the ledge was just above me, and I could see very little. I figured that the German guard, seeing me struggle uphill in his rifle's telescopic sight, must have followed orders to shoot at anything or anyone crossing his terrain.

It was quite dark by now, and I was still a few miles from the hotel. Although I knew the way, I did not enjoy skiing in the dark. Still feeling no pain, I carefully raised myself up and slowly crept up and over the ledge. My teeth were chattering, and I was shaking from the cold or perhaps from the shock. I fell into a steady pace, taking the long strides the long-distance skier favors. Back at the hotel I released the bindings and, avoiding any of the other guests, headed for my room. I removed and examined my *Tornister*. In the center was a neat hole where a bullet had penetrated the fur and several layers of cigarettes before being completely spent. Apparently the distance had been too great for the bullet to do any harm except to smash some of the cigarettes.

In retrospect I realized that I had been not just lucky but positively crazy. Yet what I had done was not unusual. For some Europeans, smuggling was not a moneymaking venture but a sport. My mother would not think of buying a fur coat in Germany when the best furriers had their shops in Poland. She simply went to a tailor in Cracow, Poland, selected the furs, and several weeks later took the night express train and wore the coat back across the Polish-German border.

Until the Swiss became concerned that destitute Jews would enter and stay in their beautiful country, crossing European borders had been done with little formality. Then Heinrich Rothmund, head of the Swiss federal police, requested—and the German government happily obliged—that the passport of every Jew be identified. On August 17, 1938, a decree was issued requiring Jews to bear first names that were listed in the directives of the Minister of the Interior. If the individual did not already have an "approved" (easily identifiable as Jewish) name, then a middle name had to be adopted: Sarah for females and Israel for males. In October 1938, Jews were required to exchange their German passports for new ones, clearly identified by a large red letter "J."[5]

2

The November Pogrom

The year was 1938 and the situation was ominous. Hitler's anti-Semitism was a constant topic of discussion in the Jewish community, and there was no end of speculation as to what could have caused his hatred of Jews. "The Jews did not care for any of his paintings," said some, though "His aunt was incorrectly treated by a Jewish physician" was by far the most popular expression.[1]

When Hitler seized power in 1933, his ideas on "national enemies" were revealed by decrees that excluded Jews from German society and supported isolated acts of violence against Jews and their property. Most German Jews were not overly concerned. I heard repeatedly: "The Nazis are a passing political phase." "This anti-Semitism is directed against the Polish Jews," the older people said, referring to those who had immigrated from Poland during the previous few decades.

To prevent Jews from taking their assets out of Germany, bank accounts were frozen, property was confiscated, and emigrants were subjected to various taxes. One such tax was the *Reichsfluchtsteuer* (exit tax) introduced on December 8, 1932, even before the Nazis came to power. It applied to all emigrating German nationals who had property valued over RM (Reichsmarks) 200,000 or an annual income of at least RM20,000. The tax effectively robbed anyone leaving Germany of his or her property. The tax laws were amended in 1934 and 1938. When the prospective emigrant applied for the necessary papers, a tax was payable in the amount of 25 percent of the value of listed assets which had not yet been sold. Consequently, many wealthy people were not inclined to leave. Some Jews who did plan to go, and who had available cash after their bank accounts were frozen, used an ingenious method in order to leave Germany with their valuables. They went to a trusted jeweler or goldsmith, who fabricated ordinary utilitarian items out of solid gold; belt buckles, dress buttons covered with cloth, handbag decorations, and the like were popular items.[2]

In April of 1938 Jews were ordered to catalogue all their possessions. The Nazis were just waiting for the right moment to "aryanize" Jewish property. Three months later President Roosevelt called for an international conference in Evians, France, to discuss the problems of Jews trying to leave Germany. When it became known that the conference was a failure, Hitler mocked the inaction of the free world: "We say openly that *we do not want the Jews*. The democracies keep on claiming that they are willing to receive them—and then they leave them out in the cold; *no one in the world wants them*" (italics added).[3] The unwillingness of the free world to accept Jews into their countries demonstrated to Hitler that political considerations were paramount in the West. Jews did not have the rights normally given to political refugees. Their fate was decided by the politics of the world's nations. The free world's rejection of the Jews provided Hitler with an additional excuse to do with them as he pleased.

In early November 1938 German newspapers reported that the secretary of the German Embassy in Paris, Ernst vom Rath, had been assassinated by a young Polish Jew, Hirschel Grynszpan. Grynszpan's parents were among the 17,000 Polish Jews caught on the German-Polish border after the Nazis had tried to deport them to Poland.[4] The German Jewish community, fearing that there might be some sort of retaliation, did not have to wait long. Josef Goebbels, Hitler's propaganda minister, seized the pretext of the assassination to initiate a pogrom of unprecedented proportions.

On the night of November 9, 1938, attempting to make the event appear as a spontaneous outburst by the German people, gangs of Hitler's Brownshirts, in a well-planned and well-organized operation, went on a rampage. They roamed the streets of the cities in Germany and Austria, and for Jews it became a night of horror. They destroyed Jewish property, looted stores, smashed shop windows, and beat, raped, and murdered Jews.[5] (According to the Nuremberg laws sexual intercourse between Aryans and non-Aryans had become illegal; still, like any other "crime," it continued. After the pogrom, in a report by a certain Major Buch of the Nazi party court, it was confirmed that indeed there were cases of rape, which the major considered worse than murder.) More than 1,000 houses of worship became flaming torches. Torahs and prayer books were defiled and burned.

The November Pogrom signaled the beginning of the horror for Europe's Jewry and gave the world a chilling preview of the Holocaust. It became the watershed, the turningpoint in German Jewry's thinking. Before the November Pogrom, individuals making a serious effort to emigrate were either young adults, those who had relatives in another country, or those few who were deeply pessimistic about their future in Germany. Overnight the discussions about whether to pack up and leave, concern about abandoning all that our parents and forefathers had worked for, became meaningless. The November Pogrom changed the views of most German Jews; there were few optimists left. We felt trapped and forgotten by the world.

Our matzoth factory was not visible from the street. It was on a corner property behind two tenements that faced the streets; gates led through archways to the back, where the factory was located. Although it had always been vulnerable to anti-Semitic vandalism, we had never experienced a serious incident. My father was held in very high regard by his non-Jewish employees, most of whom lived within a block of the factory. On the evening of November 9 my father received a coded phone call from one of his workers, alerting him to what was going on downtown. Over the years, Jews and other anti-Nazis had developed a simple warning system. A phone call suggesting that the individual "go for a walk" meant that a police or Nazi raid was in the offing. My father made his way to the factory, closed it down (never to operate again), and stayed overnight and the next day with one of his non-Jewish workers. He took with him when he left a wax paper bag with five small deli or tea matzoth, as they were called, and later passed two of them on to my brother, Heinz. Long after the war ended my brother gave one of these matzoth to me, and I kept it as a reminder of Jewish life in Germany. Now, half a century later, this matzo is still in perfect condition in its original wax paper wrapper. (Accompanied by a Jewish calendar of 1937–38, it has been donated to the U.S. Holocaust Memorial Museum in Washington, D.C.)

The next morning, November 10, I was having breakfast when I heard a commotion outside. What I saw from the window overlooking the street made me freeze. A truck loaded with men, some of whom I recognized, was parked there, and SS officers were coming out of the apartment building across the street with some of my Jewish neighbors. It was obviously a roundup of Jews, and I knew exactly what I had to do. I waited until they crossed to our side of the street, then I ran to the rear of our second-floor apartment and jumped out the window.

I was lucky. I got away on my bicycle and was not among the 30,000 Jewish men and boys throughout Germany and Austria who were routed from their homes and taken to the Buchenwald, Dachau, or Sachsenhausen concentration camps that day. Additionally, 2,000 to 3,000 women were arrested and held for several days at police stations.

At that time we no longer had a maid working for us, and no one else was at home. My sister and my mother were out, and I assumed that my father and my brother were at the factory. I rode around not knowing where to go or what to do. My brother's apartment was close by on Menzel Street, so I decided to pedal over. Since Heinz was considerably older, I had not had much contact with him and really did not know him very well. He had been working in the hardwood industry in Leipzig, about 275 miles from our home, and had only recently returned to Breslau to assist my father with the management of the factory. He was always working very hard and was rarely at home.

When I got to the apartment, I found Alice, my sister-in-law, in tears, holding her little boy, and the apartment in shambles. The young wife of one of my brother's friends had died the day before, and before going to the factory Heinz had gone to the family's home to pay a condolence call. Not long after he left, the Gestapo arrived at the apartment. Finding Alice and the baby alone, they suspected that my brother was hiding and ransacked the place, tearing the bedding and upholstery apart. In spite of the bitter cold (or perhaps because of it), they took pleasure in breaking the windows. After venting their fury, they menacingly faced Alice and the baby: "We'll be back tomorrow morning, and if the *Schweinehund* (dirty dog) Jew Heinz Heppner is not here, we will take you and the baby." The group leader turned and left. The baby, Michael, was one and a half years old, and having heard his mother cry, he was wailing loudly. I consoled Alice as best I could and left to see for myself what was going on.

At his friend's place, my brother had learned of the Gestapo roundup and had discussed with his friends the feasibility of fleeing to Berlin. They could not comprehend that the attacks on the Jews were being carried out nationwide. When he returned home from his visit and heard of the threats made by the Gestapo, he was stunned. There was no choice. He could not leave his family to go into hiding, and there was no safe place where all of them could hide. The government kept detailed records on the populace. The police knew exactly where everyone lived and worked and how many people lived in each dwelling. My brother telephoned a few friends and packed a small suitcase with warm clothing.

After leaving Heinz's apartment, I rode toward downtown. In the distance

I saw smoke rising. Instinctively, I felt that it was my synagogue, Breslau's largest, with a huge slate-covered dome. The inside of the dome contained frescoes of biblical scenes, and an enormous pipe organ stood at the rear of the altar.

Fearing a roadblock, I decided to leave my bike and take a streetcar. I stood on the rear platform as the tram approached the intersection at the Anger Platz. For a fleeting moment I could see flames engulfing the outline of the partially collapsed dome, but I could not see the rest of the huge building. For years our family had worshiped in this synagogue. I had become Bar Mitzvah in this synagogue. Now, overnight, this edifice, built of solid brick and as huge as a cathedral, had become a skeleton. I was trembling, shaking with fear. I felt totally helpless, but for the few seconds I was able to catch a glimpse of my burning synagogue, I was filled with fury and hate and vowed to survive the Nazis. Next to me I heard an elderly woman muttering to herself, "Oh, what a pity, it was such a beautiful building." Unfortunately for her, a storm trooper in civilian clothes was standing next to us. He pulled the cord, bringing the tram to an abrupt halt, grabbed the woman by her arm, and dragged her screaming from the streetcar.

I was frozen with fear and deeply concerned about the fate of this woman, wondering what was going to happen to her. Afraid that there were more Gestapo on the tram, I tried not to let my face betray my emotions. This show of brutal police power reinforced my conviction of the need to leave Germany as quickly as possible, even without my parents. But where to go? There was no place to hide and no way to fight back. I found myself on the run. I did not know how to avoid the Gestapo. I did not know what had happened to my father or to my brother. It would have been easy for me to cross the border into Czechoslovakia, but the Führer had annexed the Sudetenland on September 26, 1938, so that country was no longer a haven.

I decided to change trams and go to Göls. The firm was located in a heavily industrialized area on Lange Street where the SS would never look for Jews. The SA mobs had done their smashing of windows, looting, and beating primarily in the shopping districts. There were many places in the machinery yard where I could easily hide. I was afraid of Artur, the yard master, who was a member of the SA, the Brownshirts. Most likely Herr Michelsohn had been taken, and I would have to avoid Artur, or he would turn me in when he saw me. But when I got there, I was surprised to find that business was going on as usual. The Michelsohns occupied an apartment one floor above the office, and Herr Michelsohn was working in his office as if nothing had happened, smoking his usual black cigar. Artur must have been a very satisfied and well-paid employee, but I played it safe and stayed hidden inside a storage tank until late in the evening, then made my way home.

Nazi officials called this pogrom derisively "the week of the broken glass" and later on derisively named it *Reichskristallnacht* (crystal night of the Reich), memorializing the quantities of broken glass that littered the streets. Reasoning that world opinion would not be aroused over broken glass, they successfully diverted world attention from the killing, rape, and deportation that took place, and the destruction of more than 1,000 temples and synagogues throughout Germany and Austria. Regrettably, and most likely unwittingly, the American Jewish community adopted the Nazi term "crystal night," perpetuating the glee of the Nazis in breaking millions of marks worth of show windows of Jewish-owned stores. In New York the General Jewish Council (forerunner of the present-day Conference of Presidents of Major American Jewish Organizations) held a regularly scheduled meeting on Sunday, November 13, three days after the pogrom. The minutes show that such business as resolutions, eulogies, Jewish unemployment, the census, and the anti-Semite Father Coughlin were discussed. Finally, later in the day, the council got around to the subject of responding to the pogrom. The following resolution was passed:

> "Resolved, that the General Council was against holding, either under our auspices or under the auspices of any Jewish organization, any public demonstrations or mass meetings in any place other than a place of worship."[6]

Though the mass murder of the Jews took place in out-of-the-way concentration camps, the crimes of November 1938 were committed in full view of the German public. Yet though they witnessed crimes committed against friends and neighbors, most Germans chose to remain silent. Either they were paralyzed with fear or they were indifferent to the plight of the Jews.

In 1933 the Nazis had arrested Germans for political reasons and had taken them into "protective custody." These prisoners (some Jewish, some German political dissidents) became the first inmates of Dachau and Buchenwald concentration camps, where many suffered the most sadistic, gruesome, and unimaginable tortures ever known to mankind. In October 1938 these inmates watched the erection of many wooden barracks. It became obvious to them that large numbers of new inmates were expected. They speculated among themselves about the classification of these new prisoners until a talkative SS guard said to the Jews, "Your race comrades will come here." Thus the camp inmates learned of the impending mass arrest of Jews even before vom Rath was assassinated. On the evening of November 9, on the camp loudspeakers, the inmates listened to the voice of Goebbels telling the world of the "fury of the people" venting their wrath against the Jews' property. What he did not say was how the Brownshirts beat, maimed, raped and killed Jews. It was Goebbels, master of propaganda, who in 1933, in reference to the Jews, said, "No harm will befall them; we'll treat them like flowers, but we will not give them any water."[7]

The night of November 10 the camp inmates lay on their cots fearing the worst, a new wave of mass tortures or hangings, but they were left alone by the guards. The SS were busy preparing for the thousands of new arrivals. The next morning the camp loudspeaker blared: "All barbers report to the assembly place." What the barbers saw defied description. It looked like a battlefield. Clothing, hair, teeth that had been knocked out, shoes, hats, umbrellas, money, and suitcases lay scattered on the ground. Paper money was flying in the air. Masses of men, moaning, bleeding, in tattered clothing, tried to stand at attention. Many lay lifeless on the ground. As soon as they entered the gates the Jews had been attacked by the SS, who beat them until they had exhausted themselves. Those Jews who were still able to stand had their hair shorn by the barbers and were packed into the new barracks. That night and for several nights thereafter, the fury of the SS guards continued, and the old inmates could hear the cries of the mistreated and tortured men. Nervous breakdowns, suicides, and murders were common events until a "normal" camp routine was established.[8]

At this time the Nazis' goal was to make Germany Judenrein—to free Germany, and Austria, of all Jews. Since the extermination policy had not yet been formulated, the Gestapo would release any Jew from the camps as soon as one of two conditions was met: if the Aryan buyer of a Jewish business needed help from the former Jewish owner, or if a relative could present proof that the inmate would leave Germany. Many men stayed in the camps throughout the cold winter until a relative could find a country willing to provide a visa or was able to secure transportation to a country outside of Germany. In many cases, however, a wife, mother, or daughter would come to Gestapo headquarters with the necessary papers, only to learn that the inmate "had died while trying to escape."

On the morning of November 11, at seven o'clock, a policeman arrived at my brother's apartment, picked up Heinz, and walked with him to the police station, where a large number of Jewish men were assembled. After standing in the police station all day, 400 men were marched through the streets to the Breslau freight railroad yard. The streets were thronged with crowds of people shouting abuse. Constantly watched by the SS men, the Jews boarded a train and traveled all night, knowing neither their destination nor what would happen to them. When they arrived, my brother recognized the place as Weimar. "What an irony," he thought, "the birthplace of the republic." The prisoners were chased through the station to waiting trucks, which took them to Buchenwald.

On November 12, at a meeting of Nazi leaders presided over by Field Marshall Hermann Göring, who was also the czar of the German economy, it was decided to order Jews to pay for the removal of the rubble of the properties damaged in the pogrom. It was further agreed to eliminate Jews from the German economy, to exclude them from schools and public facilities, and to transfer all their business enterprises and property—including jewelry and works of art—into Aryan hands. All insurance payments due Jews for their damaged properties were to be confiscated by the state. Wealthy Jews who had escaped the roundup were to be picked up and held for ransom. Finally, the entire Jewish community was fined one billion marks as punishment for their "hostile attitude toward Germany and their abominable crimes." A proposal to confine the Jews to ghettos where they would be used as forced labor did not appeal to several Nazis present. At the end of the meeting, a committee was appointed to deal with the biggest problem to be resolved: how to "shove the Jews out of Germany into foreign countries."[9]

A week after my brother was arrested, Alice received a postcard from him, mailed from Buchenwald, with a short message indicating that he was well. Fortunately, prior to November 9, Heinz had negotiated with a Uruguayan diplomat for a visa. Getting it was just a question of how to meet "certain required conditions," meaning how to raise sufficient cash. There were long lines in front of South American consulates, many of which furnished visas for a fee. Jews, so often accused of being mercenary, saw the irony as others tried to enrich themselves at their expense. My brother had received written assurances that he would receive a visa after presenting himself at the consulate. Armed with this letter and mustering all her courage, Alice went to Gestapo headquarters. After keeping her waiting several hours, Sturmführer Krause inspected the letter and told Alice that the matter would be taken under advisement and that she should come back the next week. It was easier than she had expected. "You can pick up your husband at the railroad station," she was told, but an additional condition for Heinz's release was raised: the booking of a first-class passage on a German ship to Montevideo. Alice was not told on what day Heinz would be released or what train he would take.

One week later, during morning roll call at Buchenwald, Heinz's name was called on the loudspeaker. He was ordered to get his hair cut again, and he received a railroad ticket to his hometown. After some formalities, he was taken with several other men to the Weimar railroad station, where they boarded the train to Leipzig. To their surprise, they were met at the station by representatives of the American Joint Distribution Committee (JDC), who took them to the station restaurant for a meal and gave them some money. For several days and nights Alice had gone to the station, almost despairing, before Heinz finally arrived.

All Jews released from the camps were required, at regular intervals, to report to Gestapo headquarters on the progress of their emigration efforts. The letter from the consulate had served the vital purpose of getting Heinz released from Buchenwald, but the promised visa for Uruguay never materialized. Nor was emigration to the United States possible for Heinz and Alice; Heinz had been born in a part of Germany that was deeded to Poland after World War I, and the small U.S. Polish quota was filled. My brother was told at Gestapo headquarters, "If you are not out of Germany soon, you *Schweinehund*, we'll take you again for keeps."

3

"Get Rid of the Jews!"

t all looked so hopeless. We could not stay in Germany any longer, that was certain. My mother had been corresponding with her niece, Mary Weintraub, who lived with her husband in Washington, D.C. Mary had written that she wanted us to leave Germany and to come to the United States. She sent us a legal document, an affidavit that the Weintraubs would receive and care for us; it listed a summary of their assets and certified that we would not become a public burden. With that document in hand my parents went to the American Embassy. They received a slip of paper stating that they were registered on the waiting list for Germans under the number 67391-92 and were told to come back when their number was called. "How soon would that be, a few days or weeks?" they inquired. "Oh, it could be a year or so," was the reply, "because we have a quota system in America, and this year's quota has been filled."

They were also informed by the clerk that among many other documents, a good conduct certificate would be required. This was a most preposterous requirement, apparently designed to discourage German Jews from trying to go to the United States. Didn't the Americans know that the only authorities that could issue the good conduct certificate—a *Führungszeugnis*—were the German police or in some cities the Gestapo? In Berlin, Jews who went to police headquarters to apply for the *Führungszeugnis* were surprised to get the precious document without any trouble, but there was a hitch: the applicant had to leave the country within a specified period of time. When, as it all too often happened, the applicants were unable to get a visa or find a haven abroad within that time limit, they were then required to report to Gestapo headquarters three times a day: at 6:00 A.M., noon, and 10:00 P.M. without fail, and not one minute late. No excuse, not business affairs or even illness, was accepted; one complied or one risked getting beaten up.

Nightly at the dinner table my family discussed the available options. When I mentioned that I intended to go over the border, my father pointed out that I would not get very far, since the large "J" in my passport was a dead giveaway. My sister had other prospects. A few years earlier she had met a gentleman, Kurt Grundland, who also was handicapped. They had become engaged and planned to emigrate together and were negotiating with several of the South American consulates for visas.

Of course, many rumors circulated in our community. The one most discussed involved a country with no visa requirements. A check with a Jewish organization dealing with emigration problems, the Hilfsverein der Juden in Deutschland, revealed that there was indeed such a place: Shanghai, China. What we heard was not comforting: the Japanese, who were allies of the Nazis, had bombed and razed Chinese cities—especially Nanjing—and had occupied Shanghai since 1937. Furthermore, there was a war raging in the coastal areas. There would be no way for us to make a living in Shanghai and no assurance that we would be able to survive there. When we inquired about transportation to Shanghai, we were sternly warned not to attempt to go there. It was suggested that we might be unable to disembark and could be forced to return. What to do?

I had made up my mind not to stay in Germany any longer, and my mother finally decided to ask her old travel agent for advice. China was at the other end of the world: how would one get there? how would one live there? were there other people besides Chinese living there? who had ever heard of anyone but criminals going to Shanghai? how would one communicate? The agent reported that one could indeed travel to China without restrictions. He confirmed that there were obstacles, and that there was a war raging in the coastal cities. Further, very few passenger ships were going to the Orient, and those—primarily Italian and German ocean liners and a few Japanese steamers—were booked solid for the next six to twelve months. The journey would take about four weeks. Since no one would guarantee that passengers could land in Shanghai, a round-trip ticket would have to be purchased.

The agent, who had taken care of my parents' travel arrangements for many years, asked my mother whether our family did not own some impressionist paintings, hinting that the steamship agent was a collector and that there was always the possibility of a booking cancellation. As it happened, someone's misfortune worked in our favor. Shortly after the initial meeting with the travel agent, my mother received an urgent call from him reporting that a Jewish couple had committed suicide on board the luxury liner *Potsdam* as it left the Hamburg harbor. Like many others, this couple had been unable to face leaving their home and family for an uncertain life in another world. "A cabin for two is available on the *Potsdam*; could you leave on very short notice?" the agent asked. "You could take a train to Italy and meet the ship in Genoa." It was decided that my mother and I should use the tickets and go ahead. My father was still trying to sell the factory and the apartment building and needed to stay with my sister until she was able to leave.

I had had one year of Latin and a few years of French in school, and I wondered if I could use these languages in China. Would my mother and I be able to use the skills we had learned in our crash courses? Surely, tie-making and locksmithing and welding would be useful in China—or would they? Some Jews in Berlin, attempting to get additional information, had visited the Chinese Embassy. They said that they were not told much, except that it was dangerous to enter Shanghai. After crossing a guarded bridge it was necessary to crawl under barbed wire, and of course, the best time to do that would be at night. Apparently, although the Chinese government had no jurisdiction over the Shanghai International Settlement, it had no interest in encouraging additional foreigners to enter China.

It was insane to go penniless to a strange country in a war zone, leaving family and friends and all belongings behind. But my mother was a resolute, determined woman. Her instinct told her we would be better off abroad, no matter where. She also knew that I was ready to bolt, and she had made up her mind not to let me leave without her. The travel agent assisted in preliminary preparations of the detailed paperwork required by the German bureaucracy and contacted the Gestapo to expedite the processing of our documents.

Since my mother had anticipated leaving, she already had most of the voluminous paperwork completed. In the few days left we went to police headquarters and, together with the other necessary papers, received the all-important *Führungszeugnis*.[1] At the request of the Norddeutsche Lloyd, the German steamship agency, the Gestapo gave us clearance to leave Germany on a preferential basis. The bank transferred the funds for the tickets from our frozen account to the Norddeutsche Lloyd, and my mother delivered two of our paintings to the agent.

My mother had been instructed to type out an inventory of items we intended to take along, and we each packed these items in two suitcases and called the officials to arrange for inspection and to seal the luggage. At that point a crisis developed. For years, I had saved all my pocket money for my stamp collection and had received many valuable stamps as presents. I had spent countless hours on my favorite hobby, and I was proud of my collection. To me, my stamps were priceless, and now my mother reminded me that I would have to leave my prize possession behind. The two albums were not heavy or bulky, but I would never be permitted to take my collection out of Germany. It was risky business to try to hide items from the officials checking and sealing the luggage; thus it was best to leave only with the most necessary items.[2]

The taxi was waiting for us when I tried to say *Auf Wiedersehen* to my father and my sister. I suddenly became ill, broke out in tears, and suffered a severe nosebleed that could not be stopped. When my mother and I left for the railroad station, I instinctively felt that I would never see my father and my sister again. We hurriedly said *Auf Wiedersehen* to Heinz, who had brought us to the station. We almost missed the night express train that was to take us to Genoa.

Shortly before we reached the Austrian border, my mother, who always had enjoyed smuggling, told me that she had stashed a second watch in her raincoat pocket, although she was permitted to take only one watch in addition to her wedding ring. I became almost hysterical: "Don't you know that if the watch is discovered at the border crossing, we will be arrested and sent back to Germany?" I asked her. I wrapped the watch in toilet paper, and when we reached Innsbruck, Austria, I went out on the platform and tossed the beautiful watch into a mailbox.

When the train reached the Brenner Pass, the border station between Germany and Italy, all Jewish passengers had to get off the train with their suitcases to pass inspection. The rest of the passengers, many on their way to ski in the Alps, remained in their seats, and the train took off without us. We thanked our stars that we had disposed of the second watch, because our luggage had been opened and searched thoroughly. When the contents of the luggage agreed with the listed inventory and no contraband was found, men and women were separated and strip-searched, a degrading experience. Since the express train had left, we had to wait for what the locals called the milk train, which stopped at every village to load and unload milk and mail. We breathed easier once we were finally under way again, especially when we were on Italian soil.

Upon our arrival in Genoa late at night, we were told that we could not board the *Potsdam* before the next morning, so we had to find a place to sleep. We had been permitted to take only twenty German marks with us, the equivalent of eight dollars in American money. For the first time in our lives we realized that we had to worry about expenses. We found a small, inexpensive hotel and had just dozed off when we were almost jolted out of bed. My mother, who had traveled to Italy before, realized that an earthquake had struck. For me it was a new experience. We were not injured, but sleep was out of the question. When dawn broke, we made our way to the dock and waited until boarding started.

The departure of an ocean liner about to sail to the other side of the globe has always been an emotionally charged event, and this one was no exception. As usual, there was a large crowd at the dock to watch the spectacle and to see the passengers off. Once the gangplank had been removed, the passengers lined the decks, holding paper bags full of colored confetti, waiting for the traditional last blast from the *Potsdam*'s steam whistle. It was March 3, 1939; we could feel the vibrations of the mighty engines as the gap between the slip and the dock widened, and we realized that we were finally leaving Europe. My mother and I watched the other passengers throwing paper streamers to their friends below as a last symbolic handshake. It was a festive sight, all the colored streamers connecting the passengers on the ship with the people on the dock, but for us there was no one to wish us "Bon Voyage" on our journey from an easy comfortable life to an unknown existence.

On board the *Potsdam* we soon met other emigrants going to the Far East, and all of us shared the same concerns. What would we find? How and where would we live? These were some of the questions on our minds. In the meantime, we decided to enjoy all the luxuries traditionally found on ocean liners of that period. We speculated about how far the rest of our twenty marks would last in a strange country with no one to meet us at the wharf upon arrival. Fortunately for us, since we were traveling on a German ship, the bank had been permitted to deposit several hundred marks for us with the steamship company as "on board money." This enabled us to buy any item available in the ship's store; there was even enough money for us to buy a Leica camera as an investment.

When my mother and I sat down for our first meal aboard ship and were handed a huge menu with an enormous selection, we were once again confronted, though not unexpectedly, with the problem of *trefe* food—food not prepared in accordance with Jewish tradition. Since our original discussion some time before in that restaurant, during which I recognized the validity of my mother's logic, I had overcome my aversion to *trefe* food. Besides, at that moment, on the ship, we were so far removed from our normal routine that we did not even give it much thought. On this luxury liner we were exposed to some of the finest foods a master chef could concoct. We felt as Adam must have felt when he was offered and tasted of the forbidden fruit. But we concluded that as long as we remained true to our faith and did not deny our Jewishness, our observance of many of the ancient laws and restrictions was not relevant during these most difficult times, when our primary concern was to survive.

We arrived at Port Said late in the evening. Some of the other emigrants and I wanted to go ashore, but when the British officials saw the red letter "J" on our passports, they became uncooperative. They warned us not to leave the harbor area and to return to the ship before daybreak. It was obvious that they did not want penniless refugees staying in their colonial empire. I had never been that far south before, and the warm air and exotic harbor intrigued me. We were met by a group of Jews who had waited for the ship's arrival. They had presents, they said, and led us to an old house not far from the harbor. We climbed rickety stairs to the second floor, where tables were covered with all sorts of used clothing. The Jewish community in that area had been informed that needy German Jews would be passing through and had taken up a collection. I was bewildered that I now was considered poor enough to need and accept used clothing. On the street I was stopped by Arabs who tried to sell me dates, which I love. They did not understand me when I said, Ich habe kein Geld, I have no money, but after I turned my pockets inside out, I was able to barter my German cigarettes for their dates.

In the days that followed, the ship slowly made its way through the canal to the southern port of Suez and the Gulf of Suez until we reached the Red Sea. I knew geography rather well, and next to the ship's stores a map of the area was displayed, showing our daily location. I fantasized about all the places I had heard about that lay to port and starboard and that I could not see.

Life on board the German ship was in stark contrast to the anti-Semitism we had left in Germany; no sooner would I pick a deck chair to sit on for a moment than a steward would be at my side, offering hors d'oeuvres and drinks.

Our route took us through the Gulf of Aden, into the Arabian Sea, then to the Indian Ocean to the south, until the ship made its way first to Bombay and on to Colombo on the island of Ceylon (now Sri Lanka). We sighted lots of shark fins and were told that this area supposedly contained the most sharks in the world. On we went through the beautiful Strait of Malacca and to the scenic entrance to the harbor of Singapore, where the ship unloaded cargo.

We were just a few degrees north of the Equator, and in the evenings we gazed at the southern skies. From there the ship cruised northward through the South China Sea to Hong Kong, which is one of the most beautiful harbors in the world. We managed to go ashore and window-shop. I remember walking into a candy store and looking longingly at all the goodies but having no money to buy any.

From Hong Kong we headed east through the Luzon Strait to the next port: Kobe, Japan. Not knowing much about the difference between Japan and China, we wrongly assumed that this Oriental city would provide us with a preview of Shanghai. Somehow my mother had "converted" some of our shipboard money to real cash, so while the ship loaded and unloaded freight, we were able to spend the day taking a wild cab ride to Takaratzuka, the famous opera. Neither my mother nor I had ever experienced such hazardous and reckless driving as demonstrated by our cab driver.

The next morning, with mounting apprehension, we left for the final leg of our journey. The voyage had been interesting and exciting, but the overriding thoughts in our minds were of what would be awaiting us in Shanghai.

SHANGHAI

The Temporary Haven

4

A Strange and Alien World

The engines had been quiet during the night as our ship lay at anchor in the estuary of the Yangtze River, waiting for the tide to come in. While the steward finished stacking our luggage, my mother and I sat down for our last sumptuous breakfast. According to the bulletin posted daily, we would arrive at the Shanghai jetty around noon. I was excited, but my mother was very apprehensive. We ate in a rush in order to join the other passengers already lining the upper decks to watch the pilot come aboard. Like any teenager, I looked forward to the ensuing adventure. I could not fully comprehend the trepidation I heard voiced in the conversations of the adults.

As the *Potsdam* slowly eased into the muddy, winding Whangpoo River, total silence fell over the passengers. We were horror-stricken. At first, the countryside was flat farmland dotted with villages, but all along the shore we saw mounds of rubble. As we came closer, we saw a large power plant, oil storage tanks, wharves and warehouses (called *godowns* in Shanghai) lining the shore, but behind them, as far as the eye could see, nothing but buildings in ruins. Strangely, those houses that were left standing did not look anything like the houses with the upturned eaves with dragons that we had found pictures of in the books we had read on China. Certainly they were like nothing we had expected.

Shanghai was perhaps the wildest and most cosmopolitan city in the world, the Paris of the East, the city for adventurers and conmen. It was considered one of the most crime-ridden cities in the world, a place where every type of vice was available. Shanghai was the city where pickpockets and beggars were united in guilds, the city that placed scant value on human life, the city with more prostitutes per capita than any other city in the world. Shanghai was also a haven for entrepreneurs because of the laws of extraterritoriality; foreigners enjoyed many privileges and were not subject to the Chinese courts and taxes.

Since the sixteenth century, European nations had sailed their merchant fleets to China, where they saw tremendous marketing possibilities. But from the beginning the Chinese resisted the foreigners and imposed tight restrictions. British merchants began to smuggle opium into China, and addiction to the drug spread rapidly until it reached epidemic proportions. By 1836 more than four million pounds of opium had been delivered to Canton. The imperial government of China vainly tried to stop the opium trade and finally declared war on Great Britain. After three years of sporadic battles China's emperor sued for peace, and the British won many concessions, including the right to establish trading posts along the coast.

When the treaty of Nanjing was negotiated in 1842, the British demanded a small plot of ground where they could build a settlement for their traders to live in and carry on their business. One of the five sites the Chinese picked was a mud flat along the Whangpoo River, a tributary of the Yangtze. They thought it of little value because it flooded with every high tide, and unofficially the Chinese named this settlement shang-hai, the city by the sea. When one of the frequent typhoons (dah fong—big wind) struck while the tide was in, the streets would be filled with up to four feet of water. There, foreigners could live and not be subject to Chinese law.[1]

The International Settlement of Shanghai dated back to 1854, when the British, French, and American consuls drew up an arrangement for the government of the settlement and the French Concession, or Frenchtown, as it was called. The Shanghai Municipal Council (SMC) was the governing body; at a later date it included both Chinese and Japanese members. While the British were in charge, most of the business was conducted at No. 3 Bund, the Shanghai Club. After the war of 1937 the Japanese occupied the section of the International Settlement called Hongkew.

A metropolis of more than five million people in 1939, Shanghai included every conceivable nationality. In addition to the Chinese, approximately 20,000 Japanese, Koreans, Filipinos, and Indians, 4,000 Americans, 9,000 British, 2,600 French, 5,000 Germans and Dutch, and more than 15,000 Russians lived in Shanghai. Among the White Russians (some of whom were fanatical anti-Semites) who had found their way to Shanghai after the Bolshevik revolution of 1917 lived approximately 4,500 Ashkenazi Jews (those that had lived in central and eastern Europe). The most prominent Jewish families, however, were Sephardim (those that had been expelled from Spain during the Inquisition or originated in the Middle East); they included the Sassoons, the Kadoories, the Hayims, the Abrahams, the Hardoons, and others who had come to Shanghai about 1870 from Baghdad by way of India. Over the years most had acquired British citizenship, and Sir Victor Sassoon was considered the dean of this illustrious group.

As we drew closer to the city, we saw streets with a few people, bordered by destroyed wharves and rows of houses. Until 1941 the British and the French retained the International Settlement and the French Concession, respectively. The section we were passing, north of the Soochow Creek, was Hongkew, often called "badlands" by the Shanghailanders (the permanent residents of Shanghai). Hongkew was partially destroyed by bombardments during the Japanese invasion of China in 1937 and during the retreat of the Chinese army. Until then it had been a very densely populated district. In crowded Shanghai this was now the only area where land or partially demolished buildings were available at prices some of the refugees, or the relief committee, could afford. Thus most refugees congregated in these bombed-out slums. We did not realize that we were looking at the area where we would be living. We were still in shock from the destruction we had seen, when we approached the imposing row of commercial buildings lining the Bund, Shanghai's beautiful waterfront boulevard, which looked as impressive as any modern city in the Western world.

The liner's engines had become completely quiet as the ship dropped anchor in the middle of the river. It was a strange sight: on the far side was Pootung, a flat industrial area; facing us was the Bund, lined with tall, imposing, modern buildings. Hundreds of dark-sailed junks and sampans—those flat barges propelled by means of a long oar mounted in the stern—were moving up- and downstream and now circled our ship.

It seemed a long time before we were transferred to the launch that would take us to the customs jetty. We soon learned that in the Far East nothing and no one moved with any dispatch; *memetchah* (take it easy, it can wait) or *mintzoh* (tomorrow) were among the first Chinese words we learned. It was March 28, 1939, and the weather was fairly warm. As we neared the jetty, I could smell the stench of decay mixed with the strong odor of the street kitchens. Not one of us refugees on the *Potsdam* had a friend or relative in Shanghai who could help us get settled in this strange environment. When my mother and I disembarked, we counted our cash; between us we had two German marks— about 80 American cents.

Incredibly, Shanghai was free from the twin curses of passports and visas! It was difficult to believe that no one asked for our papers as we passed through the customs house. Tens of thousands, indeed hundreds of thousands of Jews in Europe were trying to find a country permitting them entry, and here Jews could just walk ashore! We were met by representatives of one of the committees that had been hastily organized by Jewish Shanghailanders. Although most of us had little luggage and were cleared through customs quickly, we still needed assistance because we were unable to communicate with anyone. Neither my mother nor I knew much more of the English language than "yes," "no," "please," and "thank you."

What followed presented an incongruous sight. Assisted by coolies in rags, well-dressed gentlemen and ladies in fur coats and hats gingerly walked up the plank of a truck that looked and smelled as if it had been used to carry livestock. (I did not notice that someone stood at the jetty and took pictures. Thirty-seven years later I came across a photograph in which I recognized myself standing on the truck.)

We were taken to a large building, facing a creek, in which two floors had been converted into emergency shelters, furnished with cots. On each floor was a toilet, and a makeshift kitchen was manned by some of the earlier arrivals. The Embankment Building, as it was called, was located near the Garden Bridge, the connecting link spanning Soochow Creek. This small creek, called by some the busiest river in the world, was the boundary between Hongkew and the rest of the International Settlement. Sir Victor Sassoon, one of the wealthiest Jews in the world, owned the Embankment Building and permitted several floors to be used as a reception center for Jewish refugees. Here, my mother and I spent our first two weeks trying to get used to our new surroundings.

From our window I could look down on the masses of sampans covering the creek. Whole families lived all their lives on these boats, cooking and eating there, washing themselves and their laundry in the filthy water. Children were born and died on these small boats. In lieu of a funeral, their bodies were wrapped in a bamboo mat and entrusted to the water. The windows of the building were screened and had to remain open for ventilation. When the wind was not blowing, the creek had a stench of its own that was quite noticeable even three flights up.

All new arrivals were issued a blanket and bed sheets, a tin dish, a cup, and a spoon. How curious, I thought: this morning we ate breakfast in the dining room of the *Potsdam*, served by uniformed stewards, at a properly set table with the silverware laid out, and now we were queuing up in a soup kitchen.

Nothing demonstrated more clearly the drastic change that had taken place in our lives than the sight of us dressed in our good, heavy European clothing, the women still adorned with fashionable hats and gloves, waiting in line with tin pots in hand for our next meal. How could this possibly have happened to us between breakfast and lunch? I almost retched at the first bowl of soup I received, and for a Chinese copper I bought a candy bar. (At home in Breslau and in Altheide, I had been spoiled by our cook, who enjoyed serving me only what I liked to eat.) In the spring of 1939, one American dollar was worth about CN (Chinese National currency) $6.50. A Chinese dollar—about 15 American cents—still had enough purchasing power for a four- to six-course meal at a good restaurant in the International Settlement. Lunch or dinner at a Russian restaurant in Hongkew would be considerably cheaper.[2]

In the reception center the immigrants were almost paralyzed. The older ones sat stunned on their bunk beds. Some cried and were near nervous breakdowns. They did not know what to do and were afraid even to leave the building. A representative of the Speelman committee—named after Michel Speelman, the chairman of the Committee for the Assistance of European Refugees in Shanghai (CFA), had given a lecture telling us all about the dangers facing newcomers.

Don't drink the water or brush your teeth with it, or you risk getting typhus.

Don't ever drink milk, or eat any raw fruit or vegetables.

Stay away from the Japanese guards at the checkpoints.

Don't go into the old Chinese city, or into the Japanese section of Hongkew.

Don't carry any valuables and don't trust policemen.

Don't walk in the sun without a pith helmet. Wear a small towel around your neck to absorb your perspiration and prevent prickly heat. If you get bitten by a mosquito, you get malaria. If you get bitten by a flea from a dead rat, it's worse—black plague.

How do you prevent catching scarlet fever? An epidemic was raging through the city at the time. The refugees could only wait to be moved out of their temporary quarters into one of the Heime (homes) that were under construction. Heime was a euphemism for former barracks, warehouses, or schools hastily converted to use as camps. As they were completed, the refugees were sent directly to one of these Heime in Hongkew, a destination more primitive by far than the Embankment Building.

The first European refugees had arrived in Shanghai from Austria in March

1938 after the *Anschluss*, when Austria accepted annexation by Germany. These early arrivals had been warmly welcomed and urged to forget their national origin, to consider themselves just as Jews. There were no professional social workers in Shanghai to deal with the many problems that arose, but the initial response of a select group of Jewish community members to the appeal for relief for the newcomers was both quick and generous. They welcomed the refugees, fed and housed them, and assisted them in finding employment or setting up small businesses. Funds were established, and everything possible was done to alleviate their suffering and restore their dignity. The board of the Sephardic Synagogue granted permission to use the synagogue as a reception center, and mattresses were placed in the sanctuary. By the end of the year more than 1,500 refugees had arrived.

In 1939, however, the trickle increased to such a flood that the local Jewish assistance committees were no longer able to cope. Even though the cost of feeding the refugees was very modest, it became imperative to send out appeals for funds to Jewish communities throughout the world. The tempo of their arrival increased with every ocean liner arriving in the harbor, with no end in sight. The majority of refugees came by ship: the large Italian liners *Conte Biancamano*, *Conte Verde*, and *Conte Rosso* shuttled back and forth between Italy and Shanghai, bringing thousands. Others traveled by train via Poland, the Soviet Union, Siberia, and Manchuria to the port city of Dairen, where they boarded Japanese coastal steamers for the three-day voyage to Shanghai.

Initially, the influx of refugees had no economic impact on the Chinese. Neither they nor the Japanese knew what a Jew was. We had landed in a country that had apparently never experienced any anti-Jewish manifestations. The philosophies of Confucianism, Buddhism, Taoism, and Shintoism never taught hatred or contempt for other religions. It seemed we had found a haven—a country without anti-Semitism! To the Chinese at first, we were just another group of *nakonings*, foreigners. But the Chinese were puzzled by us. Most of the Austrian and German refugees were well educated; they had learned their Latin and Greek well, but few knew English. They had no money for rickshas or beggars. Worse yet, in a country where no white man would perform menial tasks of any kind, many refugees, overcome by the extreme poverty in which they found themselves, would try to get jobs in manual labor, competing with coolies at coolie rates. Eventually, some of the White Russians found themselves competing for jobs with the new arrivals. This fear of economic competition accelerated the anti-Semitic feelings that already existed among the White Russians. Even some members of the Russian Jewish community, who had been faced with severe economic problems since the Japanese invasion of 1937, were heard to say: "We did not call you; we are not responsible for you."

Naturally, this situation was exploited by some members of the German colony, who had no problem playing their anti-Semitic propaganda machine on the fears of Occidentals and Orientals alike. The German colony had most of its facilities in the French Concession. There was a German church, a German club, a German-language radio station. A Nazi paper, the *Ostasiatischer* (East Asian) *Lloyd*, was published regularly. The Germans had their own chamber of commerce and a Gestapo office. Klaus Mehnert, publisher of a Nazi periodical and Baron Jesco von Puttkamer, called the Goebbels of the Far East, managed the *Deutsche Nachrichtenbüro* (German information office) for East Asia. Among the members of this group was Colonel Ludwig Ehrhardt (alias Eisenträger), chief of the German secret service for the Far East, and Hans Mosberg, who was rumored to be a former Jew and one of Hermann Göring's "honorary Aryans."

Those elements of the Shanghai international community not affected economically by the new arrivals had their own reasons not to be sympathetic. One factor was the "loss of face" suffered by the white community with the arrival of destitute refugees. This was a society where Europeans were respected for their power or wealth, where manual labor on their part was unheard of. In the "Help Wanted" section of English-language newspapers, advertisements could occasionally be seen with the notation "No refugees wanted."

Resident Jewish leaders, embarrassed by the poverty-stricken Jewish refugees and receiving little help from the rest of the world, saw no other recourse but to bring the dangers of an unlimited influx of destitute refugees to the attention of the Shanghai municipal authorities. This tragic episode even involved Eduard Kann, a very wealthy Shanghai resident of West European ancestry, who, together with his wife and a group of former Austrians, had been active in assisting the first arrivals in 1938. Yet in 1939, when refugees began to arrive by the thousands, overwhelming the Jewish community's limited resources, his greatest fear was that "there would be too many refugees in Shanghai."[3] The small Jewish community of Shanghai felt harassed; its members considered themselves unjustly burdened with what they rightly considered to be a problem for world Jewry.

Their attitude was a direct reaction to the poor response on the part of world Jewry to the committee's requests for financial aid and trained relief personnel. The response of the American Joint Distribution Committee was typical: after promising a grant of U.S.$2,500 and clarifying the JDC's world-wide commitments and limited resources, its director, Joseph C. Hyman, concluded with an assurance to Shanghai's resident Jews that it would extend its influence to help prevent any more refugees from coming to Shanghai! He proceeded to communicate this policy to various authorities and orga-nizations. Similarly, in a letter of February 17, 1939, to Roswell Barnes of the Council of Churches of Christ in America, the JDC's Herbert Katzki clearly delineated his organization's policy: "On the advice of local authorities in Shanghai we have advised the European agencies, so far as it is in their power, to try to discourage further emigration to Shanghai. To stop it altogether, as you undoubtedly know, is most difficult, for large numbers sail for Shanghai without consulting the agencies."[4]

Clearly, in 1938 and 1939 Jewish leadership in the free world was slow to awaken to the need to assist the Shanghai refugee community. Knowing of the dangers facing Jewry in Europe and knowing that Shanghai was one of the few places in the world to which a concentration camp inmate could flee, Jewish leaders had their priorities tragically out of order. At that time the Gestapo was still openly encouraging Jews to leave Germany and releasing them from concentration camps whenever their relatives could secure a visa to a foreign country or passage to Shanghai. The Holocaust had not as yet occurred, so no doubt it was difficult to raise money, but the $2,500 sent to Shanghai by the JDC was barely enough to feed 5,000 persons for about a week at 8 cents per day. A few years later, after Pearl Harbor, the allocation was reduced to about 3 cents (U.S.) per day.

It cannot be stressed enough that later on, when the need *was* finally recog-nized, Jewish organizations, especially the JDC, through their financial contri-butions enabled 15,000 refugees to survive. In 1939, however, among Jewish organizations accepting this "policy of limitations" were the London Coun-cil for German Jewry, the HIAS/HICEM (the International Jewish refugee aid society), and the B'nai B'rith. They were notified of refugee conditions in Shanghai by the JDC, which, obviously for lack of funds, was forced to admit its intention of cutting down the influx of immigrants.

Encouraged by the action of the city's Jewish leaders, the Shanghai munici-pal authorities in turn prevailed upon various world governments to inter-cede with the Germans and Italians to prevent more Jews from leaving their countries for Shanghai. In a confidential dispatch dated February 18, 1939, U.S. Secretary of State Cordell Hull suggested that the American Embassy in Berlin "mention informally to the German authorities the desirability of discouraging the travels of Jews to Shanghai on German vessels." Similar memos, sent by Undersecretary of State Sumner Wells to the American Embassy, can be found in State Department files.[5]

Through all of this the Japanese maintained public silence. This was puzzling. Japan was the real power in Shanghai. Japan controlled the harbor and permitted Jews to land without a permit until late in 1939, when the refugee population had reached about 16,000—almost three-fourths the number of Japanese residents.[6] Even then, the Japanese authorities hesitated to stop the flow until they received assurances from Sir Victor Sassoon and Ellis Hayim, the two most influential leaders of the Sephardic community, that the Jewish organizations of the United States and England would not protest such action.

Later on, the Japanese allowed relatives of Shanghai refugees to land, provided they were in possession of U.S.$400 and a landing permit, which the Japanese issued for a fee. At points of embarkation in Italy the HIAS furnished families leaving for Shanghai with the necessary funds, with the understanding that they would return $300 to the Shanghai office of the HIAS upon arrival and keep only $100. A scandal developed when thirty-seven refugees refused to surrender the $300 and insisted on keeping it. In 1942, JDC representative Laura Margolis learned from Captain Inuzuka, then in charge of the Bureau for Jewish Affairs, that a Mr. Peretz, a refugee, and a Mr. Katawa, a Japanese, were using the confusion regarding the required landing permits to instigate a black market racket, selling landing permits to refugees.[7]

On June 21, 1939, the American-owned *Shanghai Evening Post & Mercury* carried exciting news. It reported the most promising of several proposals by Jacob Berglas, an eminent German banker and industrialist, to settle 100,000 European Jews in Yunnan Province in the southwest of China. The German government of course viewed the plan favorably, and the Chinese government was eager for trained foreigners to come to southwestern territories not previously developed. The Chinese as well as the provincial government of Yunnan, located in Kunming, agreed to offer these refugees the same rights of residence, work, and governmental protection as Chinese citizens. Berglas had proposed a financing plan with provisions for participation by cooperative banking institutions.

Shortly thereafter, in an editorial referring to the Berglas proposal, the *Shanghai Evening Post & Mercury* noted: "The plan does not impress us as impossibly utopian and we hope there may be in it some fresh opportunity for unfortunate people deserving far better from the world than they are getting at present."[8] Several refugee newspapers and journals as well, including the respected *Gelbe Post*, commented extremely favorably on the prospects for the resettlement of Jews in Yunnan. Yet the files of the Joint Distribution Committee reveal that the Berglas plan was rejected by a committee of the JDC as being "too visionary."[9]

5

Now What?

I finally became hungry enough to eat at the soup kitchen and devoured whatever was offered. I remembered the aria from Humperdinck's children's opera *Hänsel and Gretel*, which contained the line "Hunger is the best cook," and now I knew it was true. I soon became friends with several other teenagers, all of whom were curious about the strange new environment and who shared the same problem. We had very little money, if any, and not one of us was able to find a job, although we wanted desperately to earn some money. With nothing to do except stand in line at the soup kitchen, we roamed the big city and took in all the fascinating, bewildering sights, getting to know almost every nook and cranny of Shanghai. Whenever possible, we attempted to communicate with just about anyone, and our ignorance of English produced many humorous incidents. "How much watch?" one refugee would ask and, after being told the time, would respond, "That much watch?" We were exposed to that universal language spoken in so many parts of the Orient, Pidgin English. The Chinese who did not speak a foreign language but who had contact with foreigners all spoke and understood Pidgin English.

Shanghai was a hotbed of opium dens, spies, and international intrigue. Kidnapping or "snatching," as it was called, was a common occurrence. Shanghai was also a heaven for entrepreneurs because of the laws of extraterritoriality; foreigners enjoyed many privileges and were not subject to the Chinese courts. Shanghai was a tax-free paradise, since only real estate was taxed. Few foreign attorneys practiced before the Chinese court, where only the Chinese language could be used and it was said that no case could be won unless the judges were sufficiently bribed.

No longer did Europeans have the power they had had under the Manchus until 1911, and before the Kuomintang revolution, yet some vestiges of the past remained. Until the 1917 influx of Russian refugees, foreigners were usually wealthy compared with the average Chinese. Newcomers to Shanghai were surprised when they patronized a restaurant or a bar and, instead of being asked to pay, got away with signing a chit, a piece of paper indicating the amount of money owed. Foreigners rarely carried cash and were encouraged to settle any purchase by signing a chit. The only exception was the small change needed to pay the ricksha coolie. Chinese shopkeepers who were fortunate enough to do business with the *taipans*, the foreign managers of large corporations, were only too happy to extend credit to such extravagant and highly profitable customers. There was never any real danger that the *taipan* would leave without paying his debts. Most likely, he worked under contract for one of the foreign companies, and the shortest period for which these people were sent to the Far East was one year. The network of Chinese employees working for foreign companies provided sufficient control, and every Chinese businessman could learn at any time the status and whereabouts of any foreigner.

Shanghai was many things in the late 1930s, but most important, it was an "open" city, requiring no papers or visas of any sort for entry. Hence, it had for many years been a haven for outlaws and for refugees from various forms of persecution. European families, fearful of embarrassment and anxious to guard their good name in society, exiled their black sheep sons to Shanghai. It was reputed to be the city in which the cheapest expendable commodity was life.

Shanghai was also the city where pickpockets and beggars were united in guilds. The more severe a beggar's body deformities, the higher his income. Since his sores and wounds always seemed to remain infected and never healed, it was assumed that they were regarded as a professional asset. No matter where one walked, there would be a beggar jealously guarding his territory, shaking his tin can with one of his diseased limbs, demanding his due. To newcomers, the sight of these unfortunate creatures was revolting. Everywhere too, begging urchins approached, chanting "no mama, no papa, no whiskey soda, no Russian sweetheart."

In Shanghai, the world capital of rackets, even the beggars were exploited. In several districts it cost them ten Chinese cents (about one American cent) a day to do business. Racketeer leaders, to protect the income of those who contributed daily, rigidly controlled the quota of beggars on each street. "Unlicensed" beggars were not allowed to "work" in their "spheres of influence," and a gang of muscle men saw to it that no outsider trespassed. More were allowed to work when daily collections of alms were on the increase. The income reported by "licensed" beggars was checked and compared with the racketeers' estimates, based on the volume of pedestrian traffic. The choice of the right quota was a most difficult decision. Allowing more beggars into a given area might provide an immediate increase in revenue, but since each one then might experience a subsequent decline in income or even be forced out of business, it could in the long run prove to be bad judgment. These problems kept the management of the racketeers busy. They even had a department for interracket affairs which was charged with the delicate task of sending appropriate presents to racket competitors in order to maintain a "good-neighbor policy." Collecting "taxes" from the beggars was just one of a multitude of sources of income for the racketeers. They also demanded—and received—substantial "contributions" whenever a new place of business opened its doors.[1]

Shanghai's pickpockets were said to be the world's best. It was reported that they received thorough training on life-sized dolls dressed in garments covered with bells, which would ring at the slightest motion. One might assume that a man's wallet would be safe in the inside breast pocket of a jacket, yet many of the immigrants discovered to their dismay that such an assumption was in error. A skilled pickpocket, standing or sitting behind a victim on a crowded streetcar, was able, without being noticed, to cut through the back of the victim's overcoat and jacket, and *voilà*, the victim's wallet was his. Unfortunately, even poor and inexperienced refugees who carried no money lost their wallets with all their vital ID cards and photographs. Eventually, they learned the hard way that the pickpocket guild maintained a code of honor. All wallets were gathered at its headquarters, where the money was removed and—provided they contained money—the wallets were returned to their owners with the rest of their contents intact.

Burglars had no such code. Except in the winter, or when a typhoon was raging and the rain came down in sheets, windows were kept open for ventilation. The fact that most windows were barred proved to be no deterrent to the skills of these professionals. Standing on a ladder or sometimes on an accomplice's shoulders, using long poles with a grappling device, burglars were able to reach almost any article within a room. When victims woke up the next morning, they found that some of their belongings had mysteriously disappeared.

There may have been more flagpoles in Shanghai than in any other city in the world. In times of unrest, flag shops did a landslide business, because raising a foreign flag in front of one's house or business usually prevented Chinese marauding soldiers from looting. Of course, the Union Jack and the Stars-and-Stripes were by far the most popular. The number of stripes or stars on some American flags depended entirely on how much the customer was willing to pay. Some wealthy Chinese who had purchased foreign passports would display more than one flag in the belief that if one flag offered protection, they would be safer with a number of them.

Since Shanghai was known as one of the most crime-ridden cities in the world, we received dire warnings about the consequences of being careless. (Violent crimes were not as prevalent in Europe in the 1930s; on the rare occasion when a murder was committed, it was the subject of discussion in every city.) We had been told not to trust Chinese or White Russian policemen but to find an Indian Sikh if we were in trouble. As members of the international police force, the Sikhs were said to be the most reliable of the security forces, and they were big, imposing-looking fellows, some weighing perhaps 250 pounds. It was on Nanking (now Nanjing) Road, in front of the Cathay Hotel, that I saw two ricksha coolies fighting over their passengers. The problem was resolved quickly when the Sikh on guard duty walked slowly up to the combatants, grabbed each one by his neck, lifted them both into the air, knocked their heads together, dropped them, and majestically walked away. A more common method used by Shanghai policemen to punish ricksha coolies for infraction of rules, or to shake them down (cumshaw, a derivation of commission, was the generic term for "squeeze money" or tip), was to remove the seat and back pillows from their vehicles. Without the pillows a coolie was grounded, since he could not get another fare and probably would not have anything to eat for the day.

This inhumane method of punishment disturbed me, and later on I tried to find out more about coolies but encountered only blank stares. Where did they come from? I asked some Chinese, but they either could not explain or I did not understand them. The Shanghailanders I questioned had never given it any thought and really did not want to know. Most likely they had left a farm after a drought or famine and somehow wound up in China's biggest city. It seemed that a coolie really was not considered human. He had neither a home nor a family. All he owned were the jacket and pants he wore, a pair of straw sandals, and a straw hat. He worked for wages and hours set by his boss. Loading and unloading ships, carrying enormous burdens on bamboo poles, or pushing and pulling thousands of squeaky wheelbarrows through the streets of Shanghai, coolies provided the machinery that kept the city moving.

A ricksha coolie was kicked when he got in someone's way, and all he could do was protest and howl if a fare did not pay him the agreed-upon price. He slept wherever his last fare of the day had taken him, between the shafts of his vehicle at the side of a road. The licenses for about 68,000 public rickshas were distributed by the SMC to a group of only 144 businessmen, whose tightly controlled monopoly was a profitable racket.[2] Three coolies teamed up to rent a ricksha for a dollar per day and took turns pulling it, around the clock. The exceptions were those coolies who pulled the shiny, polished, privately owned rickshas. Sometimes dressed in silk, these ricksha pullers were status symbols for well-to-do Chinese.[3]

The busiest intersection in the International Settlement was in front of the four large Chinese department stores, Wing-On, Sincere, Sun, and Sun-Sun, where Nanking Road connected with Bubbling Well Road. Although very few cars were on the streets, the bike and ricksha traffic was extremely heavy and the crowds very dense. The odors of the street kitchens mingled with the deafening noise of the crowd to assault the senses. The noise of the city was overwhelming; it sounded as if all its fifty radio stations were going full blast at the same time. Coolies never greased the axles of their wheelbarrows; they believed that the squeaking, ear-piercing noise would frighten away the bad spirits.

Close to this intersection stood the Hung Miao Rainbow Temple, with a constant stream of people going in and out. After encountering some misfortune, such as spending a night or longer in jail, a Chinese would visit a temple to pray for better luck "next time." The assistants in a public bathhouse could provide a vigorous scrubbing to remove dirt from the body, but only a visit to a Buddhist temple could provide a thorough spiritual cleansing to get rid of "ash-colored luck," as bad luck was called locally. Consequently, the temple was heavily frequented by Shanghai's army of girls in the "entertainment" business. Some prayed for better business, others for protection against illness; still others prayed that whatever bad luck was in store for them would be prevented. Playboys thronged to the temple to enjoy their "baths" between what they called "screens of perfumed flesh."

To the right and left of this temple stood old women escorts with their charges: "Hello Master, wantchee number one French girl? Master, short time three dollar, long time five dollar," the old amahs asked for a half or a whole hour of pleasure. After the offer of a French girl, the nationalities changed to English, American, Russian, and on down the line until the spiel ended with the *pièce de résistance*: "Master wantchee young boy, velly young?" Many of the girls were children, some maybe as young as five years: "Wantchee virgin, master, velly velly goody, master?" We learned that life was cheap, very cheap, and girls were even cheaper. The most beautiful girls were said to come from Soochow; during floods or droughts the traders supposedly bought them for a few dollars. (How many had not been bought from their parents but were "snatched" was not known, though at one time the Shanghai papers blamed snatch gangs for the disappearance of about 218 children who probably had been sold into slavery.) Most had been sold to bordellos, where the new owners recovered the purchase price many times over after a young girl spent her first night with a favorite customer of the house. They had little chance ever to earn enough money to repay their owners. One of my friends fell in love with one of these girls, but there was no law that would help him to free her, and he never succeeded in making enough money to get her released from her owners.

Every morning coolies pushed carts around the city to gather up, depending on the weather, sixty to eighty corpses from the streets. I was particularly disturbed to see the bodies of many babies and children among them. These were often baby girls whose parents either did not want them or could not feed them and lacked the money for a funeral. After one cold spell, 534 dead bodies were picked up. At the collection center they were piled up and burned. Seeing these frozen corpses, we came to the frightening realization that we were totally dependent on the Jewish relief organizations for food and shelter. We were living in a society where only one's extended family would care for a person; no one else would. Those who left their villages lost the protection and care of their families. Whoever got sick and died might as well do so in the street, where the sanitation crews would pick up the body.

The narrow side streets were fascinating, known for the unique wares sold in the stores along the way. On one street one would find nothing but incense or coffins; on another street were handbags or furs, Chinese medicine, or silks and brocades. And like our barbershops with their poles, every sort of store had its own shop sign, a colorful tablet describing the nature of its wares. Stores displaying three brass balls as a shop sign could be found on many different streets and always on a corner. These were the pawn shops, always located at an intersection with screened entrances on either street. Should a person emerging from one of the exits run into a friend, he could save face with the alibi that he was not exiting from the shop but merely taking a shortcut. These pawnshops were my salvation, and no doubt many other people's as well. After our first winter, as soon as it got warm, I pawned most of my winter clothing and my riding boots. In the following years, as inflation progressed, I paid as much as 48 percent interest per month, but by the time I redeemed my belongings, the value of the Chinese currency had fallen so much that I made money on the deal.

Carefully, my friends and I compared the Chinese street names to a list of street names we had been given before venturing into the old inner city. We enjoyed exploring the area, although we had been warned not to lose our way. Few foreigners ventured into this maze of streets and alleys, since without the ability to read the Chinese street signs and speak Shanghai dialect, an adventurer could become hopelessly lost and easily fall victim to criminals. On the rare occasions when we had a few Shanghai dollars, we would walk all the way to Yu-Yuen (now Yuyuan) Road beyond the western outskirts of the International Settlement and visit the gambling halls. It was the custom for gamblers to be given something to eat and, after losing all their money, furnished with a ricksha to take them home.

We had heard about the infamous opium dens and soon had our first opportunity to visit them. We were rather disappointed, but it was a good experience for us to see the human wrecks lying on their cots smoking the opium. The spectacle thoroughly turned us off. After this visit I was never tempted by opium, and, even though I occasionally took a drink, I made sure that I always remained in control of myself.

What many of my friends and I missed, though, were cigarettes. Whenever I could afford to do so, I tried to get American cigarettes. Camels, Lucky Strikes, and Chesterfields, which came sealed in round cans of fifty, were sold by the piece; quite often, whenever I had some money to spare, I would literally walk a mile for a single Camel. We avoided buying cigarettes in packs of twenty because they usually were moldy. Lighting a cigarette was a chore because matches usually were too soggy. Some Chinese cigarettes were the "remanufactured" kind: coolies walked along the streets with a bamboo rod fitted with a nail and picked up butts from which the tobacco was rerolled and sold.

Walking through Shanghai's streets made me regret that shortly after our arrival I had sold my camera and could not photograph these exotic scenes. Some streets and sidewalks were so crowded I had to shuffle my feet, since normal walking was all but impossible. The din of the vendors assaulted our ears, and the peanut oil from the food stalls assaulted our noses as we worked our way slowly through masses of people almost uniformly dressed in black or blue. We were fascinated by the colorful spectacle. Professional letter writers performed their task while their customers, usually illiterate Chinese, waited patiently. Customers crowded around ambulant libraries, paying a few pennies to read from the selection of available journals and booklets.

A Chinese business consortium had hit on the idea of buying up all the copper coins, the coins necessary to get on a streetcar or bus. Once the consortium amassed almost all such coins that had been minted, stalls were set up at bus and streetcar stations, where the coins were sold at a premium. Of course there were the inevitable old blind men, each one led by a child clanging a bell, each one holding his tin can, appealing for alms. And the money changers—how could the city get along without them? Invariably there would be a funeral procession trying to wind its way through the crowd, the white-clad mourners walking behind priests decked out in red and gold garments, preceded by a band banging on noisy instruments to banish the ghosts that might follow the procession. It was even more crowded in the lanes, where cobblers would make a new pair of shoes for a customer in less than a day, and locksmiths a new set of keys while customers waited. Discovering that many European refugees were destitute, some Chinese invented several trades appealing to them. Craftsmen plied the lanes calling: "Kaputie—ganz machen," which, translated from German slang, meant that they would fix whatever was broken.

While I loafed and bummed around the city not knowing what to do with myself, my mother, unaccustomed to the lack of money but as always full of energy, visited as many of the people involved in the committees as she could make contact with. She arranged for a meeting with an official of the CFA and, as fate would have it, encountered an old acquaintance, Kurt Marx, who was the executive director of the organization. Although she had no related experience, she was offered and happily accepted a job as one of the caseworkers assisting the newcomers. Her primary role was to establish communication between some of the more needy immigrants and the committee, which was in the process of getting organized.

With the money my mother earned we were able to leave the Embankment Building after a few weeks and rent a furnished room in a modern-looking Western-style house located at the end of North Szechuan Road in the north end of Hongkew, where most Japanese lived. The house had a telephone and a bathroom, which we shared with the other occupants. Close by was Hongkew Park, which boasted a large swimming pool with supposedly clean, safe, filtered water and even a water slide. The ground-floor apartment was occupied by the Nakamotos, a couple with a two-year-old son. My mother had rented the single room adjoining the apartment. On the second floor lived the Jacobys, a young Viennese woman and her mother. The other single room was occupied by a man named Groddeck, a German refugee in his sixties.

For a while I kept busy with my fly swatter. I was keeping track of the number of flies I could kill with a single hit. This activity drove my mother crazy, and in her next letter home to Breslau she bitterly complained to my father that her lazy son did nothing all day long except catch flies.

On weekends the nearby park was filled with Japanese. They played a strange game they called *bahsseballe*. One man threw a small ball to another one, who tried to hit it with a heavy wooden stick. When he made contact, some of the players started running around the field, but most of the time they just stood around. There was little action, and I found it a very boring game.

A few months after our arrival I still had not found a job. It was June, and my mother and I experienced the beginning of our first Shanghai summer, with temperatures of 95 to 100 degrees Fahrenheit and extremely high humidity.[4] Although the window was open, there seemed to be no ventilation in our room, and air movement was stifled by our mosquito netting. Lying on narrow couches, we fanned ourselves, but breathing was difficult. After a while sweat ran down our bodies in little rivulets, soaking the sheets and wetting the couches. It was just a matter of time until the couches were moldy, making the nights even less bearable. We were very fortunate to live in an exceptionally clean house, so at least we were not bothered by bedbugs—the Japanese family took care of that—but occasionally a giant roach flew into the room like a dive bomber.

I made friends with Mr. Nakamoto, the owner of the house, who was the Shanghai branch manager of the Osaka Marine & Fire Insurance Company. His English was by far better than mine, and we spent many evenings sitting outside the house near the curb, solving the world's problems. Often we were joined by Captain Groddeck who, armed with the omnipresent fan, tried to cool off. Groddeck claimed to be a former ship's captain. He lived alone and seemed to have some moderate means of support. He was a grouch, but he took a liking to me. He never talked about himself, and I did not know how to ask. There was an aura of mystery about him; though everyone called him "Captain" no one knew where he acquired that rank. I liked Groddeck, who had traveled all over the world and seemed to know just about everything an inquisitive teenager was curious about. We sat there in the dark, looking up at the brilliant southern night sky, and talked about the captain's trips and experiences. He was not only a degreed mechanical engineer but a wise man. Engineering was one of the professions that had appealed to me. It seemed to be almost as interesting as zoology. With nothing else to do, Groddeck delighted in lending me some of the books and manuals he had brought with him and insisted on giving me assignments. Fortunately, the books were in German, so in less than a year I felt that I had acquired a working knowledge of basic engineering. After my mother and I moved again, to a room on Ward (now Chang Yang) Road I lost track of my friend and never heard from or saw him again.

One evening as we sat in our chairs, facing the fenced entranceway to the house, the quiet air was pierced by a sudden shriek, followed by loud wailing. Groddeck, who was rather portly and did not move quickly, followed Nakamoto and me as we went running toward the alarming noise coming from the side of the house. Mrs. Nakamoto had turned on the lights, which illuminated a ghastly sight. The houseboy, as a Chinese servant was called, straddled the high fence that surrounded the house, impaled between his legs by an iron picket. Apparently he had wanted to avoid being seen leaving the house and had tried to scale the high fence. He must have lost his grip and slipped. As blood poured down both his legs, several men tried unsuccessfully to lift him up. It appeared that the barbed tip of the spike was lodged internally. Fortunately, his agony did not last long; he lost consciousness and appeared to have died. Mrs. Jacoby had been on the telephone trying to get help, but the police ignored her. I was incredulous that no one would bother to help an ordinary Chinese houseboy. The nearest ambulance was apparently stationed at General Hospital in the International Settlement. After several desperate attempts to get help, Mrs. Jacoby finally was forced to give up, and we resigned ourselves to the fact that the sanitation department would take care of the body in the morning.

The other tenants went away, but Captain Groddeck and I were too agitated to leave the scene and remained quietly in our chairs on the street. I had learned what little value a human life had in Shanghai, and it frightened me. We were both puzzled, occupied with the same thoughts. Why had the houseboy tried to avoid us? He was free to come and go and was not responsible to the tenants. As we were contemplating what had happened, we saw what appeared to be the figure of a woman at the entrance to the house. She stood quietly to make sure no one was around and then carried something heavy to the fence where the houseboy's body was still impaled. Without speaking, Captain Groddeck and I quietly approached the fence and found the younger Jacoby standing on a chair, removing what appeared to be an envelope from the ichang (the Chinese garment) of the houseboy. She was frightened and started to tremble when confronted by Captain Groddeck. She held a finger up to her lips, pleading for silence. Groddeck shrugged his shoulders. We assumed that the houseboy had been the messenger in a love affair. It was only after Pearl Harbor, when Miss Jacoby's boyfriend was accused of spying and arrested by the Japanese gendarmes, that I remembered the evening when the houseboy died while carrying a mysterious message that was never revealed.

One evening in mid-July 1939, I was lying on my bed and thought I was on fire. I had a high fever and was delirious. The next morning my mother telephoned someone at the CFA, who advised her to take me to the hospital as quickly as possible. General Hospital in the International Settlement was out of the question—who could pay for it?—but the CFA had cleared out a small bomb-damaged schoolhouse on Washing Road in Hongkew and converted it into a makeshift hospital.

My mother was able to get me into a ricksha for the long ride to the hospital. The coolie earned a good *cumshaw* for jerking the handles upward whenever I attempted to hurl myself forward to get out of the ricksha. A male nurse assisted me into a ward occupied by about six male patients. Most suffered from one tropical disease or another which the refugee doctors were unable to diagnose. Basic equipment, such as an X-ray machine, was not available. Although delirious, I was able to make out a doctor coming into the room carrying a syringe with a long needle, which he stuck into the spine of a young man. It was obviously a painful procedure, because the patient screamed loudly. The next morning the young man was carried out; he had died during the night. His bed was occupied by another man, and I became very frightened as I watched the spinal tap procedure repeated on this new patient. He did not last much longer, and his body too was carried out. I was delirious fighting the fever, and fearful as I lay watching men die, one after another. I lost track of time, but it must have been the next day when the doctor approached my bed carrying the dreaded syringe with the long needle. By now I had associated the syringe with dying; all I remember was that I turned over slowly in my bed, pulled my knees up to my chin, and with all the strength I could muster kicked the doctor squarely in the groin. With a scream the doctor fell backward on the adjoining bed. My mother told me later that I regained consciousness after several days. I stayed in the hospital for some weeks, suffering from double-sided pneumonia and pleurisy.

Late in August my mother brought me a long letter mailed in England from my brother and sister-in-law. At long last they had received permission to enter England. Heinz and Alice, like so many others, not knowing what to expect in a new and different country, had prepared for emigration by taking crash courses, learning trades that might be useful to them or enable them to get a visa. They had taken courses in how to be a butler and maid, and as it turned out, that was exactly what the British were looking for—domestic help! Neither Heinz nor Alice had ever been in a kitchen, and neither knew how to cook an egg, but with the skills they had acquired in the courses and with the help of friends, they pretended to be "domestics" and were able to leave Germany for England in July 1939.

The owners of the estate on the outskirts of London who hired them to help them get out of Germany were Jews. Even when they discovered that neither Heinz nor Alice knew much about domestic service, the owners treated them very well. They helped Heinz find a job in the hardwood industry and permitted them to stay in the apartment they were occupying. Later we learned that just as Heinz was starting his new job, the war with Germany broke out, and he was interned for ten months on the Isle of Man. In spite of the fact that Heinz had a family with a three-year-old baby, that his passport was stamped with a "J," and that he had spent time in Buchenwald, the British authorities insisted that as a German he was a security risk.

When I was released from the hospital and returned home, my mother gave me several letters and postcards that had arrived during my illness. All the mail was old as it had been routed via Siberia. There was a long letter from my father and sister pleading for help. We read the letter over and over; what could we do? There was—what irony—a letter from our relatives the Steins, in Spindlermühle, Czechoslovakia, where I had gone skiing. They were pleading with my mother: could she help them find a place to go, anywhere in the world? When I finished reading the mail from my father and my sister, my mother and I only looked at each other wordlessly.

After Germany invaded Poland in September 1939, letters from my family would come less and less frequently. The last communication I received was a Red Cross letter from my sister, dated November 8, 1942. She was in some Jewish home. In the twenty-five words she was permitted to write, she hoped to get mail from me and indicated that she had lost track of my father, my brother, and her fiancé.

6

Of Toys, Books, and Angels

found a job for you" my mother announced one evening when she came home. "I heard about it at the committee. It's about time you got out of this room and earned some money." I couldn't have agreed more. As directed, early the next morning I walked the seven miles or so to Avenue Joffre in the French Concession to meet Mrs. Rabinovich at the Peter Pan toy store.

The Rabinovich family was one of the many Russian Jewish families who had left their homes in 1917 after the Bolshevik revolution. The family lived above the store and consisted of Mrs. Rabinovich, her husband David, his mother, and the couple's two daughters, Ira and Alla. Mrs. Rabinovich was very energetic and businesslike. It seemed to me that she lived only for her family and her store. She greeted me cordially. "You are handy, I've been told," she said. "You'll do whatever needs to be done—clean up, wrap purchases, look after the inventory, and help out with sales, and you'll get paid every two weeks, and of course you'll have tiffin [lunch] with us upstairs." The idea of selling toys did not particularly appeal to me, but they were correct in assuming that I would be happy with any job as long as it put money in my pocket. So I did as I was instructed and began selling toys. Mrs. Rabinovich imported some toys from Japan, but most were handcrafted by a crew of Chinese woodworkers who labored in the back of the store. Tiffin was uncomfortable, because the family primarily spoke Russian. Although by then I had picked up some Chinese, a few words of Japanese, and a working knowledge of English, Russian was a language I was unable to grasp. Nevertheless, I liked tiffin because of the homelike environment. Since for the Rabinovich family it was the main meal of the day, I got plenty to eat. I even got used to borscht, a soup made of red beets which normally is not popular with non-Russians. On several occasions Mrs. Rabinovich hinted that I might take Ira, her older daughter, to a movie, but since I had never dated before, I was too shy to pursue the suggestion.

Business was very good, since Mrs. Rabinovich worked very hard and had little competition. It seemed that the whole foreign community came to the store to buy toys. She was pleased with the way I treated the customers and appointed me manager of a new branch store for which she had sublet a section of a shop called the "Home of Books," a new enterprise. Mr. Shin, the manager and one of the owners of the bookstore, had earned his Ph.D. in the United States, where he had met his elegant and artistic wife, Hsien. With the backing of several friends, they had opened a contemporary-looking, Western-style store. It was larger than necessary, and Shin decided to rent to Mrs. Rabinovich a space sufficient for a ten-foot-long display case. I was ecstatic. In a very short time I had become a manager, a title bestowed on just about every foreigner working in any supervisory capacity in Shanghai.

The new store was in the downtown business district at 204 Nanking Road, only two blocks from the Bund. Every day, Fen Lee, a young girl who had worked and lived at the Rabinovich household for the better part of her life, would come to replenish the inventory and pick up the cash receipts. Business at the branch outlet was very slow, however, and I spent almost all my time learning to read English books. As a boy in Germany I had been a voracious reader, and even though reading English was tedious, I read whenever I had a moment to spare and increased my vocabulary in a relatively short time. I became friendly with the Chinese staff, especially Mr. Liu, the bookkeeper.

Shortly after Christmas 1940, Mrs. Rabinovich came to inform me that she would have to close the branch; toys usually were purchased by women, and the branch store was too far from the residential and shopping area. Worried about the lack of business, I had anticipated this possibility and had laid the groundwork for a change. Shin was also faced with a problem. He and his wife were well read and knowledgeable in Western literature, but the other employees were not. So, despite my poor knowledge of English, I became the token foreigner, selling English-language books in a Chinese bookstore.

Rarely did an individual Chinese go into a new business by himself. Rather, several friends pooled their financial resources and selected one among them to serve as manager. The businessmen whom I met participated in many endeavors, thereby minimizing their risks and assuring themselves of their incomes. It was also customary in Shanghai not to hire strangers but to employ relatives whenever practical. Even if the relatives lived far away in a different part of China, a member of the family would be invited to travel to Shanghai and become part of the business and participate in the profits. In the rear of every Chinese store was a loft or raised platform where the employees stored their belongings and their bedrolls, which they unrolled every night and spread out on the shop floor, where they slept.

Three times a day a coolie would bring their food in trays suspended from both ends of a bamboo pole, swinging in front of and behind him. The food was excellent and was part of the minimal pay the employees received. During the time I had worked for the branch toy store, I never had eaten any lunch, because I rarely could afford to go to a restaurant. Now I was part of the bookstore staff and regularly had my lunch with the rest of the employees. At first I had serious misgivings, because many Chinese were suffering from communicable diseases and because everyone around the table dipped his or her chopsticks into the common bowls. Yet the variety and quality of the northern Chinese cuisine prompted me to forget my anxiety and enjoy the food. I became as proficient in the use of chopsticks as the Chinese and agreed with them that the Western way of eating with a fork and knife was barbaric and utterly uncivilized. The Chinese were unable to understand how anyone would accept food which had not been precut in the kitchen, leaving this task to be done while the food was consumed. I also learned to my surprise that tea was not drunk as regularly and often as plain hot water. All day long, no matter how hot the weather, I followed my Chinese friends' example. Carefully holding the hot cup with two fingers by the bottom and the rim, I very slowly and noisily slurped the scalding water. The frugal Chinese claimed that hot water quenches thirst as well as any other drink, and after getting used to it, I had to agree.

Occasionally though, I went across the street to Jimmy's Kitchen, an American-style eatery, where I splurged and had a mug of American-style coffee and a doughnut. Jimmy's was popular with foreigners and Chinese businessmen alike and usually very crowded. Once, just as I was carrying my coffee to one of the tables, bullets suddenly started to crisscross the small room, ricocheting from the ceiling and the tiled walls. I hit the floor, realizing that it was just another one of the frequent assassination attempts. I never learned the identity of the assassin or the victim. Possibly, Chinese partisans had succeeded in tracking down a Chinese member of the Japanese puppet government.

On New Year's Day the store was closed, the profits were divided, and most employees went home to visit their families in the interior of China. Liu the bookkeeper lived with his parents in the old inner city, not far from the store, and he went home every night. Liu had a very inquisitive nature, and whenever we had a few moments, he queried me about my experiences growing up in the Third Reich. I had enjoyed the unusual opportunity to work closely with the Chinese. I got to know my co-workers quite well and grew extremely fond of them. I learned how easy it was to do business with the Chinese, as a handshake would seal any contract. Those with whom I came in contact were hardworking, intelligent, reliable, friendly, and honest with their business friends. I had become very comfortable in this environment, so I was pleased when Liu invited me to spend a day with him and his family at his home. Armed with a clearly written map of the old city and its Chinese street signs, I managed to find the house. By Western standards it was sparsely furnished with straight-backed chairs, wooden tables, and the typical wall decorations favored by Chinese. The dinner that Liu's mother served, however, was memorable. Liu was a highly intelligent person and would not stop asking questions about Europe and Germany, the problems involving the Nazis and the Jews, and living in the Western world. We spent a pleasant day trying to explain to each other the environment in which we lived.

The other Chinese employees at Home of Books did not have sufficient command of the English language to be qualified to sell English-language books to foreigners. The ones we sold were highly unusual: they were "pirated editions." Kelly & Walsh, an American bookstore that primarily sold books published in the United States and the United Kingdom, was one block down the street. Very few Chinese could afford to buy these expensive imported books. One of the Kelly & Walsh salesmen was an informer for the owners of Home of Books. Whenever a new best seller arrived, especially a title on the Book-of-the-Month Club list, Shin was informed of its arrival and would send someone over to purchase a copy. Then a meeting would be held with representatives of all the other Chinese bookstores in the city so that a consensus could be reached on how many copies should be "reprinted." Since China did not recognize foreign patents or copyrights, no laws were violated when the Chinese reproduced these books by the ancient stone process (lithography). Within days, these volumes would appear on the shelves of the Chinese bookstores, minus the copyright page, printed on cheap newsprint but with a hard cover. College textbooks in any discipline, however—be it medicine, chemistry, or engineering—were printed on high-grade paper, and even the color illustrations were usually passable; unless one looked for the copyright page, it was difficult to tell the difference between the original textbook and the copy. The main distinction was the price. American and English fiction and nonfiction were sold in our store for Chinese currency—and very cheaply. One of the first English-language books I attempted to read was Ernest Hauser's *Shanghai, City for Sale.* It dealt with Shanghai's background, its economic and political composition, and everything else I wanted to learn about my new environment. In the beginning, however, I had great difficulty reading it; I could not understand how a city such as Shanghai could be sold.

I had little trouble selling books. When a foreign customer entered the store and started to browse, I would present the catalogue of available reprints and ask what book the customer had read recently. By then I had an idea of the sorts of books this individual might be interested in, and I would lead the way to the section on the shelves where they were located. I experimented with my prospective customers. As each one entered, I attempted to predict what kind of book this person might find appealing: "By any chance, would you be interested in seeing a new analysis of . . . by . . . ?"

To my utter amazement, the biggest customers for the more expensive textbooks were American sailors from any U.S. Navy ship arriving in port (before Pearl Harbor). In Germany, a sailor was rather low on the social scale and not considered to be an educated person. It was my first encounter with the American system; I learned that in America anyone could and would join the Navy in order to receive or continue an education. These sailors would come to the store in groups and pay with American dollars (also called "gold dollars"). When they left with huge packages loaded into their rickshas, the shelves were empty, and the stock had to be replenished.

When there were no American warships in the harbor, we had time to think how we could attract local customers. I had an idea how to increase business, and after consultation with Shin we developed Shanghai's first readers' club. It was an unusual system enabling readers for the small fee of CN$48 (about U.S.$7.00) to get one book a month for one year from a catalogue listing about 1,300 of the titles we stocked on the shelves. The reader could keep those books they enjoyed or return those they did not wish to keep. It took several years for the idea to catch on, but by that time I was no longer with Home of Books.

At the next corner from the bookstore was one of the hundreds of small banks and money changers. Like so many businesses in China, the bank had no window; its front was open to the street. Behind a barred counter sat several clerks, the fingers of their right hands continually moving the beads of their abacuses. The clicking produced a distinct noise, and I often wondered what it would sound like if those fingers strummed a guitar. Other clerks were at the phones calling out the constantly changing rates of exchange, which another person posted on a large blackboard clearly visible from the street. The currencies fluctuated, but not as much then as after the start of the Pacific war when China's mega-inflation started to get out of control. I learned, like everyone else, to deal in six different currencies: the old Chinese dollar, after the start of the war the new (occupational) currency, the Hong Kong dollar, the Japanese yen, the British pound sterling, and, most important, the American (or "gold") dollar. My contact with the exchange banks was quite tempting, and since I now had a little spare money, I started to speculate, buying and selling gold dollars. I did not have time to read the financial news, and if I had, it is doubtful that I would have been able to interpret it. As a rule I was just plain lucky to pick up a few extra dollars. Occasionally I would spend an evening with friends in a friendly game of penny ante poker. As inflation worsened, the game really became spirited when a player could respond to a bet: "I see your thousand and I raise you another hundred Chinese dollars."

I never had any formal English-language lessons, but I discovered a pleasant way to augment my reading and improve my English. I went to see American movies. To make them more attractive to the non-English-speaking population, the movies had Chinese subtitles and were accompanied by a handbill giving a synopsis of the story in several languages. Now and then I managed to wheedle a free pass from a Chinese friend whose father had a financial interest in one of the movie houses. There I sat, trying to understand the dialogue, comparing it with the printed synopsis. It was an unusual way to learn a language perhaps, but I found it both expedient and successful.

One day when I was redecorating the bookstore's show window, I found myself face to face with a well-dressed gentleman who smiled and waved to me. It was Kurt Salinger, a refugee whom I had met on the train to Italy and who, with his wife and child, had been a passenger on the *Potsdam*. He and a White Russian named Ustimovich were salesmen for the Royal Typewriter and Monroe Calculator agency. "Business is booming," Salinger beamed, and said he was looking for space to start his own business. Of course I introduced him to Shin, and a deal was consummated. Using the section previously occupied by the Rabinovich branch outlet, Salinger and Ustimovich opened the "Office Furnishing Company" in Home of Books, with an option to add to the space if more should be needed. Salinger, who was an entrepreneur, and Ustimovich, who was in charge of outside sales, had persuaded the shop foreman of the Royal Typewriter Company to join the new firm. Lee, an elderly Chinese business friend of Ustimovich, bankrolled the venture and became a silent partner. The shop foreman was able to buy an inventory of good used typewriters and calculators, and they were in business. Salinger was correct: business was very good—so good, in fact, that Salinger too went out to make sales calls. "Ernst, would you mind keeping an eye on things while we are out?" was the first step in the transition to my working for both companies, drawing two small salaries.

Everyone was pleased with the arrangement. Shin had reduced his overhead, Salinger got reliable help cheaply, and I not only made more money but enjoyed the varied activities. In the beginning I had a hard time. Selling books in Chinese currency and office machines in American or Hong Kong dollars or English pounds was confusing. Often, before I could ring up a sale, I sprinted next door either to confirm a rate of exchange or to change money.

I had always been interested in technology, and I watched with fascination as Wong, the shop foreman, disassembled a complex machine, washed and lubricated it, reassembled it, and made the necessary adjustments. In the store I also encountered Chinese typewriters, which actually worked more like mechanized typesetters. Their use was slow and tedious (and not widely used): first a stylus had to be moved to the selected character; then, by means of a lever, the character would be lifted up and pressed against the paper by a hammer.

For individual letter writing most offices in Shanghai still used ink and brush; however, for business correspondence, where copies were a necessity, double-sided pencil carbon paper was used. Hedging against inflation, and while still employed by his old company, Ustimovich had purchased large quantities of this popular office staple. Surely, I thought, insurance companies needed carbon paper, and armed with a sample, I went to call on my neighbor, Nakamoto. It would be great, I thought, if he would buy maybe a dozen cartons. I left the sample for the office clerks to try. Several weeks later I was utterly surprised when I received an order for 100 cartons, and I became a hero at the Office Furnishing Company. "The Japanese must be expecting a war or a shortage, to buy that much," Ustimovich exclaimed. No matter what the reason, I was jubilant. This was my first real business transaction, and it had put money in my pocket.

About that time I met two Korean businessmen who were buying supplies and who complained about the shortage and rising prices of paper products. I inquired whether they would be interested in financing a writing pad I knew about, on which one could write without using paper. After several weeks of negotiations we struck a deal giving me a cash advance and obligating me to come up with a sample of this mysterious writing tablet. I was supposed to be paid for my assistance during the manufacturing phase.

Liu, the bookkeeper, warned me to be extremely careful. Although Korean and Chinese dialects are quite different, Liu had overheard the men say that they had no intention of paying me; they intended to cheat me out of the balance of the money. I hunted around until I found a waxy substance, blackened it, and covered it with cellophane. I had duplicated the magic slate I had used as a boy. You could write on the cellophane cover with any instrument, even your fingernail; when you lifted the cover, the writing would be gone, and the pad could be used again and again. Mindful of Liu's warning, I negotiated an additional installment, and only after I received the cash did I happily turn the gadget over to the two men, never to see them again.

Whenever I was not busy, I loved nothing more than to sit near the window and read. A constant stream of pedestrians passed by our store, and one day late in 1941 when I stared out the window, I looked into the faces of two men wearing long black robes, black wide-brimmed hats, long beards, and earlocks—Yeshiva students! I had read that a group of them had arrived from Japan, but I had not seen them in Hongkew. They had been received by the Russian Jews and quartered elsewhere in the International Settlement or in Frenchtown. I waved to them and met them at the door. "You understand Yiddish, maybe?" one of them asked me. "I speak German, so I understand a little Yiddish if you speak slowly," I replied in German. "You're selling books. Maybe you're printing books too?" he continued. When I responded that indeed we did print our books, they both broke out in a big smile. "Ah, the Rebbe [Rabbi] told us here are printers that print books on stones." "So what do you want to print?" I asked. They looked at me as if I had asked a stupid question. "What book we want to print? The Talmud, of course! We have a Talmud." "You came to the right place," I assured them, and I was only too happy to provide them with the name and address of the company that printed our pirated editions.

"So what were you doing in Japan?" I asked them. Every refugee in Shanghai had a story to tell, and the Yeshiva students were no exception. These pious Jews came from Poland and had been rescued in Lithuania by divine providence: they spoke of miracles and two angels who had saved them from the Nazis. I had difficulty understanding them, and I could not know then that thirty-five years later I would hear the amazing story of their rescue and become involved with one of the two "angels" who saved their lives.

Though the majority of refugees in Shanghai came from Germany and Austria, other countries were represented as well. Some came from

Czechoslovakia and then, after the German invasion on September 1, 1939, from Poland and the Baltic countries. During 1940, with thousands of Jews from Poland trapped between the advancing German army and the Soviets who were moving into Lithuania, a miracle happened in the Lithuanian town of Kaunas. At that critical moment a Japanese intelligence agent named Sempo Sugihara arrived in the city and, as a cover, opened a consulate. At about the same time a new honorary Dutch consul, a representative of Philips Radio Corporation of the Netherlands, arrived in Kaunas to replace a consul who had been a Nazi sympathizer.[1]

One of the Jews desperately trying to leave was Nathan Gutwirth, who had been born in the Netherlands. He contacted L. P. J. DeDecker, the Dutch ambassador in Riga, about the possibility of escaping to the Dutch West Indies island of Curaçao or to Surinam. He was told that no entry visa to Curaçao was required but that only the governor of the island could issue a landing permit, which was granted very rarely. Gutwirth then went to see Sugihara, and the so-called "consul" offered him a transit visa to Japan if he could secure an end visa to some other country. Gutwirth next called on the new Dutch consul, who, not yet familiar with procedures, contacted the ambassador, who verified that entry into Curaçao required no visa, only a landing permit. To Gutwirth's surprise the new consul, who wanted to help, obligingly stamped his passport with that notation but omitted the crucial annotation that a refugee would be highly unlikely to receive a landing permit.[2] When Gutwirth discovered that Sugihara accepted this meaningless stamp and issued the promised transit visa, he of course immediately sent all his friends to these two consuls. The Dutch as well as the Japanese consul issued visas for a nominal fee or, when necessary, at no charge, evidently out of humanitarian motives alone. Sugihara ignored orders from Tokyo not to issue additional visas. When all consulates in Kaunas were closed, he was transferred to Berlin, and after the war he was dismissed from the foreign service.[3] On the strength of those visas, the Soviets permitted more than 2,000 Polish Jews to leave Lithuania and thereby to escape the Germans.

Having never learned the name of the Dutch consul, the refugees referred to him as Mr. Philips, and his identity remained unknown until 1976. The day after I gave the talk at the Indianapolis Hebrew Congregation, Gabriel Cohen, publisher of the Anglo-Jewish paper *Jewish Post & Opinion*, who had been in attendance, received a letter from a Professor Jan Zwartendyk, Jr. He stated that for years he had unsuccessfully tried to find out what had happened to approximately 1,400 Polish Jews that his father, then an honorary consul in Kaunas, had helped to escape from the advancing Nazis some thirty-five years before, and he asked the publisher's help. And so, by a remarkable coincidence, the Dutch "angel" was identified as Jan Zwartendyk.[4] Then in his eighties, he learned for the first time that his compassionate actions had indeed saved not just 1,400 but (because some visas were used by families and friends collectively) more than 2,000 lives.

In fact, 2,178 refugees arrived in Japan with forged passports, illegal papers, and the so-called "Curaçao visas." Among them were about 70 rabbis and 350 Talmudic students from the only complete institute of Talmudic study saved from Nazi destruction, the Mir Yeshiva. Among these pious Jews, the two consuls were later known as "the Angel of Curaçao" and "the Angel of Salvation." The Japanese in Kobe showed these strangers traditional hospitality; the authorities issued them bread rations and, for Passover, even additional flour rations so that matzoth could be made. To their amazement, the Japanese government extended their transit visas and permitted them to stay in Kobe until two months before the attack on Pearl Harbor, at which time they were transported to Shanghai.

After their arrival, the Yeshiva students succeeded in securing a complete set of the Talmud and had it copied almost in its entirety by the lithographic stone process in order to continue their studies. The Polish Jews developed an enormous esprit de corps and often pitted their will against the CFA (and later against the Japanese, for which some of them paid with their lives). Religiously far more observant than the German, Austrian, and Czech refugees, they flatly refused to enter any of the Heime, which they considered degrading. Instead, they insisted on, and received, cash subsidies from the CFA which enabled them to live in private rooms and get kosher meals. Foremost among factors in the Polish refugees' favor was the fact that they shared their East European heritage, Yiddish language, and religious practices with Shanghai's Russian Jews. The assimilated Central European Jews, in general, had no knowledge of Yiddish and tended to be liberal or reform in their religious practices.

7

Illo

In April 1941 I met my one and only girlfriend, Illo Koratkowski. She was from Berlin. Her father, Paul Koratkowski (who shortened his name to Korat after his arrival in the United States in 1947), a disabled and decorated World War I veteran, had decided to leave Germany quickly after the November Pogrom. He had escaped the roundup and had not been taken to a concentration camp. He had gone to Shanghai alone, intending to go on to the United States as soon as their quota number was called and to meet his wife and daughter there. Until then it would be better for them, he had reasoned, to remain in Berlin, where they were comfortable and Illo could finish school.

On September 1, 1939, Illo was celebrating her sixteenth birthday. Her mother was just lighting the birthday candles when the air raid sirens sounded over Berlin. They spent the rest of the day in an air raid shelter. Poland had been invaded; the war had begun.

It became obvious that they needed to leave Berlin as quickly as possible or they might be trapped. Fortunately, Illo's mother was able to buy two railway tickets on the Trans-Siberian Railroad to the Chinese harbor town of Dairen, and boat transportation through to Shanghai. In May of 1940 they began the long voyage to join their husband and father. They stayed overnight in a first-class Moscow hotel. The next morning they were troubled by the stares of hungry Moscovites watching them through the restaurant's window as they ate a lavish breakfast. They continued their 4,000-mile journey, crossing almost half the land mass of the earth via Siberia, from the Ural mountains to Irkutsk on Lake Baikal and from there to the Manchurian border. In Manchouli they changed trains for Harbin, where they and other refugees on the train were met by members of the Jewish community, who provided them lunch. Then they continued to the harbor town of Dairen. After an overnight stay at a local hotel, they boarded a Japanese coastal steamer for the final three-day journey to Shanghai.

Illo's father had been managing director of a commercial bank in Berlin. Before he left Germany he had been able, through his banking connections, to transfer some money to Switzerland. Drawing on that reserve when he arrived in Shanghai, he rented an office in a downtown building and started a small accounting business of his own. Within a short time he had built up a regular clientele. Illo lived with her parents in an apartment building on Hardoon Road, in the International Settlement. Most of the tenants in that building were members of the U.S. Fourth Marines and their families. There, as well as in the French Concession, the Western-style houses were larger than those in Hongkew, solidly constructed and equipped with modern conveniences, including central heat.

Heinz Egon Heinemann, owner of the Western Arts Gallery, was one of Koratkowski's clients. He bought and sold rare books and badly needed someone to assist him with correspondence, cataloguing, and sales. Koratkowski told Heinemann that shortly after her arrival from Berlin his daughter Illo had found a job with a biweekly literary paper but had lost it after two months when the paper folded. She spoke English and French and was able to take shorthand in these languages as well as in German. Koratkowski was very pleased with himself for having insisted that she take shorthand and typing classes in high school. He was a practical man and had felt they would be helpful for taking notes in college and give her marketable skills as well. Now she needed a job where she would also be able to further her education. Would Heinemann have an opening for his daughter in his store? Heinemann quickly agreed to employ her, pay her a small salary, and teach her as well. He loved to teach and promised that she would learn not only the rare book business but literature, and Western and Oriental art as well.

The store was located on Avenue Joffre in the French Concession, not far from Hardoon Road where the Koratkowskis lived. It was an easy walk for Illo to get to work and come home for tiffin. She loved her work and quickly became close friends with Heinz and his wife, Paula. Heinemann operated his business in half of a store, the other half occupied by Mr. Tsao, a well-educated Chinese curio dealer. A daily visitor in Heinemann's store was Lothar Brieger, the renowned German literary critic. Also a refugee, he lived in the French Concession and took daily walks with his little dog, Biche. In his gruff way he became very fond of Illo, whom he called *Kleine* (little one). He was occasionally asked to write an article or give a lecture at the university, and Illo

would transcribe his notes and type the articles. He taught her about literature and art, and she listened spellbound to the scholarly discussions between
Heinemann, Brieger, and other "regulars" at the store.

The inventory of rare books and valuable and unusual Chinese antiques
attracted many of the European Shanghailanders, especially members of the
diplomatic corps. Almost daily one could find members of the German colony
browsing at the Western Arts Gallery. Hans Mosberg, the alleged "honorary
Aryan," was one of those who frequently stopped in to browse and chat.
His name sounded Jewish, but he looked more like a portly German. Over a
period of time he became friendly with Heinemann and confided in him that
indeed he had been a Nazi party member. He was apologetic and claimed, as
so many others did, that he had been forced to join the party; however, he
insisted that he had never agreed with Nazi ideology and was appalled at the
mistreatment of the Jews in Poland. When he became aware of the misery of
the Jews in the camps in Hongkew, he regularly used Heinemann to channel
cash confidentially to the relief committee. Mosberg liked Illo, who reminded
him, he said, of his daughter in Germany. In the center of the Western Arts
Gallery stood a porcelain pagoda that reached almost to the ceiling and must
have been worth a fortune. Mosberg often joked that he would give Illo this
pagoda as a wedding present should she get married and invite him to the
wedding.

Illo was a member of the Haverim youth group, which had been organized by Karl-Heinz Sober, a young orthodox rabbi. Some of its members
had suggested that it would be beneficial to hold some joint activities with
another Jewish refugee group, the Thirteenth Rovers of the British Boy Scout
Association, which I had joined some time before. We were assisting the orga-
nizers of the British Boy Scouts to prepare for a charity ball to benefit refugee
youth, and I had volunteered to become the contact person with the Haverim
group—of which Illo was the representative.

I was waiting for her in the office of the bookstore and watched her enter-
ing. Her reputation had preceded her. She was nobody's girl, I had heard from
my friends. She dated no one, and her activities were strictly chaperoned by
her mother. She walked with determination, chin high, and had an innocent-
looking but intelligent expression. She wore a gray tweed, tight-fitting winter
coat with fur collar and trim and a zippered front. It was an elegant coat,
although her mother had made it over from one of hers. (Illo had been outfit-
ted with a new wardrobe before leaving Berlin, but in a final growth spurt she
had managed to outgrow most of her clothes and shoes within a year.) Illo

and I made small talk, if discussing the weather and the military situation can be called that. Depending on the season, heat, humidity, cold, or the latest typhoon was an important subject for discussion; weather played a vital role in our daily life, but nothing could be done about it. And foreign politics was of interest, but we could do nothing about that either. We quickly changed subjects and sat down to talk about the business at hand.

The dance was to be held on April 26, 1941, at the Shanghai Jewish Club, the cultural and social center of the Russian Jews. All proceeds were to be used for the establishment of a kind of community center in Hongkew, a place where refugee youngsters could congregate and play away from their oppressive home environments. The ball was supported by the entire Jewish community of Shanghai.

How ironic, but perhaps typical of the spirit that prevailed among the young adult refugees, that we were organizing the affair without ever considering that we also would be among the beneficiaries. Advertisements and "Compliments from a friend" had to be sold for the dance program, the booklet itself assembled and printed, and all the details connected with such an affair attended to. While we young people were to do much of the detail work, adults, my mother among them, did the overall planning as members of the executive committee. Illo and I were to work together on some details, and it was easiest to continue to meet at the Home of Books because of its convenient location.

The executive committee meeting at which we were to give our report was held at the Foreign YMCA, which was located halfway between Hongkew and Illo's home on Hardoon Road. Of course, I used the opportunity to take her home at the end of the meeting. I found Illo fascinating to talk with, and soon our conversation turned from planning for the ball to other topics. We discovered a mutual love of classical music. By that time I had thoroughly fallen in love but had no idea how I could possibly tell her of my feelings. She introduced me to her parents; Koratkowski was a rather authoritative, curt, and businesslike man, while his wife, Irene, was sensitive and always interested in what I was thinking or what I had to say.

As the time for the ball approached, it was only natural that I would ask Illo to be my date. Since her parents were going to attend, as well as my mother, her mother could have no objection. On the evening of April 26, therefore, I carefully dressed in my double-breasted black suit. How little we had known about the conditions we would face in Shanghai when we packed our clothes in Breslau! It felt good to be dressed up again, and my spirits soared. I escorted my mother to the club; Illo was already there with her parents. Seeing my date in her beautiful long yellow evening gown (she had brought two gowns with her from Berlin) quickly made me forget reality.

I had taken practical courses in Breslau to prepare for life in a new country, but I had not had dancing lessons. Yet when I saw that some of my friends went to Illo's table to ask her for a dance, I could not defer asking her any longer. I figured that the other guys could not possibly dance any better than I did and finally got enough courage to dance with her. After a few dances some friends asked Illo and me to join them for a drink at the bar. Someone bought a round, and I reciprocated. What I did not know was that the club bar poured imported drinks only, and when the bartender asked me to pay up, the amount was more than I earned the whole month. I hastily excused myself and made the rounds to all my friends who were present to borrow sufficient money to settle the bar bill. This episode brought me back to reality but did not stop me from enjoying myself for the rest of a most unusual evening.

8

Of Scouts, Soldiers, and Deadly Games

Many refugee youngsters had belonged to youth organizations in Austria and Germany. Consequently, there were quite a few former scouts among the Austrian refugees and some from Germany, who were eager to join a scout group when they came to Shanghai. All had taken their scout training in the old country seriously and now were anxious to continue their activities, if at all possible. Fortunately, the British Boy Scouts Association, under the dedicated leadership of Commissioner A. H. (Sandy) Gordon, was well established in Shanghai and received the refugee scouts from Austria and Germany with open arms. With few exceptions, the scouts were organized by country of origin. At one Shanghai scout parade, forty-two nations were represented.[1] Besides the French and the British troops, the Jewish troop of Russian refugees, headed by Captain Noel S. Jacobs, was very active. Fred Mittler, an old scout from Vienna, with the assistance of several of his friends, set out to organize a scout troop and the Thirteenth Rovers, which I joined.[2]

Lack of financing for uniforms and activities did not deter the refugees. Senior scout leadership quickly recognized the burning need to keep the refugee youths occupied. The Thirteenth Rovers, a troop of older teenagers, assumed responsibility for the younger troops. In December 1940 we published "Our Songs," a twenty-seven-page booklet containing forty-six popular English and German Boy Scout songs. We even succeeded, where all the other scout groups had previously failed, in holding a fortnight's summer camp at Millington Camp. It was managed by four Rover Scouts, including me. Although there were many obstacles, the camp was a great success.

Scouting in the European sense was all but impossible, and much imagination was necessary to develop and maintain activities that would keep children of all ages off the streets until the first schools, financed by Jewish millionaire Horace Kadoorie, were opened. Some of the children had little opportunity to see grass or trees. Millington Camp, a magnificent estate belonging to the British Boy Scouts Association, provided camping facilities. With the aid and supervision of a single medical volunteer, Dr. Mario Herbst, a few of us Rover Scouts supervised camping activities for more than 100 youngsters. Except for one boy's minor ailment, no one became ill, which was an extraordinary achievement considering the climate and the primitive sanitary conditions under which we were forced to operate.

One important benefit to the community was apparent only after the outbreak of war in the Pacific. It was rumored that the Japanese intended to organize the refugee youngsters into a youth organization under their control in order to indoctrinate them. Not knowing how long the war might last, we were concerned about the possible effects of such an organization. Fortunately, the committee was able to convince the Japanese authorities of the insurmountable language difficulties of their plan, and they agreed to leave the training of the youth to our small Rover group.

The International Settlement of Shanghai was policed by a multi-national force, the Shanghai Municipal Police (SMP), made up primarily of Chinese policemen, Indian Sikhs, a few British officers, and White Russians as non-commissioned officers (NCOs). Periodically, applications for the elite special police forces were accepted, and I applied. The interviews and tests lasted several days, and I got as far as the final elimination tests, which assumed a rudimentary knowledge of algebra: "If one train travels 300 miles in one direction at 85 miles an hour and another train . . ." I gave it a try, but it was hopeless; I should have realized that my lack of mathematical knowledge would prevent me from becoming a special police officer. So I decided to join that unique institution, the Shanghai Volunteer Corps (SVC), which reinforced the SMP and, under the command of British officers, provided the International Settlement with a viable defense.

The Shanghai Volunteer Corps had been founded on April 4, 1854, in anticipation of increased attacks on the International Settlement by the T'ai P'ing revolutionaries. In 1939 its strength was about 2,000 men of twenty-seven different nationalities, including 200 officers.[3] It was a gentlemen's army and not easy for a refugee to fit in, since many of its members were very much involved in the social activities of the international community. But math was not a requirement, and I knew that my training in the *Schwarze Fähnlein*, the youth group I had belonged to in Germany, would make me a useful member.

When I filed my application and presented my letter of reference from

Commissioner Gordon, I hoped that I would not be assigned to the "Jewish" infantry company, whose members consisted primarily of Russian Jews, because I did not particularly care for the infantry. I was lucky; I was accepted as a driver in the transport company, where I was assigned to drive lorries and miscellaneous armored vehicles. There was no pay, but belonging to an active company was a mark of distinction. For me, however, it was the sumptuous tiffins that made the corps especially attractive. (I avoided the bar at headquarters, since I had no money with which to reciprocate and I did not want to be put in the position of having to refuse an offered drink.)

There was one minor problem. At age sixteen in Breslau I had once found the keys in my brother's car and had driven it around the block, but that was the extent of my driving experience. When I took the driver's seat in a truck and was told to drive, I pleaded that British lorries differed from those I was used to, so I was assigned to a short refresher course. The test was tough; it included driving through an obstacle course, and the instructor was allowed to give illegal orders and use any trick to provoke a failure. Shifting gears required double-clutching; clashing gears would automatically disqualify the applicant. Nevertheless, at the end of 1940 I passed my police driving test. I was jubilant. I was measured for my uniform and greatcoat, which supposedly were tailor-made, and I was issued boots and leg straps, bandoleer, revolver holster, hat, and both pith and steel helmets. I was surprised that the uniform fit fairly well, since I had been told by some friends that the standard question of the quartermaster was "How do you like your uniform, too large or too small?" I was also issued a wooden truncheon, and during riot control training I learned how to prevent an adversary from wresting it away and using it against me. I did not relish the idea of being put into a situation where I would have to use the truncheon to hit people over the head. Fortunately, as a driver, I never was put to that test.

It felt good wearing the British uniform, even though I still held a grudge against the British for trying to keep the Jewish refugees from going ashore in British-controlled ports on my way to Shanghai. Even drill was fun, and the switch from "model" German weapons to real guns—the British Lee Enfield—made me feel good. My Black Pennant paramilitary training had prepared me quite well.

Soon, I came to the attention of the company commander during one of the rifle target practices. After the squad had shot a rapid round of five shells from prone position, the sergeant approached the targets with his wire gauge to check how many bullets had scored and how far from the bull's-eye they had

Refugees being transported to camps upon arrival. Thirty-six years later, the author recognized himself in this photo, standing on the truck.
(From the author's collection)

Section of destroyed Chusan Road as we found it in 1939.
(From the author's collection)

Chusan Road after it was rebuilt and occupied by refugees.
(From the author's collection)

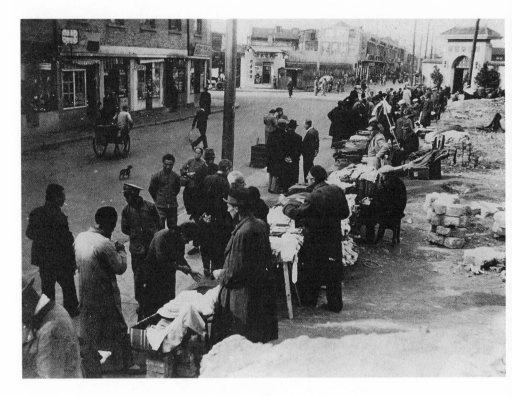

Refugees selling their belongings on Kungping Road.
(From the author's collection)

The author in 1941.

Chinese policemen "investigating suspicious goods": matzoth carried by a
Chinese delivery man. This shakedown took place on the corner of
Broadway and Wayside Road in Hongkew.
(Courtesy H. P. Eisfelder)

Japanese soldier checking Chinese ricksha passenger's ID card.
(From the author's collection)

Courtyard between lane houses serves as a community kitchen. (Photo by
Arthur Rothstein, courtesy UNRRA, United Nations Archives)

Four physicians share one consultation room. (Photo by Arthur Rothstein, courtesy UNRRA, United Nations Archives)

Transport Company of the SVC on parade in the drill hall. Author is fifth man from left. (From the author's collection)

Some of the Thirteenth Rover Scouts. Alfred Mittler, organizer of this group,
is in the center in full uniform; the author is at right in the second row.
(From the author's collection)

CARD OF IDENTIFICATION
No. 2649D
Date of
Issue 13 DEC 19

Photo with Signature of Bearer
ISSUED BY
THE INTERNATIONAL COMMITTEE FOR
THE ORGANIZATION OF EUROPEAN
IMMIGRANTS IN CHINA
SHANGHAI
2B 12, 41.-200

THE INTERNATIONAL COMMITTEE FOR
THE ORGANIZATION OF EUROPEAN
IMMIGRANTS IN CHINA
Certifies that   D.P.

ERNST
HEPPNER
is duly registered as a *bona fide*
Emigrant with us.
Born at   BRESLAU
Country   GERMANY
Date of Birth 4TH AUGUST 1921
Passport No. H922/36
issued at   BRESLAU
by   POLICE
Any further information will
be given by applying to our
Office at
SASSOON ARCADE—SASSOON HOUSE
NANKING ROAD

The author's IC or "Komor" pass,
a Jewish refugee's identification card.

AUFRUF

an alle juedischen Maenner und Frauen Shanghais

In ernstester Stunde wendet sich die JUEDISCHE GEMEINDE mit einem Notschrei an Euch. Eine furchtbare Not ist ueber einen grossen Teil der Emigranten hereingebrochen. Wie die Joint-Vertreter veroeffentlicht haben, hat die amerikanische Hilfe zur Zeit ausgesetzt. Hunger und Krankheit bedrohen viele unserer Brueder und Schwestern. Es muss deshalb alles unternommen werden, um rascheste Hilfe zu schaffen. Wir fordern deshalb alle Glaubensbrueder auf, sich mit den zunaechst Betroffenen solidarisch zu erklaeren. Um **SOFORTIGE** Hilfe zu bringen, fordert die JUEDISCHE GEMEINDE vorerst:

1. Jede Familie, die eigene Kueche fuehrt, soll taeglich mindestens **einen** Hilfsbeduerftigen mit einer Hauptmahlzeit versehen.

2. Familien, die eigene Kueche nicht fuehren, zahlen eine ihren Verhaeltnissen entsprechende monatliche Abloesung von mindestens Sh.-Dollar 30.- (dreissig).

3. Restaurateure, Kaffeehausbesitzer und Barbesitzer erheben von jedem Gast einen an die JUEDISCHE GEMEINDE abzufuehrenden Notstandszuschlag von 10%.

4. Lebensmittelhaendler (Provisions-Stores) erheben von jedem Kunden ebenso einen Notzuschlag von 5% fuer die bedraengten Glaubensbrueder.

5. Es ist Ehrenpflicht eins jeden vermoegenden Emigranten, seinen bedraengten Glaubensbruedern **SOFORT** mit einem grossen Geldbetrage beizuspringen.

Alle, die hier aufgerufen werden, werden ersucht, ihre Bereitwilligkeit unverzueglich in die Tat umzusetzen und dies der JUEDISCHEN GEMEINDE, 805 East Seward Road, Tel. 50192, persoenlich, schriftlich oder telefonisch mitzuteilen.

SHANGHAI, den 11. Januar 1942.

**Vorstand und Repraesentanz der
Juedischen Gemeinde**

The AUFRUF (Emergency Proclamation)
from the Jüdische *Gemeinde* to residents of the ghetto.

Japanese naval forces parading up Nanjing Road on Pearl Harbor Day,
December 8, 1941. Note swastika in window.
(From the author's collection)

Ghoya, "the King of the Jews," inspecting a ghetto checkpoint.
(Courtesy H. P. Eisfelder)

Refugee member of the Pao Chia checks the pass of another refugee
returning to the ghetto. (Courtesy H. P. Eisfelder)

Our wedding day.
(Photo by Gert Friedrichs)

Lane houses bombed by American B-29s on July 17, 1945.
(From the author's collection)

Members of the author's scout troop saluting the American
flag after our liberation on September 3, 1945. Author is between second
and third scout from left. (From the author's collection)

American officers saluting. Manuel Siegel of the JDC is fourth from left.
(From the author's collection)

Entrance to a *Heim* after V-J day. The flags were painted on the wall
by refugee artists. (Photo by Arthur Rothstein,
courtesy UNRRA, United Nations Archives)

Recreation hall in one of the *Heime* is operated by the refugees. Walter Koratkowski, uncle of the author's wife, is leaning against the wall at left rear. (Photo by Arthur Rothstein, courtesy UNRRA, United Nations Archives)

Room in a *Heim*. (Photo by Arthur Rothstein, courtesy
UNRRA, United Nations Archives)

Searching lists for names of survivors of Europe's extermination camps.
(Photo by Arthur Rothstein, courtesy UNRRA, United Nations Archives)

Ghoya's return to the ghetto: "So sorry, so sorry."
(Photo by Gert Friedrichs)

Personnel of A-4, Air Corps Supply, JUSMAG.
Col. Harry W. Atkinson is fourth from left; the author
third from right. (From a set of photographs by a U.S. Air Corps
photographer, presented to personnel leaving the command)

hit. Usually this took him only a few seconds, but when he came to my target, he stopped for quite a while and took repeated measurements. Shaking his head, he walked over to the lieutenant and consulted with him. Shortly, both of them went back to the target and repeated the measuring process. With an unbelieving look in their eyes they removed the target cover and came back to my position. "Jolly good show," they proclaimed, congratulating me on the unusual feat. All five bullets had scored in the center of the bull's-eye, making a single, large, almost perfectly round hole!

Small arms practice proved to be a challenge of a different sort. We were issued heavy, long-barreled Webley revolvers and learned to aim while raising the heavy guns, rapidly firing double action. The lieutenant watched. No matter how hard I tried, I could not coordinate the timing to start pulling the trigger while raising my arm to be ready to aim and fire when the gun reached the horizontal position. "What's the matter, driver? Your hand is shaking like a leaf," the lieutenant called out. I was embarrassed, but I got my chance during left-handed practice, when my score improved considerably. Being a southpaw, I had been forced by my teachers in Germany to write with my right hand. Although I became ambidextrous, my left arm remains the stronger one.

"Spit and polish" reigned of course, but it was the corps' coolies who did the polishing. After rifle drill, the company lined up with rifles held horizontally, and specially trained coolies would go from soldier to soldier, reaming out the rifle barrels.

One day the call came: "Rice riots in the city." The police could not control the population. The phone call that reached me in the store ordered immediate mobilization of the SVC and assembly in the drill hall. I rushed home to get into my uniform and within two hours reported to the company sergeant. About fifteen lorries were lined up inside the hall, machine guns mounted on their cab roofs. A squad of infantrymen, rifles at the ready, climbed onto the truck; the sergeant took his seat next to me. I started my engine and waited my turn as one lorry after another slowly made its way out the gate and into the street. I tried not to show my excitement, but I had a difficult time concealing it. When my turn came, I put the engine in gear, gave it a little gas, slowly let out the clutch and—the lorry lurched and the engine stalled. I heard rumbling from the soldiers behind me and noticed the frown on the sergeant's face. I restarted the engine, repeated the maneuver, and stalled again.

The company commander had kept a close eye on the lineup and now, riding crop under his left arm, came to my lorry and climbed up on the step.

As I nervously started the engine for the third time, the captain shouted, "You got the bloody hand brake set, driver. Don't you know what you're doing?" By that time I was not at all sure of what I was doing. I released the brake and once again tried to make a go of it. I was so nervous by then that my feet were shaking on the clutch and the accelerator. The lorry lurched forward in spurts, and the soldiers standing in the back yelled and swore at me, while the fellow at the machine gun on top the cab kept pounding on the roof.

Somehow I made it out of the drill hall, and under the direction of the sergeant I headed for the inner city, where most of the rice shops were located. Floods and hoarding had caused another of the periodical shortages of rice with a commensurate price increase, and the poor people had become restless. Thousands thronged the streets, pushing and shoving, preventing the rice shop owners from closing their stores and lowering the shutters. The task of the SVC was "to show the flag" and control the crowds should the police be overpowered. I carefully inched the lorry through this mass of humanity. I had to stay in the center of the narrow streets to avoid hitting any of the shop signs that hung in front of all houses and storefronts, leaving only a few inches of clearance between them and the roof of the lorry's cab. I leaned on my horn as I drove slowly through the crowds. Occasionally I would depress the clutch and hit the accelerator. The resulting engine roar usually scattered the people sufficiently for us to make some headway. Given my lack of experience, this turned out to be a most nerve-racking situation, and after several hours of driving, when things had quieted down, I was happy to get the squad and my lorry safely back to the drill hall.

Although we were not infantry, our company was not excluded from guard duty at the Garden Bridge, where Japanese and SVC soldiers stood guard, separated by perhaps 100 feet. At regular intervals I reported for my stint to stand at attention without moving a muscle or to parade back and forth. Parading for two hours in the summer heat caused more than one soldier to faint. The Garden Bridge carried perhaps the busiest foot traffic in the city. During the morning and evening hours thousands crossed this bridge to and from work, among them many of my friends. Seeing me, they made it a point to call out jokes or pull faces, trying to make me laugh. When I returned to the guard shack after my tour of duty, I learned that nothing quenches thirst better than a cold glass of beer.

One day during drill, Pit, one of my closest friends, a Rover Scout, and also a member of the SVC transport company, told me that Patrick Goharty (not his real name), one of our British members, wanted both of us to join him for tiffin after drill. Pit's full name was Heinz Bergmann, but his friends called him by his nickname. We had a lot in common, since he too had been a member of the *Schwarze Fähnlein*. He was often moody, and even though we were close, he would never confide in me what was bothering him. After the war ended, while I was in Nanjing, I learned that Pit had committed suicide, apparently in distress upon learning that the Nazis had murdered his whole family.

On this day, however, we left the drill hall and walked the few blocks to Patrick's office on Kiangse Road. He owned an import-export company and was evidently well off. Though many of the well-to-do owned their rickshas, Patrick owned a Vauxhall, and his chauffeur drove us to a restaurant in the inner city, overlooking the Whangpoo River. Typically for Shanghai, the restaurant had no great ambience but superb food. The three of us sampled five dishes, and Pit and I, hungry as we usually were, ate as much rice as possible. The conversation drifted to politics, and Pit and I found it easy to voice our opposition to the hated Japanese military government.

After the meal Patrick invited us for a boat ride, which was a real treat for us. The car took just minutes to get to the jetty, where we boarded a small but beautifully designed houseboat. Constructed of solid mahogany with brass fittings—polished immaculately by Liang, Patrick's boatman—it slept four, and the bar was well stocked with imported spirits. Liang expertly steered the boat away from the jetty, working his way through the maze of junks and sampans. I kept wondering why Patrick had invited us for tiffin and now for a boat ride on the Whangpoo. Pit had not told me that he had seen Patrick previously, or why, but it was obvious that they knew each other well and that Pit knew the purpose of this meeting. It didn't really matter; I had had an excellent meal, and Patrick was an exemplary host. Fascinated by the traffic on the Whangpoo, we sat in the bow of the boat, nursing our drinks.

Since Pit and I had both been members of the *Schwarze Fähnlein*, I was not surprised that the talk narrowed sharply to focus on my activities in Germany and my feelings toward Nazi Germany and its Japanese partner. As our conversation continued, however, it became apparent to me that I was being carefully but skillfully interrogated. How well did I know two specific persons, Patrick wanted to know. I was taken completely by surprise when he revealed that these two were suspected of being informers on the payroll of the Germans or the Japanese. Patrick was particularly interested in their movements, and I readily agreed to assist in keeping the two under surveillance and to report on their whereabouts and actions. Pit grinned at my almost furious reaction when Patrick offered a reward. "I told you he wouldn't take money either,"

Pit laughed. He knew that I would consider such an assignment a matter of honor and would not accept compensation for any anti-Nazi or anti-Japanese activities.

After Pit and I parted from Patrick, we quietly walked back to Hongkew, involved in our own thoughts. "We better not discuss this matter, and I mean not even between the two of us," Pit said, and I readily agreed. Thereafter, I met with Patrick occasionally, and the conversation centered primarily on the few known informers within the refugee community.

An easy way to ferret out informers was to invent and circulate a carefully worded *bonke* (slang for a rumor that was nonsensical or hard to believe) in order to incite the Kempetai, the feared Japanese secret police, into action. It was noteworthy that even Japanese civilians were duly respectful and apparently afraid of the Kempetai's rough behavior. On one occasion one of my friends circulated the *bonke* that a uniformed Japanese had been discovered shot to death and covered up with garbage in a residential area of Hongkew populated by Japanese civilians. *Bonkes* spread in Hongkew like wildfire, and it took little more than an hour for trucks loaded with gendarmes to arrive and encircle an entire block. The Kempetai obviously were dumfounded that there was no corpse, and since they had surrounded a residential block in which Japanese civilians lived, they could not follow their established procedure of starving out the entire block until the culprit could be found. These planted *bonkes* proved that the Japanese had paid informers within the refugee community; regrettably, so did the Nazis. By following the path of the *bonke* and by tracking the persons who heard and repeated it, we could often trace the leak.

At one meeting, after discussing the threat the Japanese posed to world peace, Patrick had a special request. Would I try to report on Japanese military checkpoints and movements on the outskirts of Shanghai? It was important to confirm the location and number of military camps reported to be east of Hongkew, near Woosung. Patrick did not have to ask me twice. As a nineteen-year-old, I found this work exciting and the height of adventure.

One Sunday, a group of the Thirteenth Rovers and some of the older scouts borrowed bikes to take a ride out into the countryside to play a popular scout game called "fox hunt" or "follow the hare." In Europe, we had loved to play this game on skis. One player, the "fox," would try to shake off the hunters, who were trying to separate the fox's ski tracks from those of the rest of the skiers. In summer, we used paper confetti or cut-up sheets of newspaper to mark the trail, but in Hongkew paper was often in short supply, even for sanitary purposes.

This time the fox, one of the younger scouts present, had decided to use rice instead of paper and had stuffed a few handfuls in his pockets. Heading out along the Whangpoo in the general direction of Woosung, we gave the fox a ten-minute lead and then tried to track him. Pedaling along, we peered down at the road surface, carefully checking every intersection to determine which direction the fox had gone. Passing through a small village where none of us had been before, we found chickens fighting over some scattered rice. We saw nothing but typical rice fields, with open spaces to the right and left of the road. Then, coming around a bend, we saw what must have been the ruins of warehouses and, suddenly, barracks and tents stretching from horizon to horizon. Unable to read road signs, we had entered a restricted military area. We could not turn back, because we had to find the fox. We found him soon enough—at a checkpoint, surrounded by a squad of Japanese soldiers. My friends and I had gotten ourselves into a precarious situation, and we all knew it. We were in the middle of nowhere, at the edge of what appeared to be a military installation, surrounded by soldiers, and with little means of communication.

In addition to arresting suspicious foreigners in their area, the guards, as we found out later, were incensed that our fox had thrown rice on the road. Just as bread, the basic food, has strong symbolic meanings for Europeans, so has rice for the Orientals.

A truck arrived, and unceremoniously our bikes were tossed up into it. We jumped in too, without any prodding from the menacing bayonets. The truck took us to a military building and rolled to a stop in a field behind it. Finding foreigners in their midst must have been a highly unusual event. As soldiers came running from all directions, I turned around to a very frightening sight. We were standing in front of the targets of a rifle range. An officer brought a Chinese to talk with us, and Fritz, who spoke the best Chinese, tried to explain that we were Boy Scouts, just playing a game. It was hopeless to try to communicate with the Chinese man, probably a prisoner of war from a distant province, whose dialect was not familiar. Fritz did finally understand that the Japanese, assuming we might be spies, were trying to ascertain our nationality.

We normally carried identification cards issued by one of the refugee committees, but never our old German passports. The swastika on the cover page had prompted many of us to get rid of those passports, and many of them had expired anyway. Furthermore, consular protection was meaningless in Shanghai, where a Japanese soldier could stop an individual on the street for any suspicious act, pull his automatic pistol, and fire a shot through his head with no questions asked. My knowledge of what could happen was based on a story about one refugee who, riding his bicycle along Yangtzepoo Road, was accidentally hit by a military truck. Foolishly, he attempted to write down the vehicle's license number, whereupon the truck stopped and then backed up over his bike. A soldier got out, grabbed him, and forced him into the truck. A day later his body was seen floating in the Whangpoo.

When the sergeant motioned us to empty our pockets, either by watching what Fritz was doing or by instinct, we did not turn over our ID cards. Fritz, knowing we had no options, decided to say that we were Germans. As soon as he said the word *Deutzkahs* (Japanese for *Deutsch*), the expression on the face of the officer changed. We were told to wait, all the while surrounded by the soldiers, rifles at the ready. It seemed we waited an eternity, standing in the boiling sun. I tried to stand erect, but my knees were almost buckling and my stomach was doing flipflops. Despite the unbearable heat, I was shivering. How did I get myself into this situation? Most likely the Japanese would use us for target practice. Was it worth it all? I knew nobody would ever find out what had happened to our group, and no one would ever find our bodies. Of course, if I got out of this mess I would go straight to Pat and report my discovery. But was that really worth it? There must be a way out. We were not permitted to speak to one another. As soon as one of us made a sound, a soldier would point a bayonet at his stomach. Running was hopeless; we would not get far. Any thought of overpowering them was silly. But Fritz had played his cards correctly, bluffing that we still were German citizens. After an hour or so, which seemed much longer, a staff car pulled up, and two officers emerged.

Many Japanese field-grade officers had been to Germany for advanced training, and these two spoke German haltingly. After a lengthy interrogation held in German, the officers seemed satisfied that we indeed were who we claimed to be. I noticed that during the interrogation one officer issued some whispered instruction to a lower-ranking officer. Apparently he was dispatched to the headquarters building; he returned shortly and, reporting to the colonel, repeatedly shook his head. We were able to explain the nature of the "fox hunt," and after repeated promises to the colonel that we would meet again and teach him German, he ordered our bikes returned, and we got out of that area as fast as we could pedal. Later on I learned from Patrick, who obviously had a contact in the German consulate, that the Japanese lieutenant had phoned there in an attempt to verify our group's identity. Luckily for us it was a Sunday, and there was no one in the office who could understand the Japanese and thus deny our German citizenship.

In its issue of December 21, 1945, the *North China Daily News* published a story headlined "Local Neutral Boy Scouts Worked Underground for City, Official Discloses." The paper described how some scout groups and individual scouts "had largely contributed to the welfare of Allied civilian camp internees and Shanghailanders residing outside the camps. Working under the British Boy Scouts Association, the scouts carried on throughout in a splendid manner and the work they did for the good of the community can never be wholly recorded." The paper was not privy to the incident with the Japanese, but my friends and I who were involved in it, as well as some of the other Jewish scouts, at the end of the war received a commendation and a medal for "services rendered during occupation."

9

Survival

Although the shock of the transition from comfortable, well-to-do conditions in Europe to a far more primitive existence was understandably great, most of the refugees retained their optimism and good spirits. "We are here only temporarily, we have relatives in America, and our immigration quota number will be called up soon," they often repeated to themselves.

More than half the refugees made every possible effort to reorganize their lives on a self-supporting basis.[1] Everyone who possessed more than he or she needed for sustenance was rich, and everyone who had an income to cover basic needs was well off. Some refugees found living quarters in Hong-kew in partially destroyed houses that were hastily rebuilt by the owners or, quite often, by the refugees themselves. Out of the rubble a new settlement emerged. Entire streets and lanes were cleared and the houses rebuilt with material from the ruins. Grocery stores and delicatessens, sidewalk cafés and tailor shops opened. An area of several blocks around Chusan Road became known as "Little Vienna."

Most of these houses had originally been built for low-income families. Each house had, on the average, about ten rooms, the largest ones downstairs and the rest on the second floor. Some rooms measured no more than eight by eight feet.[2] The houses belonged to foreign investment corporations, which had built and then leased them at fairly reasonable prices. Until the bombardment by the Japanese in 1937, each one had been occupied by two or more Chinese families. Now, with shelter at a premium, the refugees rented rooms for U.S.$1.50 up to $15 a month. Rental prices did not keep up with inflation, because the Shanghai Municipal Council had adopted rent control.

Still, whole families lived in a single room, with several families in one house sharing the primitive facilities. The walls were paper thin, and you whispered unless you wanted the whole house to hear what you were saying. Standards of etiquette were impossible to maintain when men and women were forced to meet in the narrow hallways at all hours of the day or night, in all stages of undress, on their way to or from the "honey bucket." Few houses in Hongkew had a toilet; close to the entrance of most houses was this ubiquitous bucket with a seat on top. Every morning a coolie would go noisily from door to door with a pushcart and empty the smelly buckets, the contents to be sold as fertilizer or "nightsoil," as it was called.

The general atmosphere of hopelessness caused some errant behavior that resulted in an increase in the number of divorces. The majority tried to maintain a level of decorum, but quarrels and fights were unavoidable in these close living quarters. On the other hand, it is noteworthy that this environment led to a high degree of camaraderie and interdependence. In cases of need or sickness, help was always available from a neighbor.

The houses were not freestanding, and only the front row faced the street. There were houses behind houses, connected by a grid of narrow "lanes" or alleys. Refugee children played in these lanes with Chinese children, picking up Pidgin English and Chinese. The houses had been built for a population with minimum physical needs and even fewer expectations. In summer, when the sun beat on the roofs and reflected from the walls, the lanes and the houses felt like ovens. Still, they did provide minimum shelter for a large populace.

The water supply came from the Whangpoo River and passed through a purification plant, yet in too many places raw sewage seeped into the joints of the water pipes, and everything that had come in contact with water had to be washed in potassium permanganate. All drinking water had to be boiled; it was purchased from a neighborhood Chinese water shop. Laundry and dishes were washed with cold water and soap substitutes.

How were we able to make a living? Some refugees received financial help from abroad, but quite a few succeeded in becoming economically independent and accomplished this almost entirely by their own resourcefulness and energy. It took lots of ingenuity. For instance, a gadget that sharpened razor blades provided its owner with a source of income. Few men could afford to buy razor blades, and I, like many others, would take him the half-dozen blades I owned and get them sharpened again and again. Other enterprising refugees discovered a different moneymaking scheme. Relatives writing to their loved ones in Shanghai usually enclosed one or two international reply coupons that the recipient could exchange at the main post office for an air mail stamp or an air letter. In the post office they encountered refugee traders offering a small amount of cash for the coupons. The trader then would sell these coupons in Hongkew at a premium.

Many refugees spread a blanket on the sidewalks of Kungping Road to sell their belongings to the Chinese public, who had never before dreamed of being able to acquire such European "treasures." Like every Bar Mitzvah boy in Germany, I had received several Mont Blanc fountain pens. I did not have to stand around very long before my fountain pen became a new status symbol for a Chinese businessman. After I had sold my camera, my mother was able to sell her custom-tailored Persian lamb coat to the Far East manager of the Standard Oil Company. The money we received paid for our rent and food for about three years.

Our community was unique in other ways. Against all odds, in the face of insurmountable obstacles and the never ending struggle for a meal, the demand for cultural activities was constant. Several dozen periodicals were published by enterprising refugees. There were literary gazettes, two monthly medical newsletters for physicians (in German, English, and Chinese), numerous Yiddish publications, and three daily newspapers. Those of us who were lucky enough to work and earn enough money not to have to live in one of the camps had opportunities for various diversions. We attended countless lectures, literary and musical recitals, and chamber concerts and could listen to German-language radio programs. Over the years we had our choice among the more than sixty plays produced. We especially enjoyed the operettas that were performed by actors who once had been well known on the stages of Vienna and Berlin.

A variety of cafés served excellent Viennese pastries. When it was not too hot, one gentleman made a modest living peddling an assortment of these pastries. He purchased them early in the morning, stacked them in a wooden case, and made daily rounds of his established customers in downtown office buildings. Café Louis, the Corso Garden, and the Roof Garden were three of the many popular places where one could sit and have a cup of coffee while reading a newspaper provided free for the patrons. In the evening the more affluent refugees could go for dinner to any number of restaurants, such as the White Horse, which was patterned after the famous inn by the same name in Austria.

Schools and educational institutions were established. A craftsmen's guild and the Organization for Rehabilitation through Training (ORT) trade school trained almost 400 students, with tutoring offered in almost any subject. The Jewish Educational Society, which had been founded in 1922, supported approximately 120 refugee pupils and provided school fees and breakfast. There were schools for children of all ages. I, however, belonged to the "lost" generation; I was of an age at which schooling was no longer available, so I was unable to continue my formal education.

The Embankment Building, which had served as a temporary reception center, filled up quickly, and refugees arriving after the spring of 1939 were transported directly to one of five camps, where conditions were extremely primitive. These camps, euphemistically called by the German name Heime, meaning homes, eventually housed and supported about 2,500 destitute refugees who could not afford to rent even a little room. Most of them were over forty years of age and without marketable skills, or they were in ill health. Among these poorest of the poor lived Walter Koratkowski, Illo's uncle. He literally owned nothing more than what he had brought with him in his two suitcases. Whenever he came to his brother's home for a meal, the primitive living conditions in the Heime dominated the conversation.

The Heime housed up to 150 men, women, and children in one large room, divided by sheets strung on ropes and furnished with double steel bunks. Each "personal" area was no larger than the aisle in front of the bed. The committee that operated the camps had furnished each person two sheets, a blanket, and a tin pot. Suitcases were used as tables, and some families had a stool, but there were not even nails in the walls to hang up clothing. The Heime had showers, but some had no washbasins or lavatories. Those facilities were outdoors, and it was a long walk to wash or use the latrines. The atmosphere and the general conditions were depressing. Light and air were at a premium; there were no facilities to clean or repair clothing, and no storage was available for the residents' few precious possessions. In order not to break up their families, men, women, and children lived together in the same room. The immediate transition from a cabin on an ocean liner to these large crowded dormitories of the Heime was traumatic.

Fearing that inflation would continue to rise, the refugees tried to hold on to their personal belongings, selling only enough to satisfy their immediate needs. They watched helplessly as the mildew created by the hot, humid climate caused continuing deterioration of their clothing. As time went by, their possessions dwindled to their last shirt and pair of shoes.

Also as time went on, the three Hs—hunger, heat and humidity—took their toll. In August 1942 thirty-one persons died of heat prostration. Death was caused not only by poor environmental and sanitary conditions but also by inadequate nutrition. The inmates were hungry, and not just for a day or a week or a month; since their arrival in Shanghai they had not received sufficient nourishment. Fathers and husbands became desperate when they sold the last item of their personal belongings and realized they would no longer be able to supplement the food their families received from the committee.

Eventually there were inmates who could no longer leave the *Heime* because they had neither shirts nor shoes to wear. Cut up burlap bags served as pants. During the summer months, when the heat would melt the asphalt, some were forced to stay indoors because they did not own even straw sandals like those worn by ricksha coolies. It was scandalous to see these poor people in tattered rags, barely able to walk, slowly moving about in the vicinity of the *Heime*. It reflected very badly not only on the refugee community but also on all foreigners.

The inmates of the *Heime* found themselves on the bottom of the social ladder. All of them had led productive lives in Europe, many were well-known and respected professionals and intellectuals. To be idle was destructive. They were constantly arguing and blaming the relief committees for the sad state of affairs. It was unavoidable, under the circumstances, that as time wore on many of the inmates grew careless about their appearance, sullen, and impassive; a few became disciplinary problems. Although there was complete individual freedom, provisions were made to provide separate housing facilities for those unable to comply with even minimum community standards.

At night the *Heime* were patrolled by refugees who acted as security guards. Though I do not remember ever seeing a drunken Chinese on the streets, drunken Japanese, especially among the military, were a common sight. One of my friends, a security guard at the Seward Road *Heim*, told me that on more than one occasion Japanese soldiers, stone drunk, came singing loudly down the street and made their way through the entrance. Inside, they became rambunctious, threatening people with their guns or bayonets. The guards had learned that it was useless to try to get rid of them in a friendly way, so they neatly solved the problem by stepping behind each drunken soldier and whacking him over the head with a club wrapped in rags. One at a time they would carry the drunks outside the gate and prop them up against the wall. The soldiers usually woke up the next morning with a king-sized headache, not knowing what had happened to them.

The *Heim* population did not remain static. Some inmates found jobs and, craving privacy above all else, left the camps and rented a room. Some who could have left stayed on—afraid to leave the food kitchens and medical care—and did nothing. Others who had lived in rented rooms and then lost their jobs, or who could no longer afford medical services, moved back into the camps. Used to being productive all their lives, some refugees became sullen and dehumanized by the process of trying to obtain help. Eventually they were forced to resign themselves to becoming *schnorrers*, a Yiddish term for someone asking for a handout.

Throughout history, Jews have been threatened and felt the need to band together and organize. Some Shanghai Jewish organizations had been in existence since the influx of refugees from the Bolshevik revolution after 1917. The oldest was the *Chevra Kadisha*, the burial society. Its members were volunteers who prepared the bodies for burial and carried out the details of funerals according to Jewish laws. There was also the Hebrew Relief Society (formed in 1916), the Jewish Education Society (1922), and various Zionist organizations. In addition, there was the WIZO (Women's International Zionist Organization) and a Council of Jewish Women, as well as an active B'nai B'rith (Sons of the Covenant, the largest Jewish service organization). Once an organization had been founded and funded, its operation continued even if the original cause or purpose no longer existed. When the refugee influx started, all the existing organizations tried to help in one way or another, but none was prepared for the number of arrivals or the length of their stay. Though well intentioned, neither these groups nor newer ones were equipped for the task.

Depending on one's perspective, three to six organizations with their committees and subcommittees, each with its own political or religious orientation, became involved in assisting the refugees. One of the first newly established major organizations, the International Committee for the Organization of European Immigrants in China (called the IC, or the Komor Committee after Paul Komor), was originally organized to assist refugees from Austria. In 1942 when German and Austrian passports were no longer renewed and all Jews lost their citizenship, the IC became their intermediary with the consulates. The IC attempted to register all refugees and issue its own identification cards.

Subsequently, the CFA (Committee for the Assistance of European Refugees in Shanghai) was organized under the direction of Kurt Marx and a few assistants and chaired by Michel Speelman, a prominent Shanghai Jewish resident. Its purpose was to assist the newcomers with food, shelter and medical help on a temporary basis until they were able to continue their journey to their final destination, or until they were able to get settled. But there was no professional staff, and the caseworkers were usually people who happened to stop by looking for work. When Dr. Marx left for the United States late in 1939, the committee staff grew to three managers as well as additional assistants and caseworkers. A bureaucracy was created that wallowed in superfluous paperwork and did not function well; favoritism and nepotism were unavoidable.

The maintenance and direction of these organizations was wasteful, chaotic, and counterproductive.[3] A subsidiary of the CFA, called the "Kitchen Fund," was established and charged with feeding the refugees but unfortunately did not improve the overall operation. Its staff increased until it numbered almost 500, and staff members became callous and careless. Sometimes incorrect quantities of ingredients were calculated, and recipients who normally stood in line with their bowls for hours had to wait still longer until another batch of food was prepared. Complaints were heard that the food ran out because the staff had hoarded too much to take home to their own families. Forgetting that they themselves were recipients, staff members acted as if they were the donors and had been entrusted merely with the management and distribution of the food. Their attitude became one of self-importance, and the people they were supposed to serve had no one to appeal to. The kitchen staff regarded the food lines as an unavoidable nuisance, to be suffered only in order to keep their jobs. And this attitude not only prevailed among the workers but unfortunately permeated into management. It was miserable for recipients to stand in line either in the broiling heat or in the rainy season. It was a waste of time especially for those who were job hunting or had to be at work at a specific time. This intolerable situation led to strife, abuse, and arguments between the committee personnel and the recipients and eventually caused cheating for food. Some refugees, afraid of what might be in store for them in the future, asked the committee for assistance even though they did not yet need it. Consequently, some caseworkers viewed every applicant as a swindler, and the committee was forced to increase its staff of investigators.

Naturally, the refugees themselves were eager for jobs in any of these organizations, preferably with the newly created Kitchen Fund. Caseworkers usually had spare food. Caseworkers investigated families who had requested extra assistance, which meant finding out if indeed, hidden in their suitcases, they had any belongings they could sell. A refugee needing a pair of shoes really had a problem. Socks were not difficult to obtain from the committee, but shoes required an investigation. Shoes were considered a major commodity because large sizes were not available in stores; they often had to be hand-made by a cobbler. Since my mother was employed by the CFA, she was in charge of some investigations involving children and persons in ill health. Though she had no background in social work, she was an extraordinarily efficient business-woman with a lot of common sense. Nightly she would tell me the stories of bungling and inefficiencies she encountered. She was very upset with the mismanagement and was biding her time until she could find another way to make a living.

A nursery, laundry, shoe repair shop, tailor shop, and bakery were badly needed. The approximately 8,000 loaves of bread needed daily were furnished by two privately owned bakeries. The committees claimed that they would have liked to find innovative means to reduce spending by assisting refugees to start small businesses but that they were never able to attract sufficient capital for these ventures. In fact, Sassoon had given money to a revolving fund, some of which was supposed to be used for this purpose. But enterprising refugees who lacked sufficient capital to start small businesses of their own often found their proposals rejected by the early committee; clearly, some of the local Jewish residents did not want competition. Thousands of Jews living in poverty received subsistence, shelter, and food for nine cold winters and ten hot, humid, disease-ridden summers. If the wealthy resident Jews or the Jewish organizations in the United States and England had made venture capital available, more refugees could have become self-sufficient instead of languishing in the Heime.

A refugee medical association had a roster of 200 members who cooperated with the committees in setting up three hospitals: the first one on Washing Road, a second in the Ward Road Heim, and an isolation ward in the Chaoufong Heim. Considering the lack of equipment and medication and the primitive conditions (there was not even hot water for bathing), the hospitals were run well and staffed by dedicated professionals.

Despite the unavoidable quarrels between individuals caused by the primitive living conditions and despite their different backgrounds and origins, the religious, social, and economic ties among the refugees brought about the need for the development of a community organization. These fearful, suddenly impoverished, and varied people, the majority middle-aged or older, many having had traumatic experiences in concentration camps and having lost all their possessions, tried to recreate the structures of their past. In October 1938 the Jüdische Gemeinde (Jewish Communal Association) was formed and succeeded in establishing an organization of persons elected to represent the interests of various elements of the community. Democratic elections for the board of directors were held early in 1941. Twenty-one representatives were elected, including my future father-in-law; they in turn elected from their number the board of directors with seven members. Kurt Redlich was elected chairman of the board. These elections have historic significance because, according to historian David Kranzler, they were probably the first democratic elections held anywhere in East Asia.

In the beginning, the primary function of the *Jüdische Gemeinde* was to provide for the religious and secular needs of the three factions—orthodox, conservative, and liberal—of Judaism. Later it was expanded to provide basic Jewish educational services and, most important, a legal department that operated an arbitration court. Disputes were brought to this court, and arbitration was binding on the parties involved, though provision was made for appeals. The arbitration board became the legal backbone of our community.

On the basis of the Chinese civil code, the legal department provided for birth and death certificates, marriage and divorce certificates. Since the legal requirements for a wedding ceremony according to Chinese law did not coincide with those of Jewish law, the *Jüdische Gemeinde* provided its members with a civil ceremony as required by the Chinese civil code, performed by one of its lawyers, and a religious ceremony performed by a rabbi. The legal department issued a very colorful Chinese document certifying that the wedding was performed in accordance with Chinese law, which governed the stateless refugees. This document was recognized by the authorities in Shanghai and supposedly all over the world.[4] The *Jüdische Gemeinde* did not perform weddings for mixed marriages, or for those who declined a religious ceremony.

The refugee community originally had two orthodox rabbis, Karl-Heinz Sober and Josef Zeitlin; a Russian Ashkenazi rabbi, whose name happened to be Meier Ashkenazi, retained the post of chief rabbi. In time they were joined by two liberal rabbis, Georg Kantorowski and Willy Teichner. Rabbi Ashkenazi presided over the Beth Din, the Jewish religious court, and one of the orthodox refugee rabbis became a member.[5] The Russian rabbinate did not approve of liberal services as practiced in Germany; however, despite their veto, the liberal-conservative groups planned religious services for the first High Holy Days. Although one of the seasonal typhoons had just dumped torrents of water on Shanghai, the services, held in a movie theater, were well organized and attended by an overflow crowd. A dozen or so rickshas were kept busy ferrying the people across the flooded streets. The income from the ticket sales was used to defray the cost of the services and to support the functions of the *Jüdische Gemeinde.*

For two years Shanghai's Jewish leaders repeatedly pleaded with the JDC to dispatch a social worker to Shanghai. The pressing needs of great numbers of Jews desperately trying to leave Europe, however, left Shanghai's refugees with very low priority. Eventually, the criticism leveled against the local committees reached the JDC in the United States. Finally, in May 1941, at the request of the U.S. State Department, the JDC sent one of its most capable staff members, Laura Margolis, to assist the American consulate in Shanghai and try to speed up the processing of applications for emigration to the United States. Margolis was also charged with investigating refugee complaints and reporting on the general situation.

Arriving about three years after the first wave of refugees, she immediately realized that it was imperative to try to make order out of chaos. Most important, she needed to check the disbursement of funds previously transmitted by the JDC. The JDC office in New York at first denied her requests for permission to set up a temporary office and to assume the responsibility of coordinating the relief effort; only after repeated reports and ultimatums was permission granted. It was a hopeless task for one person, however, no matter how skilled, to sort out the mess caused by the local relief organizations, and an uphill fight against Shanghai Jewish leaders who wanted to retain control of the funds and resented any attempt to reorganize the committee structure and to streamline operations. Upon Margolis's insistence, therefore, the JDC dispatched an assistant, Manuel Siegel, who arrived at the end of November 1941.

One day in the summer of 1941 my mother came home and told me about meeting an extraordinary woman whom she admiringly called "the American lady." She readily recognized Margolis's skills and her sensitivity to the refugees' plight. My mother decided to leave the Speelman Committee, as the CFA had come to be called, and go to work for the JDC. She considered it a great tragedy that Margolis had not been on the scene in 1939. With her insight and experience, the JDC surely would have assisted more refugees to become productive rather than existing on handouts for many years.

Despite her wealth of experience in dealing with refugee problems in other parts of the world, Margolis had never encountered conditions as chaotic as those she found in Shanghai; it was a community in despair. She declared that the struggle to earn a living which confronted the refugees was probably unparalleled in the world. There was not a single professional social worker to direct the relief effort and no strategic plan. The committees were reluctant to relinquish their authority and to follow one of her first suggestions: namely, to pool their resources. She was also faced with groups of hostile and frightened Heim inmates. These refugees were not only malnourished but had been humiliated and deprived of self-respect by the methods employed by the CFA. Margolis was quite outspoken about Captain A. Herzberg, who had been employed by Michel Speelman to run the CFA. Herzberg was accustomed to working with Chinese coolies, and one of Siegel's reports states that the refugees had been treated worse than coolies.[6] The salary of a kitchen employee was about U.S.$1.00 per month, so it was not surprising that hunger and poverty caused some of them to help themselves to food supplies from the storeroom.

While there were many Russian individuals who cared deeply about the refugees, after the arrival of the Polish Jews from Japan, some of their leaders insisted on giving more relief to the Polish and less to the German and Austrian refugees; in fact, they refused to consider any plan to aid the Germans and Austrians. This issue split the Ashkenazi community, and feelings became so heated that in some instances brothers were not talking to each other. The group that differed with Boris Topas, chairman of the Ashkenazi community, organized itself into yet another committee, called Central Jewcom, which assumed the responsibility for raising funds to feed 500 German children.

Under Margolis's guidance the camp kitchens slowly turned the most repellent rations into something minimally palatable. Early in 1942, with all of Shanghai occupied by the Japanese, a Mr. Levenspiel came to see her. He was an engineer who had observed the terribly inefficient ovens used to cook the food. He had calculated that out of every 60 Chinese cents, 50 were spent on coal consumption, leaving only 10 cents for nutrition. For two years he had tried to tell the CFA that their kitchens should be scrapped and more efficient ovens installed. Typically, until he met Margolis, no one had listened to him. Levenspiel had a plan ready for a simple, efficient kitchen with the capacity to feed 10,000 people at one time. The key ingredient for the construction of his kitchen was a special type of steam boiler, and Levenspiel, who had lived in Shanghai for many years, knew of such a boiler lying unused on the grounds of a British company. When Margolis asked the British employee in charge to make the boiler temporarily available for the kitchen's operation, he refused. Knowing that all British property was going to be confiscated by the Japanese, she enlisted the help of a Mrs. Nogami, who not only was a friend of Fritz Brahn, a wealthy local Jew, but also had a very prominent position as interpreter to the chief of the Kempetai. Nogami procured the necessary removal permit, and the Japanese supervisor of the British company gave Margolis permission to "borrow" the boiler. The redesigned kitchen was dedicated in December of 1942.

After Pearl Harbor, as an enemy alien, Margolis had to register with the Japanese occupation forces. She recognized the need to get to know the Japanese mentality and accepted the fact that she would have to work within this framework. She established an excellent working relationship with Captain Koreshige Inuzuka, chief of the Japanese Naval Landing Party in charge of the Bureau for Jewish Affairs. Inuzuka offered his full cooperation and help in her efforts to aid the Jewish refugees. Indeed, Margolis once remarked that her main problem was not the Japanese; it was trying to deal with the leaders of the Shanghai Jewish community.

Until the outbreak of hostilities in the Pacific, the JDC had on a regular schedule cabled funds to Michel Speelman of the CFA. Fortunately, anticipating the possibility of a war, Laura Margolis had made it one of her priorities to "sell" the financial power of the JDC to the local Jewish leadership. Repeatedly, she attempted to persuade this group of local leaders to advance funds in order to provide a cushion until the arrival of the cables, personally guaranteeing the resources of the JDC. Her foresight paid off, for a short while at least. When cables ceased to arrive from the JDC, some money was advanced by several wealthy members of the Shanghai Jewish community.

Incredibly, however, it appeared that only vague contingency plans had been made by the New York office for the impending war. Unlike other American Jewish organizations, which maintained communication with the Jewish community in Shanghai via neutral countries, the American JDC felt bound to honor the restrictions on communications imposed by the U.S. State Department under the "Trading with the Enemy Act," which prohibited all communication and transmission of monies to countries under enemy occupation. After Pearl Harbor the JDC ceased to transmit funds and did not dare to take a hint from a sympathetic U.S. Treasury Department official to send cables via neutral countries. No more JDC funds and no more loan guarantees were cabled to Shanghai.[7]

This strict interpretation of the letter of the law had catastrophic effects on the 8,000 refugees still dependent upon the committee for food. The staff of almost 500 refugees serving the camps was discharged. Yet most continued to work, without pay, presumably to retain their food ration. A special committee, the Kitchen Fund Consortium, was organized to deal with this emergency.

By that time, Margolis was faced with the fact that money had completely run out, and she encountered constant resistance to her attempts to borrow money against future payment by the JDC. Since most members of the wealthy Sephardic community were British and therefore enemy aliens, their bank accounts had been frozen, so Margolis was unable to get any more help from them. One of the leaders of the Sephardic community commented that since the Japanese had taken Shanghai, they should also be the ones to worry about the refugees.

In January 1942, Margolis called an emergency conference at the Jüdische Gemeinde and told its leadership that there was only enough food to feed 8,000 persons on relief for four more days or 4,000 people for eight days. This decision, she said, should be made by the refugees themselves. The refugee leadership agreed, and on January 10, 1942, 4,000 refugees were categorically cut from the relief rolls.

The Jüdische Gemeinde began to play a more important role than before, and on January 11, 1942, its board of officers issued an Aufruf (an emergency proclamation or summons), which was posted throughout Hongkew.

To All Jewish Men and Women of Shanghai

In its darkest hour the Jüdische Gemeinde is turning to you with a cry for help. A dreadful emergency has arisen affecting a large number of emigrants. The representatives of the JDC have announced that aid from America has ceased. Hunger and diseases are threatening our brothers and sisters. We have to do whatever is necessary to come to their immediate aid. We therefore call on our brothers in faith to declare their solidarity with the victims. To provide IMMEDIATE aid, the Jüdische Gemeinde issues the following challenge:

1. Each family that cooks its own meals shall daily provide a main meal for at least one needy person.
2. Families that do not cook their own meals shall pay a proportionate share of at least CN$30 (about U.S.$1.25) per month, depending upon their circumstances.
3. Owners of restaurants, coffee houses, and bars shall collect from each guest a 10 percent emergency surcharge payable to the Jüdische Gemeinde.
4. Owners of provision stores [groceries] shall collect from each customer an emergency surcharge of 5 percent for the needy coreligionist brothers.
5. It is the duty of honor of each emigrant with means to help impoverished brothers in faith IMMEDIATELY with a sizable donation.

All persons called upon by this summons are asked to prove their compliance by writing, telephoning, or appearing in person at the *Jüdische Gemeinde*, 805 East Seward Road, Tel. 50192.[8]

Though the response to this proclamation was quite favorable and helped alleviate the problem for a limited number of refugees, it was insufficient to improve the conditions for all those who had been receiving their food from the committee's kitchen.

To economize further, the staff of the committee was reduced drastically, and in April my mother received a letter:

28. April 1942

My dear Mrs. Heppner,

With reference to our conference we herewith confirm your discharge as of 1. May, 1942.

As agreed you will receive the extra loaf of bread and your food card for an additional four weeks. After that period, would you please contact your case worker for any assistance needed. We want to thank you very much for the services you have rendered the committee and remain,

very respectfully yours,
(signed) Laura L. Margolis, Manuel Siegel

The people in the *Heime* grew more restless, and the situation became extremely serious. It was pointed out to Margolis that should the situation get out of hand in Hongkew, the Kempetai—which was responsible for the security of Hongkew and was an especially brutal military unit—would be called in to quiet any riots. Inuzuka expressed his concern to Margolis and hoped that the Jewish people would help her feed the refugees. He promised cooperation and released some of the previously frozen JDC funds. He also took an unusual step and released 5,000 sacks of cracked wheat that Margolis had earlier requested from the Red Cross. Margolis stated that by taking this action the Japanese had done more for the refugees than for any other group in need of help. Of course, they were not willing to take any special responsibility for the Jewish refugees at this point, since Shanghai was filled with hundreds of thousands of poor of all nationalities. But the Japanese were most anxious to avoid any trouble at a time when they were responsible for controlling the whole of Shanghai.

Help also came from the Quakers, who worked with the residents of a *Heim* housing approximately 1,000 people; they taught them English and took over the clothing distribution. Margolis reported: "There was an unbelievable amount of activity and life within the refugee community at a time when they were hungrier than they had ever been before."

There was no love lost between Inuzuka and either the leaders of the International Committee or members of the Speelman Committee, so the *Jüdische Gemeinde*, the only organization really representing the refugees, was thrust into the foreground. One of its directors, Lutz Wachsner, conceived of a project he called *Patenschaft* (sponsorship). He figured that it cost about three cents (U.S.) per day to feed one refugee and began working on a plan to canvass the whole Jewish community to assist in the relief effort.

Margolis realized that something very dramatic would have to occur to stir the Sephardic and the Ashkenazi Jews out of their lethargy. She and Siegel had avoided any publicity, realizing that the Japanese military would be embarrassed and frown on it. But now, despite the risks to their own safety, they decided to break the story. According to their report to the JDC, on January 16, 1942, the *Shanghai Times* ran the full story, headlined "Hungry Starving Refugees in Hongkew."[9]

The Kempetai was outraged and issued an order for the arrest of Margolis and Siegel. Even Inuzuka phoned Margolis to express his anger that any news about "disorder" in Shanghai had been published. The two JDC representatives were called to the Japanese Consulate to explain their actions, and only through the intervention of Mrs. Nogami was the order for their arrest rescinded.

To complicate the financial situation further, not only for the relief effort but for everyone living in Shanghai, in June 1942 the Japanese puppet government under "President of China" Wang Ching-wei took all Chinese National currency (*loh fapi*—old money) off the market and issued its own Central Reserve Bank of Nanking notes (*sin fapi*—new money) at a 2 to 1 rate. As expected, the cost of living doubled overnight.

During this critical time Margolis had earned the respect of the Japanese authorities, and when many enemy aliens were arrested and sent to a POW camp, her internment was delayed until February 25, 1943. The following July, she feigned illness and was sent to Shanghai General Hospital. Although the hospital was under Japanese supervision, she managed to stay in touch with the refugee committee.

In the short time she was in Shanghai, Margolis accomplished much of what she had set out to do. She was finally repatriated to the United States in September of 1943. In her detailed report to the JDC she not only described the grave situation in Shanghai but also explained that she had guaranteed half a million dollars of the JDC's money to the Shanghai Jewish leadership to repay them for monies they were advancing until communication could be reopened. She immediately went to Sweden to continue her work.

Conditions among the refugees in Shanghai remained critical, however. Their desperate situation is confirmed by a letter of June 15, 1943, from the Geneva office of the International Committee of the Red Cross to its delegation in Washington, D.C., citing a report from an ICRC field delegate:

This report clearly indicates that the conditions [of the civilian population in Shanghai] are very grievous and steadily becoming worse. . . . The worst distress exists undoubtedly amongst the German-Jewish immigrants, of whom at least 6000 are on the point of starvation and about 9000 more are not far better off. The local Jewish Committee told our delegate a fortnight ago that they can raise local contributions to an amount of maximum CRB$10 per capita per month and which is next to nothing when you take into account the high cost of foodstuffs at Shanghai, even a Chinese coolie requiring CRB$150 a month to feed himself. For the moment the Jewish committee have still some of the 3000 bags of flour left which was donated last July, but even that will be exhausted by the end of next month, when the Committee will no longer be able to provide the one slice of bread daily which at present keeps precariously body and soul together of thousands of these poor wretches. It need hardly be mentioned that medical care is practically non-existent because to furnish even the most necessary medicaments would cost more than all the money which the Jewish Committee can raise. The comfort of heating can be dismissed as a dream, and the little threadbare clothing gives no protection against the coldness and humidity of the Shanghai winter climate. . . .

There are several hundred destitute persons who either have no nationality or who have no Consular representation at Shanghai, such as former citizens of Danzig, Latvia, Esthonia, Lithuania, Jugoslavia, Iraque, also Germans, Czechs and Slovakians who cannot obtain any support through the German relief society, either because they refuse to acknowledge their political affiliation with Germany or because they are of mixed ancestry and are therefore not considered as Aryans, whilst the Jewish Committee also does not recognize Protestants, Catholics or Orthodox as Jews. There is some truth in the remarks made by some of these destitute people that even the dogs have someone to care for them in the

Shanghai Society for the Prevention of Cruelty to Animals, whilst human beings are just left starving and freezing to death.[9]

It was not until the spring of 1944 that cables from the JDC guaranteeing funds finally arrived in Shanghai; they had been routed through neutral countries. After the war it was discovered what had prompted the State Department to permit the cabling of funds. Added to the JDC's continual pressure for permission was the work of Rabbi Abraham Kalmanowitz, spiritual head of the Mir Yeshiva and head of the orthodox rescue organization. Knowing of the critical conditions in Shanghai, he too had worked tirelessly to collect money, and he prevailed upon Treasury Secretary Henry Morgenthau, Jr., to reverse the official position regarding communications with countries under enemy occupation. Thereafter, the JDC received permission to cable funds via neutral countries, and the resumption of money transfers saved thousands of lives.[10] Including assistance in the postwar period, the sums of money sent by the JDC to Shanghai totaled approximately five million (U.S.) dollars.

There is no doubt in my mind, however, that without the professionalism, the dedication, the persistence, and the nerve—the chutzpa—displayed by Laura Margolis, thousands of refugees would have slowly starved to death. If there is one deserving hero in the whole Shanghai episode, it certainly is Laura L. Margolis.

10

War in the Pacific

On November 29, 1941, the Central Press Service reported that the German Consul General in Shanghai had informed the Shanghai Municipal Council that Jews living outside Germany had lost their citizenship. The *Jüdische Gemeinde* received the following statement, which stunned us when we read it a few days later in the *Shanghai Jewish Chronicle*:

> By order of the German Government, a Jew who is living abroad cannot be a German citizen. The Jew will lose his citizenship if he presently lives abroad or if he moves abroad after this proclamation. The assets of a Jew who, according to this proclamation loses his citizenship, are taken over by the Third Reich.

I was one of the many refugees who threw away the worthless passports. "Good riddance" was the general consensus, notwithstanding the fact that we had acquired an uncertain status. We were now considered stateless; we had no consular protection, and in Shanghai that meant that we had no rights whatsoever. It meant that there would be no questions asked by anyone if, at any of numerous checkpoints, the Japanese guard who checked ID cards with his left hand and pointed a Mauser automatic at your chest with his right hand happened to pull the trigger.

On November 14, 1941, I had stood among the Chinese in front of the Home of Books, watching silently as the 4th U.S. Marines marched down Nanking Road to the Bund. The regiment was being evacuated and shipped to Manila. Many of the families of these men lived in the apartment building on

Hardoon Road where Illo lived. She had made friends and sometimes gone to the movies with some of them.

The departure of the marines was not a good sign. The city was uneasy. The news was frightening. How long would it be before America and Japan would go to war?

In Shanghai (on the western side of the international dateline) it was 4:00 A.M. on Monday morning, December 8, 1941, when a phone call from the American gunboat *Wake* woke Lieutenant Commander Columbus D. Smith at his apartment with the news that the Japanese air force had attacked Pearl Harbor. He rushed down to the harbor to carry out his orders to scuttle his gunboat but was halted at the pier by Japanese guards, who arrested him and announced that the Imperial Navy had seized the *Wake* and had already renamed it *Tatara*. The British gunboat *Peterel*, having received a warning phone call from the British consulate, refused to surrender, and at about 5:30 A.M. we awoke to the roar of heavy naval artillery and saw the skies ablaze as the *Peterel* was sunk in the harbor by Japanese warships.

The attic room in which my mother and I lived faced the direction of the Whangpoo, and the concussion from the blasts in the harbor shook both of us physically and emotionally. One windowpane cracked. I was stunned for a moment, trying to decide what to do, and then I did something very stupid. I quickly dressed in my SVC uniform, put on my greatcoat and helmet, grabbed my truncheon and revolver holster, and proceeded to walk in the direction of the Garden Bridge. I intended to report for duty at SVC headquarters. The streets were deserted, but when I approached Yangtzepoo Road, I encountered long columns of Japanese infantry and armored vehicles all moving in the same direction: toward the Soochow Creek bridges leading to the International Settlement. The Japanese were occupying the settlement and consolidating their hold on the rest of Shanghai. I realized how naive I was when I saw the Japanese army and naval units on the march one short block away going in the same direction as I was. I knew I had better get off the street damn fast and out of my British uniform; I would not last a minute if I were spotted. I quickly disappeared into a corner of the nearest lane and removed my hat and helmet, dumped the revolver holster, tore off all uniform insignia and stuffed them into my pockets.[1]

The outbreak of hostilities did not come as a surprise to us, yet as stateless refugees without consular protection, we had dreaded the possibility. How would the war affect our relationship with the Japanese? It did not take long before we realized that the start of war in the Pacific had indeed ended our temporary residents' status, and we worried whether communications would continue with the rest of the world or whether we would be isolated. Of course, all Allied business establishments were closed, and many refugees once again lost their jobs and their livelihood. It was galling to see swastikas hanging from the windows of business establishments in the International Settlement.

The strangely benign attitude of the Japanese toward the Jews deteriorated after Pearl Harbor. Until then, we had often speculated why the Japanese had treated us as well as they did. It was impossible for us to know at that time the reasons for the pro-Jewish policies prevailing within Japanese government circles. We could not know that, ironically, this position was strongly influenced by some highly placed Japanese officials with strange views about the Jewish people.

It is not well known that during the Russo-Japanese war of 1904, Jacob Schiff, an American Jew and partner in the investment company Kuhn, Loeb & Schiff, made several very substantial and crucial loans to Japan and refused a similar loan request from Russia's anti-Semitic Czar Nicholas II. Subsequently, Schiff was decorated with the "Order of the Rising Sun" by the Japanese emperor himself, and he still is spoken of with respect by educated Japanese.[2]

Also, according to David Kranzler, during 1918 and 1922 the Japanese armed forces staged military expeditions into Siberia to help the remnants of the White Russian forces prevent the advancing Bolshevik army from reaching the Far East. An unfortunate result of the contact between the White Russians and the Japanese officers, one of whom was Captain Inuzuka, was the inculcation of the latter with the crudest form of anti-Semitism. They were introduced by their Russian mentors to writings such as Sergei Nilus's fraudulent *Protocols of the Learned Elders of Zion*, which had previously been translated from the original Russian into Japanese. The Japanese officers subsequently circulated this material within selected government agencies. These Japanese, who had never encountered a Jew and knew nothing about Judaism, honestly believed every word they read in the *Protocols*. They believed that these mythical Jews were involved in a world conspiracy and that Jews controlled the banks, the economy, and the governments of the Western world. Therefore, aiming for the conquest of the eastern areas of China as well as sparsely settled Manchuria, some Japanese were looking for ways to entice these powerful Jews to settle in Manchuria.[3]

When unexpectedly in 1939 thousands of Jewish refugees arrived in Shanghai, some of these Japanese officials, considered by their government to be the "experts on Jews," were transferred to Shanghai. Captain Inuzuka of the Imperial Japanese Landing Party was appointed chief of the Bureau for Jewish Affairs in Shanghai and was placed in charge of all Jewish affairs in Japanese-occupied China. This group argued forcefully that favorable treatment of the Jews under Japanese control would have a tremendous impact on the "powerful Jewish plutocrats" who controlled America's and England's destinies. Believing in the all-pervasive power of Jews and possibly fearing Jewish retaliation for any abuse, on March 2, 1939, Foreign Minister Hashiro Arita declared in the Japanese parliament that Japanese policy aimed at no discrimination against the Jews.[4]

In November 1941, before Pearl Harbor, Captain Inuzuka pressured the leaders of the Ashkenazi Communal Association to send a telegram to Henry Morgenthau, Jr., President Roosevelt's Jewish secretary of the treasury, imploring him to prevent the impending war.[5] (Even near the end of the war the Japanese still believed the Jews to be so universally influential that early in 1945 the leaders of the Jewish community in Tientsin were asked to broadcast an appeal to their brothers in the United States to use their influence on the American government to stop the conflict.[6]

In Germany, Gestapo chief Heinrich Himmler's plan for the total annihilation of not only European but world Jewry was under discussion in the Nazi party's upper echelons. This plan led to the official policy of the "final solution," which was revealed in January 1942 at the Wannsee Conference in Berlin. No matter in what country Jews were living, schemes were developed to single them out from the general population and to attempt their extermination. The plan proceeded with typical German efficiency in many European countries, but Japan, the Nazis' Axis partner, resisted dealing as requested with the Jews under its jurisdiction.

In the spring of 1942, however, a series of anti-Semitic articles appeared in the Chinese press. Persistent and frightening rumors circulated in Hongkew (which later proved to be true) that Himmler had dispatched Colonel Josef Meisinger, chief of the Gestapo in Warsaw, Poland, to Japan. Meisinger had been responsible for the murder of the Jews in the Warsaw ghetto and was called "the Butcher of Warsaw." He was accompanied by Hans Neumann and Adolph Puttkammer, who was alleged to have performed medical experiments on Jews in concentration camps.[7] After spending some time in Tokyo but finding no one receptive to their plans, the emissaries boarded a submarine for the trip to Shanghai. They were said to have brought with them canisters of Cyclon gas, and this supply of poison gas was found after the end of the war in the Shanghai warehouses of two German firms, Siemens and Bayer.[8]

In July 1942, Ellis Hayim, one of the most prominent and influential Sephardic Shanghailanders, received an urgent call from Mitsugi Shibata, a Japanese vice-consul, requesting that Hayim urgently convene a confidential meeting of Shanghai's Jewish leadership. Shibata had attended a meeting at the consulate with Tsutomo Kubota (a former naval officer who had succeeded Inuzuka as director of the Bureau for Jewish Affairs), members of the Naval Landing Party, members of the Kempetai, and the three Nazi emissaries, who allegedly were accompanied by Baron Jesco von Puttkamer (no relation of Adolph Puttkammer), chief of the German Information Bureau in Shanghai— the "Goebbels of the Far East." The following day found Shibata relating the essence of the meeting to the frightened and worried leaders of Shanghai's Jewish community:

> Meisinger, the spokesman for the Germans, had made several proposals to annihilate the Jewish refugee community. As enemies of Germany they were potential saboteurs against Germany and Japan. The best time to round up the Jews would be at Rosh Hashanah, the Jewish New Year, when most of the Jews would be assembled in the movie houses and other places that served as houses of worship. Meisinger was said to have offered two of several choices: To strip the Jews of all their belongings and load them on several old, unseaworthy barges. The barges then would be towed out to sea, their rudder cables cut, and the Jews would be set adrift to die. As an alternative Meisinger had offered to build a concentration camp on the island of Tsungming in the Yangtze delta and simply starve the Jews to death.[9]

Meisinger had gone on to describe several medical cases that Neumann had supervised in one of the concentration camps.

Shibata was concerned that for security reasons some of the young hotheads in the military would go along with Meisinger. As a matter of policy, military officials were not required to obtain approval from Tokyo for any actions taken under their jurisdiction. They did not find it necessary to notify Tokyo of their intentions. Shibata concluded that because he was an honorable man with many friends in the Jewish community, he had been compelled to bring this matter of life and death to the attention of its leaders. He was determined, he said, not to let this catastrophe happen, regardless of the consequences to his own safety or to his career.[10]

The assembled group agreed to attempt confidential contact with persons who had connections to the Japanese government and, if possible, to the chief of the Kempetai. The meetings with Kubota went very well. Unfortunately, Fritz Brahn, who met with the Kempetai, inadvertently revealed the nature of the meeting with Shibata and his knowledge of Meisinger's plans. Furious, the Kempetai chief arrested all the leaders present at that meeting. Boris Topas, who before the war had made unfriendly statements about the Japanese, was severely beaten; his fingernails were pulled out, and he was burned with cigarettes during the interrogation. Headfirst, he was thrown down a long flight of stone stairs, then repeatedly pulled up and thrown down again until he lost consciousness.[11] Following several weeks of interrogation, Fritz Kaufmann, the last one of the group, was released after being subjected to a lecture by a Kempetai officer: "How could you Jews possibly believe that the Japanese would harm you? The Japanese always have treated you well."[12] Until that time the refugees had not been aware how much Japanese people despised rumors and gossip. Even Shibata's position as vice-consul did not protect him. After weeks of confinement he was sent back to Tokyo in shame. Once the secret plans had leaked out and reached Tokyo, however, Meisinger's alleged plot to exterminate Shanghai's Jewish communities was apparently doomed to failure.[13]

Nevertheless, as the Japanese military machine advanced and the Allied forces retreated, our despair grew. Every day the papers reported new Japanese victories in the Pacific theater of operations, and the mood of the refugees bordered on hysteria. At first we refused to believe the papers, which, after all, were under Japanese military control. Yet the bad news was confirmed by persons who had access to a hidden shortwave radio able to receive the BBC. We could also listen to Radio Moscow (Tass), but we did not have much faith in news from the Soviets.

Horst Siegmund, one of my friends, worked as an electrician, and we considered him an electronic genius. When he needed an antenna for a friend's radio, he went downtown to the rest room in a Japanese office building and removed the copper float from the toilet (thereby effectively disabling the flushing mechanism). Back at his friend's home, Horst inserted a wire into a thin bamboo rod and fastened the wire to the copper ball. The whole assembly was hidden in the building's chimney and became a powerful antenna that enabled some of our friends to listen to the BBC and sometimes even to an American station. Horst also hit upon a scheme to sabotage Japanese factories. Electric meters were especially important when they were used to operate equipment measuring production in Japanese-occupied factories. Horst managed to cross-wire the meters in one plant so that the counters ran backward, causing endless confusion. When a replacement was requisitioned, he discovered the storage place for the meters and was able to sabotage several plants in this fashion.

We simply could not accept the bad war news. We were not prepared mentally or physically for a long war or the possibility, however remote, of a Japanese victory. The Allies must win the war quickly; we could not survive a long war. It was devastating to accept the reality of the Allied retreat. As the news reports became worse from week to week, our morale deteriorated. What had happened to mighty America? The Allied forces? Only our strong instinct for survival kept us going as we read the bulletins:

December 25, 1941: The British garrison of Hong Kong surrenders.
February 15, 1942: The British command in Singapore capitulates and loses this key to the southwest Pacific.
March 1, 1942: Allied naval power is smashed when the HMS *Exeter* is sunk.
April 9, 1942: American Forces surrender in Bataan.
May 6, 1942: Corregidor is overrun and General Wainwright forced to broadcast the surrender of the Philippines.

Late in 1942 new rumors made the rounds—"real" rumors, and not the *bonkes* started by my friends. These were persistent and they were frightening: the first news began to trickle to Shanghai about the shipment of German Jews "to the East" and the "liquidation of the Polish ghetto" by the Nazis. But no one seemed to know the real meaning or the implications of these unsubstantiated reports. Then the story of the meeting at the Japanese consulate with Meisinger and the imprisonment of the Jewish leadership in the Bridge House leaked out. No one was willing to corroborate these rumors, but they were passed throughout Hongkew as what they actually were: facts. We were frightened as never before. All of us had questions that no one was willing or able to answer. What was the Gestapo doing here in Shanghai? For what purpose was poison gas stored in *godowns* owned by German companies? The refugee population was near panic. Was this why we had fled the Nazis and faced starvation and deprivation and disease here in China—to be murdered by the Japanese? The suicide rate increased as more and more refugees were unable to cope with the present and face the bleak future.

Japanese military control became oppressive. Occasionally, groups of Japanese soldiers would enter our lanes, pound on doors or break them down, and ransack the houses for hidden shortwave receivers. The soldiers acted threatening and destroyed the few possessions of the family unfortunate enough to be chosen at random. Public gatherings and meetings were under military surveillance. Several refugees had the misfortune of being picked up for interrogation by the Kempetai. They joined other foreigners and Chinese and even Japanese in the lice-infested cells of the Kempetai's headquarters, the infamous Bridge House.

The prisoners there were a mixed group, without distinction as to nationality, race, religion, or social standing. All of them had been arrested for alleged or real political crimes or for security reasons. Among these unfortunates was a very popular refugee, the soccer referee Hermann Natowic. Accused of spying and operating a radio transmitter, he refused to cooperate with his interrogators and was subjected to months of torture. When he was close to death, the Kempetai told his relatives to send a doctor to take him away. A highly regarded physician, Dr. Didner, volunteered to pick him up, and against all odds nursed Natowic back to health.

Some cells in Bridge House held about thirty-five prisoners—men and women—with enough space to squat but not enough room to lie flat. A hole in one corner of the cell served as a latrine. Even when it was used by thirty-five people, it was cleaned only once a day. The prisoners suffered injuries caused by torture and developed tropical diseases. Inside their cells they were required to sit in the prescribed Japanese way, squatting on the floor with legs crossed. They were not permitted to lean against a wall, to stretch, or to talk. At nine o'clock they were allowed to curl up on the floor to sleep, if their nerves, hunger and thirst, heat or cold permitted. Even in winter, despite the cold, the prisoners had no option but to undress completely to kill the hordes of lice that infested the cells. Many of the prisoners who survived the torture of frequent interrogations contracted one of the prevailing diseases and did not survive their imprisonment. Relatives would receive a call to come and pick them up; in several cases their backs had been broken.[14]

11

The Ghetto

llo and I had been dating ever since she first visited me at Home of Books. We shared many interests including classical music and books, and found many topics to discuss in our daily telephone calls. I was a frequent guest at Illo's home in the Hardoon Road apartment. Whenever possible, I visited Illo after work and had dinner with her and her parents. Illo's mother did not want her daughter to date anyone she did not know. A strikingly beautiful woman, she was very forthright and tolerated no nonsense. It became obvious to me that she liked and approved of me, since she repeatedly invited me for return visits. For the first time since I had come to Shanghai, I felt comfortable in a "real home" environment. Illo even had her own "room," a small alcove adjoining the living room, which was a luxury I had not seen since leaving Germany. There we would sit after dinner and talk until it was too late for me to catch the last bus to the Bund.

My walk home was through deserted streets, along the race course, past the YMCA, along Nanking Road to the Bund, and across Garden Bridge into Hongkew. There the streets were narrower, and I was obliged to observe the standard precaution of walking in the center of the street, so that it would be more difficult for anyone to jump me. By the time I arrived home, I had covered about eight miles.

I was living with my mother, and life was awkward but bearable. I had a girlfriend and I had a job. I even had some spare money for amusements. Many couples went to the movies as a means of securing some privacy, but Illo's mother did not permit us to go to the movies unless another couple went along on the date. Since Illo was earning money too, her parents insisted that dates be "dutch treat." We were able to have a good time; we took long walks in beautiful Jessfield Park, and in the summer we attended outdoor con-

certs there or in French Park, where the Shanghai Municipal Orchestra under
Maestro Mario Paci regularly performed symphonic works. We would lean
back in comfortable lounge chairs and listen to the great classical works, sip-
ping a Greenspot orangeade and looking up at the star-studded semi-tropical
sky while furtively holding hands when we thought no one was watching.
French Park had a small zoo, and to this day, when we hear a performance
of Tchaikovsky's Fifth Symphony, we expect to hear the roar of lions in the
background. In the winter, besides symphony concerts, we would attend per-
formances of the ballet, which, thanks to the presence of such a large Russian
community, were first class. There were also ballrooms, huge dance halls
where, for a small cover charge that included one glass of tea, we could dance
a Sunday afternoon away to the sound of "big band" dance bands.

Early in 1943 I felt a desperate need to get out of the city and see some
green spaces, so I planned a visit to the scout camp, Millington, in Lunghwa.
Before Pearl Harbor this beautiful estate with its small rolling wooded hills,
manicured lawns, and great stone lodge had been in constant use. Now, with
British citizens in POW camps, the Boy Scout movement was inactive and the
camp unused. In weather unusually warm for February, I borrowed a bike
from a friend and rode out there. The camp was neglected and deserted, but
I managed to find enough gear to pitch a tent. I was used to living outdoors,
and as I lay on my back studying the southern skies, a dog approached and lay
down next to me; it kept me company for two days and nights.

On the third day, I saw a girl on a bike approaching my campsite. I was absolutely dumfounded when it turned out to be Illo. Perspiration was running
down her face. "You had better come back to the city," she said breathlessly.
"The Japanese have issued a proclamation that will force all of us to move to
Hongkew, into what they call a 'designated area.' "

"What about Heinemann's store and what about our jobs, and what about
your apartment and what about the Office Furnishing Company?" The questions just poured out of me, but Illo only shook her head. "No one knows
what is going on. You had better come back home." She had biked to Millington during her lunch hour, and she had to return to the store. We parted, and
I promised to pack up and come back.

On February 19, 1943, the day after the proclamation had been issued, I returned to Hongkew. I had been away for only a few days. It was obvious that
the proclamation was a very serious blow for our community. People were
standing in small groups on street corners and in cafés, discussing the news.
All were asking questions; no one had answers. Arguments were heated,

sharply dividing the pessimists who advocated resistance from the pragmatists who adopted a wait-and-see attitude.

I found a newspaper and stared at the headlines. The Japanese military occupation authorities had officially proclaimed the establishment of a "Designated Area for Stateless Refugees"—a euphemism for ghetto. The English version of the proclamation read as follows:

18. February, 1943

I. Because of military necessity, the residential and business areas of stateless refugees in the Shanghai area will be restricted to an area within the International Settlement east of the line connecting *Chohoro, Mokairo* and *Todotsudo,* Chaoufong Road, Muirhead Road and Dent Road; west of *Yoyuho Yangtzepoo* Creek; north of the line connecting *Toshikobairo, Mokairo* and *Kaisanro,* East Seward Road, Muirhead Road and Wayside Road; and south of the border of the International Settlement.[1]

II. Stateless refugees presently residing and/or operating businesses outside the area mentioned in the preceding paragraph shall move their residence and/or places of business inside the above prescribed area by May 18, 1943. Those desiring to buy or sell or rent houses, stores and other installations located outside the above area which are home and/ or business places of stateless refugees shall obtain prior approval of the authorities concerned.

III. Those other than stateless refugees may not move into the area designated in paragraph I without permission.

IV. Any person who violates this proclamation and interferes with its enforcement shall be liable to severe punishment.

It was signed by the commander in chief of the Imperial Japanese Army and commander in chief of the Imperial Japanese Navy in the Shanghai area.[2]

The Japanese military authorities claimed that the establishment of the ghetto was a military security necessity. Within the refugee community it was generally assumed that this measure was intended to limit our movements and to give the Japanese forces greater opportunity for surveillance. Another possible motive might have been to soothe the hurt feelings of the Nazis who had been stung by the rejection of Meisinger's proposal.[3] It is significant that the words "Jew" and "ghetto" were never mentioned in the proclamation, even though it was directed at European Jews who had come as a result of the Nazis' effort to expel them from the Third Reich. None of the Jewish Shanghailanders or the Russian Jews were affected; though many of them were also stateless, it was generally assumed that many of them had some kind of passport. Even those who were not legal citizens of one of the larger Western countries had at one time or another purchased a passport from a consul of one of the smaller nations.

On January 22, 1951, the former German Consul General of Tientsin, Fritz Wiedemann, shed light on the proclamation of the ghetto by releasing a statement confirming that

> the internment of Central European emigrants, as a rule primarily Jews who had emigrated from Germany and Austria to China, had taken place upon the instigation of the German government then in power. The Japanese themselves were not anti-Semitic, and we were under orders to instruct the Japanese authorities about the racial policies of Germany and to suggest appropriate measures. There was no doubt in my mind that the internment of the Jews in the Shanghai ghetto had been instigated by German authorities. From my work with Hitler I know that as a matter of policy, pressure was exerted upon friendly governments in that direction.[4]

It is doubtful that any one gave much thought to why the Japanese had chosen this particular area for the ghetto. What we did not know was that one of the reasons for selecting the site was its proximity to the jail that held some POWs, the wharves, the fuel dumps, and a powerful radio transmitter. The Japanese assumed that the Allies would not bomb the ghetto, so placing it in this particular area would provide a measure of safety for their military installations.

The refugee community was totally absorbed in dealing with the problems caused by the establishment of the ghetto. All refugees who lived or did business outside of the designated area were forced to exchange their homes with Chinese or Japanese living inside the area or to try to find housing there at vastly inflated prices. Several White Russians set themselves up as agents and did a profitable business, exchanging apartments in the rest of the International Settlement belonging to refugees with rooms in Hongkew belonging to Japanese. The proclamation included the peripheral Jews, those who had tried to hide the fact that they were refugees by posing as Shanghailanders. Thus, about 8,000 refugees who had somehow managed to overcome great obstacles and find a means of livelihood and residence in the International Settlement or the French Concession were forced to leave their homes once more and move into the ghetto.

My mother and I were lucky again. Two years before the proclamation we had moved out of our room in the Japanese house and found a small, very narrow attic room—about six by fourteen feet—at 24/13 Ward Road, which was located within the borders of the newly created ghetto. Our room was in one of the few European-style houses with more than two stories. We even had a scenic view, since the window faced the Whangpoo River and also over-looked Corso Garden, a Viennese-style tea garden. But most important, on every floor was the most valuable and highly prized asset: the W.C., which was considered a lifesaving rarity.

Illo and her parents were less fortunate; it was impossible to find within the ghetto anything nearly as comfortable as their Hardoon Road apartment. Despite their many friends, it took Illo's father almost two months to find a room on the second floor of a row house in the *Gemeinde* lane of 416/35 Tong-shan Road (so called because the *Jüdische Gemeinde* had its offices at 416/22). The room was small, about ten by twelve feet, with barely enough space for two narrow Chinese couches, a bamboo table with two chairs, and their steamer trunk. Illo slept on a folding cot, which was stored on top the trunk during the day. When she wanted to go to bed, the table was put on top the trunk. One small shelf by the door held dishes and cooking utensils, and the trunk was used as a base for the Chinese stove. There was a one-burner electric plate but not enough electricity to use it with any regularity. The small house had its advantages, however, in that it had four rooms for only three families, who shared a "real" bathroom with a tub (cold water only) and toilet.

The ghetto area totaled less than three-quarters of a square mile. It housed more than 18,000 refugees among perhaps 100,000 Chinese—twice the popu-lation density of Manhattan!

The proclamation took effect on May 18, 1943. The Japanese dissolved the board of the *Jüdische Gemeinde* and appointed "commissioners." The Japanese did not permit us to leave the ghetto without a "pass," a special ID card issued by the Bureau for Stateless Refugees. Getting this pass was often a humiliating experience, and the applicant risked mistreatment. In charge of this bureau was Kubota; two of his assistants, Ghoya and Okura, were responsible for the passes. Barriers were erected at some of the checkpoints, and the exits were guarded by Japanese soldiers, White Russian police, and Jewish members of the Pao Chia—auxiliary police—under their supervision. The Pao Chia was an old Chinese institution. According to law, the city mayors were empowered to organize able-bodied male citizens between the ages of eighteen and forty-five as an auxiliary arm of the police, with limited functions. Originally the

Pao Chia had been organized by the Shanghai Municipal Police; now the Japanese military authorities used the organization for civil air defense, and we used it for the self-protection of the ghetto. I was one of approximately 3,500 Jews forced to join the Pao Chia. I managed however, to become an assistant fire chief, thereby avoiding the onerous task of guarding the ghetto.

The Pao Chia guards never knew when they were being watched by one of the Japanese or Russians and were therefore forced to report any irregularities, such as a refugee returning a few minutes after the time stated on the pass. Anyone caught by one of the White Russian policemen was subject to merciless extortion. Although dangerous, it was not difficult to sneak in and out of the ghetto. Several of my friends, including my good friend Seppl, never once bothered to get a pass; he knew exactly where to sneak out and back in and took his chances of getting caught at a checkpoint or by one of the roving military patrols that checked ID cards.

Since the proclamation affected only stateless Jews who had arrived after 1937, the German consulate offered the Christian wives of Jewish refugees the opportunity to divorce their husbands in exchange for consular support and financial aid. It is to the credit of these "divorced" Christian wives that they used their financial aid to provide extra food for their families, whom they visited regularly.

If you could provide proof of employment outside the ghetto and were willing to wait for hours or days to see Ghoya, the self-proclaimed "King of the Jews," you might get a temporary pass allowing you to leave the ghetto for a limited time and a specific geographic area. It was pure torture to wait in line in the broiling sun for hours or sometimes the whole day just to apply for a pass. When the people finally got into the building and slowly wound their way up to the second story where the "king" had his office, many became unnerved by his ranting and raving and turned back rather than risk confronting him in one of his ugly moods.

Ghoya was a very short man who seemed to be full of complexes when dealing with the taller foreigners. His antics bordered on the theatrical, and many funny as well as tragic stories circulated about him and his crazy behavior. When Ghoya became angry, he would jump up on his desk and slap the face of the hapless applicant who happened to be there. He fancied himself a violinist and several times forced a noted musician to accompany him on the piano. When the "king" made a mistake, he would call out: "If you don't beat proper rhythm, Professor, I'll kill you, you dirty swine." Another anecdote that made the rounds of the ghetto quoted his pronouncement: "You are a grave-digger. Very honest profession. I give you blue pass. All districts. But first you bring me list of customers." And one of his more common tactics, depending on his mood, was to say to one applicant, "Your English is too good. You better go to America. No pass, get out!" and to the next applicant, "Your English is too poor. No English, no business, no pass. Get out!" After the end of the war, the artist Fritz Melchior produced a hand-painted booklet depicting these scenes.

Okura, the other Japanese who issued passes, was not as irrational as Ghoya, but he was more dangerous. The unlucky applicant who had to deal with him might be slapped, beaten, and kicked and ran the risk of being sent to the bunker, a lice-infested jail within the police station. A sentence to spend a night in this place could be equivalent to a death sentence. Not until several weeks later would the unfortunate person know whether he had contracted typhus from the lice and whether he would live or die.

After the ghetto proclamation, Illo's father had to close his downtown office. A resourceful man, he started working out of their single room, keeping books for small refugee enterprises. Illo kept her job at the Western Arts Gallery until the struggle to obtain a pass from Ghoya to leave the ghetto became too much of a problem.

My mother meanwhile had conceived of a means to earn some extra money. Drawing on her experience at our Altheide hotel, and being an excellent cook and careful shopper, she provided the main noon meal in our room for a few single paying guests. As changing conditions necessitated, she also occasionally augmented the soup kitchen's food. Given the size of our room, the number of guests was limited—one of them was Eugen Schönwald, my sister-in-law Alice's father, whose wife, Martha, had passed away in 1942. Until his death in 1945, "Father Schönwald," as I called him, was a welcome guest in our room.

I was offered a new job as night manager at the Dah Tung bakery. It was located on Dent Road, right on the border of the ghetto and around the corner from Illo's room. Under the circumstances, I was not altogether unhappy about leaving my job at the Office Furnishings Company.

"Dah [great] Tung" could mean several things: union, harmony, or even peace. Freely translated, Dah Tung could stand for "Ideal World." The bakery had been purchased by one J. Wallach, a Russian Jew who had interests in several businesses. He would visit the bakery office a few times a week to check on the cash receipts. We baked one kind of bread only. It had a delicious crust and looked and tasted something like Italian bread. A portion of the production was sold to the refugee committee to supplement the camp inmates' diet. Besides the night manager and day manager (both refugees), ten bakers and their trusted foreman worked there.

The bakers fired the oven with wood, kneaded the dough, removed the wood ashes, and with long paddles pushed the bread in and pulled it out of the ovens. As was customary in many Shanghai factories, only the foreman's name was known to the owner and the managers; the other workers were called by numbers according to seniority.

I liked my job at the bakery for several reasons. First and foremost, as part of my pay I received two nine-ounce loaves of warm, freshly baked bread daily. They made for good eating, even without peanut butter, which was the cheapest and most nutritious spread available. Second, I worked within a stone's throw from where Illo lived with her parents, which made it convenient to visit. Finally, I enjoyed my independence and responsibilities, and I had to answer to no one except Wallach, the owner.

12

"Let's Get Married!"

n July 1944, Illo's mother suddenly fell ill and was taken to the Ward Road hospital. She did not suffer long. No medication was available for bacillary dysentery. After three days, she passed away. I had admired and loved her very much. Illo was devastated.

The cemetery was located on Columbia Road at the opposite end of the city, ten miles away. There was no hearse; dedicated members of the Chevrah Kadisha pushed the makeshift casket on a handcart the long distance through the whole city in the July heat. The mourners, with special passes, rode the bus to the end of the line, then walked from there. After a short service under the blazing sun, Irene Koratkowski's body, wrapped in a straw mat that did not quite cover her, was eased out of the side of the casket into a shallow grave in which ground water could be seen. The casket was only for transportation; it was used over and over again for other funerals.

I had been dating Illo ever since the Great Charity Ball on April 26, 1941, and her mother's death brought us closer than ever. She needed my support, and I found myself spending less time with my friends in the Thirteenth Rovers and more time with Illo's Chaverim friends and Rabbi Sober. Nightly, the group got together to talk about our chances of surviving the war and the ghetto.

Among the couples who had been dating for years, talk turned more and more to marriage. Although we grew progressively more pessimistic about our future, we were normal young people whose sexuality could not be denied. Strict upbringing combined with total lack of privacy mandated marriage. For better or for worse, Illo and I wanted to be together. We had "gone steady" ever since our first meeting in 1941, and as the war progressed, there were times when we held little hope for our survival. "For worse," we said, should the persistent rumors be true that the SS had come to Shanghai and, in cooperation with the Japanese military authorities, had plans to kill Shanghai's Jewish community. "For better," should we be lucky enough to survive diseases and the war and make it out of the ghetto to start a new life together.

Although the obstacles were numerous, Illo and I decided to take the first step and officially announce our engagement. What date to pick? Since it was already October, Illo chose October 28, 1944, the birthday of the beloved grandmother she had left behind in Berlin. Rose Peril was to have followed the Koratkowski family to Shanghai but was not able to leave Germany in time. After the war we learned that she had died in 1944 in the Terezin ghetto, fortunately without knowing that her favorite daughter had died in Shanghai.

In true German tradition, Paul Koratkowski inserted a notice in the refugee paper announcing both his daughter's engagement and an open house to be held on October 28. Friends came to express their good wishes. No one gave a thought to the absence of refreshments. I wanted my fiancée to have a real token of our engagement, an engagement ring, but who could afford a ring? Then by chance I happened to see in a pawnshop a thin gold ring with an antique setting that I could afford. Instead of a stone it had a piece of glass which, later on in New York, I replaced with a white sapphire. Now that we were engaged, there were more obstacles to overcome before a wedding date could be set. The major problem was to find a room, a place for us to live, and once we found a place, how to finance it.

During those times of galloping inflation no one kept cash one minute longer than absolutely necessary. The employees of Dah Tung invested in flour on a regular basis, a commodity with which we were familiar and which was easily bought and sold. Whenever I had some money to spare, I participated in the purchase of a fifty-pound bag. At the time of our engagement I owned a whole bag of flour. Selling it would provide the money to buy a room; however, a room for a couple, in a house with a W.C., was impossible to find. After a few months of searching I was able to locate an acceptable room in the same lane in which Illo lived, but it was only large enough for one person. I offered to buy it for Illo's father with the thought that he could move into it and I could move in with Illo. He did not like the idea at first, but friends of Illo's mother persuaded him to agree, provided he could still take all his meals with us. We were now able to set the wedding date for April 8, 1945.

Illo's mother had brought with her from Berlin a pair of white voile curtains that did not fit any window in Shanghai. A friend of my mother's, a well-known Viennese dress designer, took these curtains and, as a present, designed and made a beautiful wedding gown. This, along with her mother's wedding veil, made Illo such an elegant bride that I was glad I had not yet sold my black suit and was able to redeem it from the pawnshop. To perform the required civil ceremony we chose Kurt Redlich, the good friend and neighbor of Illo's parents. The religious ceremony would be performed by our friend Rabbi Karl-Heinz Sober. The wedding present Illo asked for and received from her father was enough hot water (brought by a coolie to the house) to take her first hot bath in years. She was almost late for the wedding because she refused to get out of the tub! The wedding would take place in a large room in the Kadoorie school, which was also used as a makeshift synagogue and was located just across the ghetto border. It was understood that no invitations could be sent, and no one expected any; any one of our friends could come to the religious ceremony. We applied for and received a "collective" pass for 150 persons and were scared out of our wits when about twice as many people showed up at the ghetto checkpoint. The problem was solved neatly: the group of guests was divided, and the same pass was used for two crossings.

For a lark, Illo decided to invite her customer Hans Mosberg to the wedding ceremony, never thinking that he would dare to accept. Surely Mosberg could not possibly risk being seen at a Jewish function. Most of the guests were already seated when the door opened and, to our surprise, Mosberg entered, carrying a large box. There were no ushers, so he seated himself in the front row. The box contained a large, beautiful Ming plate. After the ceremony Mosberg told Illo jokingly that Tsao had refused to sell the pagoda, the most precious piece in his store, so he had had to substitute the Ming plate. Today it decorates the mantelpiece in our living room.

After the war we were not surprised to learn that Mosberg had been arrested by the U.S. War Crimes Commission in Shanghai. According to documents in the National Archives, Mosberg was charged and convicted by the War Crimes Court of being a member, agent, and employee of the Bureau Ehrhardt (an intelligence agency of the German High Command, operating in Shanghai), for violation of the German unconditional surrender of May 8, 1945, and for engaging in military intelligence activities. On January 17, 1947, he was sentenced to twenty years in the Landsberg Castle prison in Germany. On May 10, 1947, the judgment was approved. But strangely, on July 6, 1950, the case was reviewed, and "after due consideration and in exercise of the powers conferred upon me, I hereby order: 'That the unserved portion of the approved sentence be remitted, and that said Hans Mosberg be released from confinement forthwith.' (signed) Thos. T. Handy, General, U.S. Army."[1]

Our wedding was beautiful, with Cantor Max Warschauer and the choir chanting the ancient liturgy as well as some special music we had chosen. No one paid any attention when the sirens sounded an air raid alarm, and we were duly married without further interruption. The service completed, my new bride and I were driven in a pedicab, a bicycle-driven ricksha, to the home of a close friend where there was enough room for about eighteen of our family and friends, who were served tea and cake. As a wedding present, our friends had gotten together and pooled ingredients, and Edith Teichner, the widow of Rabbi Teichner and a family friend from Paul Koratkowski's hometown, had baked two cakes in Dah Tung's oven for the feast. We also received other gifts. "Father Schönwald," who stood up for me, gave us an American five-dollar bill that he had saved and that constituted a small fortune for us. Rabbi Sober gave us a very welcome gift, a small jar of plum jam. We decided to save it for another special occasion. The most welcome and utilitarian present, however, was a wet mop a friend had made from rags and a bamboo pole.

Getting settled in married life was easy. I had my job; I received two loaves of bread daily; we had lots of good friends; and no matter what might happen, we had each other. We felt we were luckier than many other refugees and did not mind the relatively primitive living conditions. Most landlords rationed necessary utilities; especially after Pearl Harbor, very little electricity was available for cooking or heating. Some families received an allotment of one and a half kilowatt-hours per month, which provided for some light but was insufficient for electric hotplates. Illo, like most others not living in a Heim, cooked on a Chinese stove, which looked something like a flowerpot crossed with a hibachi. Since charcoal was a luxury, everyone used a mixture of coal dust and river mud.

Cooking a pot of rice was a tedious process. First, Illo had to take the dry rice in a pot to the water shop and purchase boiling water to be poured over the rice. (The water was purchased by the ladle and paid for with bamboo chips. Because of inflation, the lowest denomination of coins—called the copper cash—was no longer available; it had been replaced by one cent, which equaled ten copper cash. Since a ladle of water cost less than one cent, the clever water merchants substituted marked bamboo sticks to be used as tokens for the discontinued copper cash.) After carrying the pot home she had to start the fire and fan the coals continuously until the rice was partially cooked, then quickly wrap the pot in blankets and pillows to keep it warm; this was intended to finish the cooking process. The fumes from the coal-mud fuel were toxic, and ventilation was a problem. During the violent downpours that accompanied typhoons, windows had to be kept closed, and once I found Illo unconscious on the floor, overcome by the fumes.

One day, one of Illo's recurrent throat infections developed into a serious case of abscessed tonsils, and she had to go into the refugee hospital. The chief surgeon, an old family friend, told her that he had no choice but to lacerate the tonsils. Anesthetic was too precious to be used for such a minor procedure; three nurses held Illo's head and shoulders while the doctor pleaded with her: "Please try not to spit on me—this gown is sterile and still has to last all day." Ignoring the pain, she complied.

13

B-29s Overhead

May 10, 1945, was an extraordinarily joyful day. Great news! The papers were full of reports of the German surrender. But the joy was short-lived, replaced by ominous questions. Where were all our loved ones? Where were my father and my sister? Where were Illo's two grandmothers and aunts and the rest of the family? The papers began to print unbelievable stories, horror stories—were they believable? They could not be true. Knowing that the Nazis had finally been defeated buoyed our spirits considerably. We were especially hopeful for a quick victory by the Allies when in the spring of 1945 the first American bombers appeared over Shanghai. The tide apparently had finally turned, and the Allies had penetrated the Japanese sphere of influence. Sometimes the Flying Fortresses, as the B-17s, B-24s, and B-29s were called, would fly very low over the ghetto area, and I would stand on the windowsill, leaning out to cheer them on. Once I could even see the cockpits of the planes. It became a standing joke that the air raid sirens, instead of signaling a precautionary alert, would not start wailing until the planes became visible. Shortly thereafter, when from the distance one could already hear the concussions of the bombs, the sirens would sound the red alert.

In July the air raids became more frequent, and the explosions of the bombs and the antiaircraft fire came closer. The early morning hours were the coolest, the best time to sleep during July and August, though sleeping was always difficult. Window screens were unknown, and mosquitoes were plentiful. The walls radiated heat, and if mosquito netting was available, it cut off whatever little air circulation there was. From the adjoining roof tops we could hear the incessant, noisy shuffling of Mah-Jongg tiles accompanied by

Chinese five-tone music. Real beds were a rarity, and Illo and I, like many others, slept on Chinese couches that were not much more than narrow wooden frames padded with rice straw and covered with upholstery fabric. After sleeping for a few hours we had to get up to "go hunting" for bedbugs and wring out the sheets, which would be sopping wet from perspiration.

Now the bombers added a new dimension to the hot and wet nights and kept everyone awake and worried. Common wisdom assumed that the Americans would not bomb the ghetto; I was unconcerned because we had learned through underground channels that the U.S. forces knew its location. The powerful radio transmitter the Japanese operated in the ghetto, however—very close to Tongshan Road, where we lived—was used to direct Japan's naval activities along the coast. They had also stored synthetic fuel and munitions in several locations in our area.

On Sunday, July 15, around eleven o'clock in the morning, the bombers attacked the wharves a few blocks from the ghetto. Though I did not fear the bombers, we took precautions against the antiaircraft shrapnel that rained down over parts of the ghetto. This was a major attack that lasted till almost midnight. It is amazing how human beings are able to adapt to almost any conditions. After several hours, life just continued as usual despite the roar of planes and bombs and the "ack-ack" of antiaircraft guns.

On Monday, July 16, it was reported that President Truman had boarded the USS *Augusta* to travel to Potsdam for a "Big Three Conference." No matter that earlier in the war the Japanese had claimed they had sunk the *Augusta*, a ship well known to the refugees. Before the war it had been the flagship of the American fleet at anchor in the Whangpoo, giving the refugees a tremendous feeling of security. "As long as these big guns are here in the harbor, we have nothing to fear," it had been said.

Tuesday, July 17, 1945, dawned as an especially hot and humid day. The air was oppressive and felt like a wet blanket. There was not the slightest breeze, and simply moving about became laborious. The temperature was normal, about 95 degrees, with humidity almost to match.

The day before, the refugee who normally was the bakery's day-shift manager had asked me to switch shifts with him. On the morning of this fateful day, then, I busily counted out the loaves for each delivery route before returning to my office on the second floor—the top floor of the building. The delivery boys stacked the loaves into baskets over the front and rear wheels of their cycles and left on their routes to the camps and grocery stores. The bakery was located on Dent Road in one of the crowded lanes where many hundreds of Chinese lived. For a few minutes I lay down on top my desk to rest. I had gotten used to the stifling blanket of wet heat, but it was made even worse by the ovens. Then, munching on a piece of bread, I double-checked the production figures and deducted from the inventory the amount of flour used. The storerooms were crammed full, as on the previous day the mill had delivered the monthly allotment of white wheat flour. Before going home for lunch, as I went to padlock the storeroom, I noticed one of the large Norwegian rats sitting on the edge of a shelf with its back turned and its tail hanging down. Sneaking up as quietly as possible, I grabbed the rat by the tail and passed it on to the cleanup boy for disposal.

The lanes were always full of rats, and mangy cats and dogs that never seemed to belong to anyone. These animals were so plentiful that as long as they were able to scrounge up food, they ceased to bother each other. The slum dwellers constantly fought the rats. It was a tossup: did the humans seal the cracks quicker, or did the rats gnaw through the walls faster? After several bombing attacks it was interesting to watch the behavior of the cats and dogs: before an alarm had sounded and before we could hear the faintest humming of the planes, cats acted nervous and tried to hide, while the dogs barked incessantly. For some reason the Chinese do not care for pets except those that can be caged. Chinese gentlemen loved to take their birds for walks or hang their cages in rows in a park in the hope that their birds' singing would improve. Caged crickets were also very popular pets.

I carefully selected two nice, well-baked, crisp loaves from the table and headed home to my bride. Illo had just returned from the water shop with her thermos, and she poured the boiling water over a few tea leaves. We were hungry. We had not had enough for breakfast, so we eagerly ate one of the loaves for lunch. Eating bread by itself did not fill us; when we finished, we were not much less hungry than before. It was about time for me to head back to the bakery. There would not be very much work until the night-shift manager arrived.

In the manager's absence, the foreman usually took a rest on the desk. It stood between two windows, and with a little imagination one could conjure up some ventilation. That's what I planned to do, at least for a little while, before the paper work for the night shift had to be completed. But as I got up to return to the bakery, Illo pleaded with me to stay a little while longer and keep her company. She was extremely nervous and had premonitions of danger. Being a brand-new husband, I decided to humor my bride.

It was almost two o'clock. A few high clouds were in the sky. We were relaxing, sitting on our cot, when we heard first the humming and then the deep roar of the approaching bombers. I jumped up and as I had done in the past, climbed onto the windowsill, trying to get a glimpse of the bombers and wave to them.

Only this time it was different. This time we were in the target area. The noise was deafening as the bombs exploded all around us. The house shook and swayed, and the floor and the walls seemed to tilt back and forth. I was flung into the room, and in a flash Illo and I were hurtling down the steep stairs to the ground floor with debris crashing around us. The sound of the air raid siren added to the confusion; the raid must be over. How did we get down the stairs? We felt our bones; nothing appeared to be broken. Miraculously, no one in our house suffered more than a few scratches.

One of the houses in our lane fronting Tongshan Road and belonging to a Chinese was on fire. Amazingly, just as had been practiced, my Pao Chia civil defense group appeared. We never had taken the fire drills seriously, but now it was for real, and we went to work. We succeeded in opening the hydrant to get water. As assistant chief it was my job to be first in line for the bucket brigade. A friend and I tried to get into the burning house and to climb to the roof. We soon realized how ridiculous our attempt was. No one could stay inside the burning house and pass the buckets, and we had no rope to haul the buckets up the side of the house. Quite a few children had brought their buckets and were ready to assist us, but we were unable to get to the base of the fire, which threatened to get out of control. We took up positions at the adjoining houses to try to prevent the spread of the fire. It would have been hopeless had it not been for a fire truck coming down Tongshan Road, trying to pass our lane. The Pao Chia members crowding the street in front of the burning house stopped the fire truck and asked for help. An argument erupted because the firemen expected payment, but we prevailed, threatening to take over the fire truck.

Another lane was not so lucky. Several fires went out of control, and the refugees as well as the Chinese were forced to evacuate and abandon their homes. More than 700 refugees and thousands of Chinese were again left homeless. Many of the fragile houses had simply collapsed under the air pressure of the explosions. Their inhabitants, some refugees but mostly Chinese, lay buried under the rubble. Casualties were heavy: in this attack 32 refugees, about 300 Japanese, and an estimated 4,000 Chinese were killed, though it is doubtful that the number of dead and injured Chinese has ever been established.

Many of the refugees worked selflessly to help both Jewish and Chinese victims and in some areas totally disregarded the danger from the shrapnel raining down on them. They ran from house to house, looking for survivors. They commandeered ricksha coolies and moved some of the injured to the first aid station. They assisted everyone in need. In the first aid station lay rows of casualties, some of them already dead.

There were no signs of panic among the refugees. The Chinese received medical aid along with the refugee victims. Camp inmates brought their last shirts—literally—and bed linens to be used for bandages. Women carried out the instructions of doctors, giving up their pillows and blankets for the wounded, making tea, helping with bandaging. Doctors operated in the streets, and one of them, a close friend of Illo's parents, related later that all he used was a pocketknife.

He also told us of an incident that later drew considerable attention. Hundreds of injured Chinese were taken to the hospital of the Ward Road prison (at that time called the largest prison in the world) but were left lying in the hospital yard and did not receive any medical attention. A prison official went to the owner of the coffee shop across the street and asked him for help. Could he possibly get a few of the Jewish physicians to come to the jail and treat the injured? The Chinese doctors at the prison hospital had refused to help because they would not get paid. Within minutes, eight refugee doctors arrived, including Dr. Kneuker, a surgeon. They requested surgical instruments from the Chinese doctors and the assistance of two nurses for every doctor. Both requests were denied, since no one could pay for the services. For almost half an hour the refugee doctors stood around, unable to do much. Finally, Dr. Kneuker entered the office of the Chinese physician in charge and repeated his demands for the instruments, which were on hand in the hospital. When the chief again refused, Dr. Kneuker locked the door, turned to the Chinese, and repeatedly hit him in his face. The instruments became available immediately, and the refugee physicians started to treat the Chinese patients who were lying on the stone floor of the hospital yard. The refugee doctors did admire the stoic behavior of the injured Chinese who had to endure the pain of the operations. Neither pain-relieving medication nor anesthesia was available, and even amputations were performed without them.

Apparently, helping strangers simply was not done among Shanghai's Chinese. All their lives their concerns centered only on their friends and extended families. The mercenary attitude common to Shanghai's Chinese was evident even in this situation. While one refugee doctor amputated a leg, the patient pulled his wallet from his garment and asked, "How much?" This was not an isolated incident. Another case was reported by refugees working to free a Chinese buried under the rubble of a collapsed house. Once his head and shoulders were uncovered, the victim had the same question: "How much?" The Chinese people did not move a finger to help any strangers, Chinese or refugees. They would not even provide a drink of water when asked to do so. While the refugee doctors were trying to complete their exhausting work at the hospital, they again requested assistance from the Chinese doctors, who all this time had sat in another room, smoking cigarettes and playing Mah-Jongg. They now refused to help on the grounds that half of the instruments were missing.[1]

The extraordinary and often courageous behavior of the refugees astounded the Japanese and was recognized by the whole city. Their actions were reported favorably and in detail by all of Shanghai's newspapers, including the American-owned Shanghai Evening Post & Mercury. Apparently not used to care and concern by strangers, many grateful Chinese brought food and fruit to the bombed-out refugees.

Earlier in the day, before the fires were extinguished, many residents had carried their precious belongings out of their houses, through the crowded lanes, to a vacant piece of land. There you could find all kinds of "treasures" that were left untouched all afternoon. Fearing the spread of the fire, Illo too had gone back into our house and brought some of our belongings outside. It was absolutely unbelievable that not one single item disappeared. Normally, things would vanish if you turned your back for a second. It was a miracle that the refugees in this particular area suffered little loss of personal property.

Ironically, this air raid had been directed from the ground by the "caretaker" of one of the synagogues, who actually was an intelligence agent trained by the OSS (Office of Strategic Services). His portable transmitter was hidden behind the ark that held the Sefer Torah, the scrolls with the five books of Moses![2]

Later in the afternoon I decided to look in at the Dah Tung bakery. No sooner had I left home than Heinz Heinemann, who was a Pao Chia section chief, came by on his bike, having heard of the damage to our particular area. He was relieved to see that Illo was all right. "Where is Ernst?" he asked her almost casually. When she replied, "Over at Dah Tung," Heinemann's face turned ashen. He did not know how to tell Illo that the lane in which the Dah Tung bakery was located did not exist any more. He just turned around and wordlessly left. Illo wondered about Heinemann's reaction, but who acted normally at a crazy time like that?

Meanwhile, I was crawling over the rubble that had once been the bakery.

I glimpsed brown fragments of the wood from my desk in a crater, our fore-man most likely buried beneath it. I searched for any of the other bakers but found no one. The delivery boys had left before the raid and apparently had survived. Of course, I could not see the ovens on the ground floor, but I could see the flour in the second story storeroom—which was all that remained of the building. Except for an occasional fire truck, disaster assistance from any government or military agency did not exist, and the lane crawled with hun-dreds of crying and wailing people trying to reach family members buried underneath the rubble.

Then two trucks loaded with soldiers of Wang Ching-wei's Chinese "pup-pet" government came slowly down Dent Road, and one truck stopped in front of the bakery. It was not likely that they had come to help, and I was sus-picious of their intentions. It looked as if they were searching for something. The soldiers apparently were a band of marauders looting the area. They made their way into the bakery and systematically loaded one bag of flour after the other on one of their trucks until the storeroom was empty.

The streets were crowded, and the truck drove slowly up Tongshan Road through the heart of the ghetto. The bakery was my responsibility, and I de-cided not to let these bandits get away with our flour, so I jumped onto the rear of the truck to find out where the flour was being taken. As we rolled east and then south, I started worrying that they might leave the ghetto. I had no pass, and if caught by one of the Japanese guards, I really would be in trouble; I would be turned over to Okura and sent to the bunker, and that would be the end. As I was moving a few of the flour bags to make room to hide among them, I spied Manfred, one of my fellow scouts, walking along the street. I called out to him, and he quickly understood the situation. He jogged after the truck, and I told him to phone Wallach at his office, the Hwa Mei Trad-ing Company. By the time the truck slowed down at the ghetto checkpoint, I was safely hidden among the flour bags. I could hear my heart pounding, and my body was shaking violently as the truck temporarily stopped and then rolled on.

The truck continued on its way, and not long afterward I could hear the steel gates of the Chinese garrison open and close behind me. Now what? I decided not to wait until they unloaded but to try to sneak out. As soon as I moved a few bags, however, a group of soldiers surrounded me. This was the second time I had been taken prisoner. I was still shaking, thinking back on how close I had come to being shot by the Japanese during the fox hunt. Now I smiled and tried to make some excuse for being on the truck, but these soldiers were not locals and did not speak Shanghai dialect. I protected myself as much as possible from the few blows I received before they pushed me into a filthy cell stinking of excrement. I stood around for a while until I was exhausted enough to sit down on the dirt floor with some Chinese prisoners and ponder my predicament. I was not overly worried. I knew I could rely on Manfred; he would get word to Wallach, who would surely want to get his flour back.

In the meantime, after Heinemann left Illo, he had gone back to Dah Tung and, with the help of some Pao Chia members, started to look for my body. To his surprise and relief, when he made inquiries, some Chinese told him that the *nakoning* (foreigner) had come back after the raid and then had left on the truck with the flour. At home, Illo had gone out to retrieve our belongings and bring them back home. Shortly after her return Manfred appeared and told her what had happened to me. There was little to worry about, he said; he had tracked down Wallach in his office, and Wallach assured Manfred that he would do whatever it took to get me back along with the flour.

Wallach was a wealthy "wheeler-dealer" who had many connections. While Illo sat at home worrying and I sat in the cell and tried to catch some sleep, Wallach started the wheels in motion to get his substantial property returned. First he telephoned some of his Japanese contacts, who assured him that looting would not be rewarded, that I would be released immediately, and that the flour would be available the next morning. Next, concerned that there would be a bread shortage, Wallach contacted his competitor, the owner of European Bakery. Mr. Wolf, who normally baked the bulk of the bread for the *Heime*, agreed to bake additional bread for the refugees and to purchase Wallach's flour. As it turned out, the looters got into trouble with the Japanese military for stealing the flour, so Wallach had to shell out only about CRB$250,000 (U.S.$123) as *cumshaw* for the flour and my release. I was dozing when late at night the door to our cage was opened; a guard motioned me out and pointed in the general direction of the main gate. I could take a hint and did not stand around. Finding myself on Hochien Road, I walked to the ghetto's eastern boundary, managed to cross it unnoticed, and found a ricksha that took me home. I was relieved to find that Illo had checked with her father and my mother and found that both were unhurt.

The next day the Shanghai papers reported that the air raids were expected to continue to increase. Around noon we had another bombing attack, lasting about an hour and a half and coming close enough to the ghetto to assault the nerves of everyone further and to delay the cleanup efforts. People were still buried under the rubble, and corpses were still lying on the streets. A few days later, on the way to another part of the ghetto, Illo and I had to pass the so-called sanitation department compound. Though we walked as quickly as possible, the stench was unbearable. There in the heat of the day was a huge pile of the rotting corpses collected from the streets; it must have been more than fifteen feet high. All we could do was to hold our handkerchiefs in front of our faces and get away as quickly as possible.

With the destruction of the bakery I had lost my job, and the following days and weeks were difficult. I did get a letter of commendation from Wallach testifying that thanks to my efforts, bread production for the refugees was not unduly delayed.[3] But Illo and I no longer had bread to supplement our insufficient diet, and we did not have any money for rent and food. Our meager resources quickly came to an end; with my job literally bombed out, we had no more income. It was unavoidable that we joined the ranks of those getting a meal a day from the Kitchen Fund. We had to get used to going to bed hungry, knowing that there would be no breakfast and that we would have to wait for our next meal until the following noon. Once a day Illo or I would carry a pot to the soup kitchen in the Seward Road Heim and stand in line to get a meal. It was not much to eat, and it was not tasty, but what were the options?

We were hoping that the weather would cooperate for a while, as the air raid had left a gaping hole in our room's ceiling. When it rained, we placed bowls on the floor to catch the water and slept with an umbrella over our heads. We were worried that the increased humidity would ruin the rest of our belongings.

The next week, on the morning of July 24, we heard the first of three separate waves of bombers approach. This time we were better prepared. I had picked up a discarded steel helmet with a bullet hole. I gave it to Illo to wear over a quilted tea cozy, while I wore my SVC pith helmet. The best protection, we reasoned, was in a ground-floor door frame. Both of us, wearing our headgear for protection, stood there for what seemed like forever. This attack lasted about three and a half hours and was carried out by about 100 airplanes. The whining, howling noise was nerve-racking. Every time the pitch of the whine hit bottom, we cringed in anticipation of another bomb. Shrapnel splinters and bomb fragments fell at our feet, missing us by inches. I picked one up, still red hot, and threw it into a pail of water to cool; later I engraved the date on it, and we still have it to remember that day by.

Hans Jacoby, an artist and book dealer who kept a diary and whose wife was a physician in charge of one of the aid stations, reported that after our

liberation he met and talked with several of the pilots who attacked our area
on July 17. They confirmed that the ghetto had become a primary target because the Japanese had many military installations there. Several large buildings, including a wing of the Ward Road prison, were used for the storage
of munitions. If the war had continued just a little while longer, the air raids
would have intensified, and the central part of the ghetto would have been
destroyed.[4]

The prospect for our survival was dimming. In addition to the air raids, the
papers reported cases of cholera in the city. The mood of the refugee community steadily deteriorated. A woman who claimed to have survived 168 air
attacks in London stated that the attacks on Shanghai were worse. In London
the people were able to sit quietly in solid cellars, which gave them a feeling of security. She said that this did not compare with the terror of facing
the bombs and the shrapnel in Shanghai. The roofs and walls of Hongkew's
flimsily built houses offered little protection and shook whenever a bomb
detonated in the distance.

What we did not know was that the end was much nearer than we had
hoped for. On July 27, 1945, the evening papers reported that America, England, and China had given Japan an ultimatum: surrender or face the total
destruction of Japan. Was it true? Could the war be almost over?

14

Peace and Gold Dollars

n one of the Shanghai papers of August 7, 1945, a small notice appeared, issued by the *Domei*, the official Japanese news agency. I have been unable to locate a copy of that newspaper, but I vaguely remember the wording of the terse announcement: "A new type of bomb was dropped over Hiroshima. Little damage resulted."

Two other short articles appeared on August 8 in the *Shanghai Times*:

Hiroshima Hit.

Osaka, August 7, Central Press Service (CPS) A small force of B-29s at 8.20 o'clock yesterday morning, August 6, raided the city of Hiroshima with high explosives and incendiaries.

Atomic Bomb.

Tokyo, August 7 (CPS) President Truman and Prime Minister Attlee announced simultaneously yesterday, Monday, that American aircraft on Sunday afternoon dropped an "atomic bomb" on Hiroshima, according to the United Press and Reuter newscasts recorded here.

After the first cryptic announcement we speculated as to the nature of this bomb. "It's like a cluster bomb," common wisdom had it, "a bomb that disintegrates into smaller bombs, and so on and so forth." Only a day later did we learn what sort of bomb had been used and read of the enormous destruction it had caused. The news that the Allies could successfully bomb Japan was reassuring and made the rumor that the war was over believable. We did not know that the Allied military had charged the Japanese to keep order in Shanghai until their arrival. A group of hotheads marched to the hated police station on Muirhead Road, where Ghoya was headquartered. To their surprise the Japanese had not left, and the group was ordered to stand in the sun for a whole day. Rumor had it that the ringleaders wound up in the bunker for the night.

Finally, a week or so later, the ghetto lanes exploded with people shouting and crying, and the news was passed from person to person that on August 14, 1945, Japan had agreed to surrender. The war indeed was over! We were ecstatic. We had survived! Everyone, Chinese and refugees alike, poured into the streets, hugging one another, dancing and shouting. Illo and I decided to celebrate and go to a bar for a drink. Everybody had a good time until a brawl broke out, and things got so nasty that we beat a hasty retreat out the back door. I was just a little tipsy, but I had to steady Illo, who was not used to gaoliang, the cheap, powerful Chinese rice wine. When I stopped to tie my shoelaces, I had to prop her against a lamppost for support.

The next morning we continued our celebration by opening the precious plum jam we had received from Rabbi Sober as a wedding present. Overnight the swastikas had disappeared; Allied flags were flying again from buildings, and the Japanese gendarmes were nowhere to be seen. The Pao Chia went into action to protect our community and our meager possessions against looting. August 18, 1945, finally marked the end of the ghetto when an American army rescue mission arrived at Kiangwan airport. Word spread fast: "They are going to the POW camp, and then they will come to the school compound." On August 30, they arrived in a strange-looking vehicle, which they called a Jeep. The GIs (as we found that the soldiers were called) were accompanied by Manuel Siegel, Margolis's assistant, who had been freed from his internment. It was, beyond doubt, the greatest moment in my life when I stood with the Rover Scouts and saluted the American flag as it was hoisted in the school compound. Spontaneously, the crowd burst into song: "God Bless America," followed by the British national anthem.

A few days after the surrender, my photographer friend Gert Friedrichs and I were walking along a ghetto street and came upon a crowd milling around a Japanese. It was Ghoya. He was shabbily dressed, and his clothes were torn and in disarray. When we came closer, I saw that the "King of the Jews" was saluting and bowing to the crowd around him, continually saying, "So sorry, so sorry." He had foolishly returned to the ghetto, supposedly trying "to be friends again with the Jews," and had had the misfortune to run into a group of teenagers who found his idea somewhat preposterous and proceeded to beat him up. That he was not killed on the spot is surely indicative of the upbringing of these young adults. It is fair to say that his life was saved because of the sanctity in which Jews hold a human life. This was the last time we saw Ghoya.

At that time the United Nations Relief and Rehabilitation Administration (UNRRA) established offices in the liberated areas to aid the 260,000,000 Chinese who had lived under Japanese domination and were urgently in need of assistance. UNRRA began to administer a fund of U.S.$535 million. The first UNRRA shipment brought canned foods, clothing, and medical supplies. The JDC cooperated closely with UNRRA to aid the European refugees and, most important, to make new medicines available. Illo and I were delighted to receive two U.S. Army blankets and some of the food rations.[1] We savored every bit of Spam and canned fruit cocktail, and a Hershey bar was a delicacy beyond description. The JDC established massive assistance programs, gave cash loans, and in cooperation with the HIAS started the process of assisting the refugees in their efforts to migrate to their final destinations.

In October 1945 a new rumor swept like wildfire through the ghetto—but it wasn't a rumor; it was a fact. The American army was hiring civilian workers! One could get a job and make money—gold dollars. I joined the crowd streaming to the small frame building standing on an empty lot and already surrounded by hundreds of men. I jogged around the building to survey the situation. Everyone seemed to be trying to get to one small side door, which was guarded by American soldiers wearing white armbands reading "MP." I did not know what that meant. Near the door I could see civilians wearing red armbands, signifying their former POW status.

Apparently the Chinese had heard about the hiring too, and as the crowds grew, the pressure became almost unbearable. There was no *Entschuldigen Sie bitte* (Excuse me, please) as everyone jostled for elbow room and tried to get closer to the door. I could hear the men with the MP armbands shouting, asking the people to form lines, but no one paid attention.

As I was trying to figure out a way to get to the building, I saw a couple of soldiers with the MP armbands elbowing their way through the crowd escorting a few more civilians who were also wearing the red armbands. As I glanced toward the group, I immediately recognized one of the men, even though he had grown a heavy reddish beard. "Pat," I shouted at the top of my lungs, "Pat!" I wildly waved my arms as Patrick Goharty turned. He had been a giant; he was over six feet tall, and before his internment by the Japanese he must have weighed about 200 pounds. Now he looked thin and haggard. But he had retained his high spirits. As he made his way toward where I stood, he grinned from ear to ear, swung his arms around me, and almost lifted me off the ground. "Come on, let's go!" Patrick shouted to the amazed MPs, and holding tight to my wrist he pushed through the mob to the building's entrance. Once inside I took a deep breath, and there two men, one Irish and the other a displaced Jew, stood and cried and hugged each other.

The civilians with the red armbands were British, released from the nearby Woosung POW camp. As Allies they were given preferential treatment and offered jobs by the Americans. Patrick half pulled and half pushed me to one of the tables where an American NCO was conducting interviews. Patrick explained that I had been a member of the Shanghai Volunteer Corps and that I had been helpful to the British during the occupation. Immediately, the sergeant let go with a salvo of questions: "What kind of job can you fill? Can you drive a truck? Can you type in English? What do you know and what else can you do?" I excitedly told the sergeant that I had passed the SVC police driver's test and could drive any vehicle and that I was also a mechanic, but he offered me a job as a cargo checker at the wharf. This was a job I had never even heard of, and I was understandably excited to learn something new. While the sergeant filled out some forms, I told him that my wife was a librarian and also needed a job. He said she could come and see him.

The next day Illo went for an interview and was told, "Yes, we could use a librarian, but only at a later time, since we have not yet received any books. Right now we need secretaries with a good command of English and perhaps shorthand." When Illo told him that she took shorthand in three languages, the sergeant's mouth popped open. "You're hired. Can you start tomorrow morning?" The next day Illo reported to a Major Pozzaro, adjutant general of the Shanghai Port Command at the Astor House Hotel, and became his secretary. Such positions were usually held by WACS, since it was the rare foreigner who was able to qualify for them. The major, who was from Florida, barely opened his mouth when he spoke, and Illo, being used to British English, had a difficult time getting accustomed to his accent and understanding his dictation. But Bill Shaeffer, a young sergeant from Reistertown, Maryland, who was a stenographer in her department, noticed Illo's predicament and helped her decipher her notes and the military jargon, which was new to her.

The GIs working with Illo in the adjutant general's office were a pleasant bunch of men and usually shared with her some of the canned goods they received. At five feet four, Illo weighed ninety-four pounds at the end of the war, and someone in her office evidently decided to fatten her up. Every morning she found chocolate bars and cookies in her desk and never found out who put them there. When Illo learned about the unique American holiday called

Thanksgiving and that all the men wanted the day off, she volunteered to work with the skeleton crew. She was invited to the dining room for Thanksgiving Dinner. While the men grumbled that they had been promised fresh and not canned turkey, Illo feasted on the canned turkey with all the trimmings she wanted.

Sometime in 1946 Illo learned from one of the officers in the legal department that war crimes trials had begun in Shanghai. She made inquiries and was shown a set of plans said to depict extermination camps located on Tsungming Island in the Yangtze delta.[2] She volunteered to work as secretary or translator for the Shanghai War Crimes Commission but was rejected because she was not an American citizen and could not get clearance to work with classified documents. Captain F. T. Farrell, USMC, the chief prosecutor, was quoted as saying that he avoided any mention of Jewish refugees, since there may have been a few spies among them, working on behalf of the Bureau Ehrhardt. I knew of two collaborators, one of whom was named Drucker. At the end of the war he was caught by some refugees. After he was severely beaten and his arms and legs broken, he was taken to the refugee hospital.

In the meantime, I reported to Lieutenant Harry A. Hampson at the office of the Shanghai & Hongkong Wharf Corporation. I joined a group of thirty civilians for a briefing. "Soon," we were told, "a flotilla of ships will arrive, and it will be the checker's job to count every item being unloaded and possibly loaded." That sounded simple enough, and indeed it was, provided that the members of each team of ten men cooperated fully with one another. On September 19, 1945, an armada of approximately 100 Liberty ships, which had been waiting on the high seas for the planned invasion of Japan, arrived in Shanghai.

My team comprised men of nine different nationalities which was not unusual for Shanghai. We worked hand in glove and became known as the best team on the waterfront. The checker teams used conventional methods, a pad on a clipboard and a pencil, to count every item, while the supervisors of the coolies used their own ancient system, which consisted of about fifty bamboo spikes fitted in a bamboo case. To check unloading, the spikes were sent up the gangplank to the supervisor in the cargo hold. When a bag or box was lifted onto the coolie's back, he was also given one of the bamboo spikes. At the bottom of the gangplank the coolie gave the spike to another supervisor, who, when the bamboo case was full, knew exactly how many items had been brought down from the boat. All this took place to the long-drawn-out constant singsong *Aeihcho ohaii*, which supposedly aided the coolies' breathing while they carried their very heavy burdens.

Illo and I came home evenings smiling happily at our new-found riches.
We earned enough money to move out of the ghetto and to rent a furnished
room in the attic of a European-style three-story house at 843 North Szechuan
Road. The room was unusually large, and it had a coal stove. In the morning I
rose first and got the fire going. One floor below was a large bathroom—and,
oh joy, occasionally warm water was available.

After a while I became bored with my job, and when I heard of a better paying one as a mechanic, a "grease monkey," I applied for it. I enjoyed working
on trucks in the motor pool and quickly learned how to pack wheel bear-
ings, replace brake linings, change tires, and make minor engine adjustments.
In one of the vehicles I found a book titled *Maintenance Manual: 2½ Ton Truck*.
Across the cover in bold letters was stamped "CLASSIFIED." I took the book
home to read and eagerly studied it. Although I had worked in a bookstore, I
had never learned how to classify a book. Working on a Jeep, I found another
manual, *¼ Ton Truck*, and again on the front cover—CLASSIFIED. I looked for
a classification number but could not find it. The foreman was an Austrian.
He knew his job and ran the motor pool very efficiently but could not answer
my question about what CLASSIFIED meant. It was some time before I found
out that it referred to restricted and secret material.

This job, too, became a bore, and after four weeks, when I was offered a
promotion to heavy vehicle operator, I was ready. I joined a group of expert
drivers who were able to handle every type of army vehicle, no matter what
condition it was in. The truck assigned to me was a monster, a model 50SD6
Corbitt eight-ton artillery prime mover with an 855ci, six-cylinder Hercules
engine. The problem with it? A nonfunctioning horn—and the lieutenant
refused to understand that in Shanghai it was next to impossible to drive a
vehicle with a defective or missing horn. Normally, when one hand tired
of leaning on the horn, the driver changed to the other hand. The superstitious Chinese had a disconcerting habit of crossing the road right in front of
the truck's radiator, believing that the vehicle would kill the evil spirits that
closely followed them. A foreigner accidentally injuring or killing a Chinese
ran the risk of being stoned to death on the spot by the angry mob. This job
had its risks, and I was relieved to get home in the evenings. After the war the
Chinese rediscovered their nationalistic pride, and one could sense their old
anti-foreign sentiments. After all, had not the papers proclaimed that it was
the Chinese who had won the war?

Sometimes our trucks had to pull the forty-foot flatbed trailers on which
we hauled crated 6 × 6 trucks from the wharf to the motor pool lot. Uncrated
6 × 6 trucks (perhaps carrying Jeeps as cargo) were drivable in some fashion;

these we would pick up at the wharf, get them started, and drive them to the motor pool. We even had to drive vehicles with missing seats or, worse, maneuver a heavy truck with defective brakes through traffic, relying on horn and handbrake.

On one of our first trips, my Corbitt was loaded with ¾-ton weapons carriers. We were crossing over a rickety old wooden bridge when the truck following me broke through and plunged a few feet down into a muddy ditch. The driver was my friend Hans Gumpert, who fortunately was not injured. Hans was an easygoing, jovial fellow, always able to make the best of any situation. With his truck and cargo sitting deep in the mud, he climbed on top the cab and with full voice burst out singing the old song, popular with the British Boy Scouts, "Pack up your troubles in your old kit bag and smile, smile, smile."

I backed up my truck, and after a steel cable from Gumpert's winch was attached to my rig, I put my mighty Corbitt into a low gear (it had ten gears) and started forward. The power of this truck was simply amazing. I could barely feel it pulling, but after a few minutes the other truck and trailer were back on the road.

Pulling long trailers through the narrow streets of Shanghai required constant careful maneuvering. I almost got into an argument with the lieutenant over the defective horn, but I could not afford to lose my job. Then I remembered the powerful substitute I had used when driving a British lorry during the rice riots. Whenever necessary, I simply depressed the clutch and stepped on the gas. The mighty engine roared, heads turned, people stared, and pedestrians scattered.

I really enjoyed this job, and Illo and I made a lot of money; between us we earned almost U.S.$100 a month. I felt secure enough to follow my mother's example. In March she had repaid the JDC a loan of CRB$4,950, and in July I visited the JDC office and proudly repaid the cash allowance of CRB$7,500 that I had received. Fortunately, the loans had been in Chinese currency. Since Illo and I now earned gold dollars, it was easy to repay them. For several years we had spent money as fast as we could, because it constantly lost value. Now Illo and I could afford a few necessities or even luxuries that we had done without for so many years. When we heard about a place in the western outskirts of Shanghai that had a swimming pool with safe water, we did not give the cost a second thought. On one glorious Sunday, Illo and I enjoyed a plunge into the pool and the extremely rare luxury of a glass of lemonade served with a straw. That pleasure cost us twenty American dollars, but it was worth every penny. For about the same amount, I bought a Chinese lamb fur coat for Illo's birthday.

Despite our new-found riches, and more or less regular income and food, we were delighted and embarrassed when a large package arrived from America. It contained good used clothing which had been mailed by a Jewish family in Framingham, Massachusetts, as part of a drive organized by the B'nai B'rith to send clothing to needy refugees in China.

Frequently, Illo came home for dinner loaded with all kinds of goodies she received from her colleagues at the office or bought at the PX. The cans came with a tiny can opener, which worked surprisingly well. Spam was great and Hershey chocolate bars even better! One carton was labeled "icebox cookies," and they were most delicious, but Illo and I were puzzled by that name. "Beetle cookies" would have been more descriptive, since the cartons and the cookies were crawling with these tiny insects. Nevertheless, these cookies were so good that we devoured them after carefully breaking them apart to avoid eating these nasty little beasts.

When Illo and I came home from work together one evening, climbed the four flights of stairs, and sat down to talk about our day, both of us started scratching our legs. At first neither of us gave any thought to it; we were used to insect bites. But then I felt something crawling around my ankle. When I caught one of the fleas, we hurriedly undressed and examined every bit of clothing until we were positive that we had killed them all. We were upset and shaken by this discovery; quite a few cases of black plague had been reported throughout the city. After a rat died from the dreaded disease, its fleas would leave the corpse and jump on another live body. We dressed as quickly as we could and walked to 695/5 Tongshan Road, the home of our physician and good friend Dr. Kurt Wolff. "There is nothing that I or anyone can do about it," he said, but he tried to calm us by insisting that not every flea bite would bring on the fatal disease.

We went to our favorite Chinese restaurant, located in our block of North Szechuan Road. We ate silently, horrified at the sudden turn of events. We had survived the Nazis, we had survived the air raids, we had survived the Japanese Kempetai and all the hardships, we were free, really free for the first time in our lives. No Nazis, no Japanese, and best of all, we were working for the Americans. We were making a real living at last and had already reapplied for our visa to the United States. But now—would we make it alive? Or would we be buried soon, barely below the surface of the soggy mud of Shanghai, wrapped in a straw mat? Maybe we would not even be given a funeral, because no one wants to get close to a black plague corpse. Deep in thought, we silently walked back to our room and climbed the stairs. No sooner had we unlocked our door than we were itching again and had to undress once more and get rid of the pests.

It did not take me long to discover the source of the fleas. The W.C. was located on the third floor, and the fleas jumped on us whenever we went down to the toilet. A rat must have died under the staircase. What to do? I got up early the next morning and found a lively cat in the alley. With the help of some Spam and a neighbor, we repeatedly chased the cat up and down the stairs between the third and fourth floor and then chased him out of the building. It worked. The dead rat was still under the staircase and the stench remained, but who cared? We had gotten rid of the fleas and had survived once again.

One evening in 1946 Illo came home with the news that soon there would be less activity for the Shanghai Port Command and that she had been asked to transfer to the newly activated Air Division of JUSMAG-China (the Joint United States Military Advisory Group) as soon as possible. Its headquarters were located in Nanjing, (then called Nanking), about 165 miles northwest of Shanghai—a distance of one hour by air, seven or more by train, and two and a half days by river boat down the Yangtze. Its mission was to assist the Generalissimo, General Chiang Kai-shek, with the reorganization and modernization of the Chinese armed forces.

During her year at the Port Command, Illo had established herself as a highly efficient administrator. She had become almost indispensable to the operation, so when she was asked to transfer to Nanjing, she replied that she would not be able to go without her husband. "What can your husband do, besides driving heavy equipment?" she was asked. "Can he type? If so, we'll find a job for him." I could type, and that's how I became a "clerk-typist" in the A-4 section of Army Air Corps Supply. In typical army fashion, my presence in Nanjing was requested immediately, while Illo was told that she could not accompany me because the billeting for married couples was not yet completed. It was good that Nanjing was only one hour's flight from Shanghai, but the mere thought of separation frightened us both.

Not knowing how long our new jobs would last, we did not give up our room. We owned one piece of real furniture, a so-called Peking chest, which we had bought in an antique shop for ten gold dollars and carted home in a ricksha. It was a beauty, made of rosewood and lined with camphor wood, and the top, front, and sides were inlaid with jade and semiprecious stones.

For a few thousand CNC dollars (the new Chinese National currency) a carpenter made a solid crate, so that we would be able to transport the chest safely to the United States when our turn to emigrate arrived.

To guard against the looting of our belongings during our absence in Nanjing, we made arrangements to have our few belongings stored, and through a refugee agent Illo purchased an insurance policy to cover them in storage. It was issued by the Shanghai agents of Firemen's Insurance Company of Newark, New Jersey, in the amount of CNC$48,000,000, and the premium was CNC$57,960. When we had started working for the U.S. Army, we were paid in gold dollars. Apparently someone in the Chinese hierarchy complained, and now we were being paid in CNC dollars. Again we found ourselves having to spend Chinese currency as fast as we received it, since it continued to lose its value. Three years later it took about 2,325,000,000,000,000 (that is, two thousand three hundred twenty-five trillion) CNC dollars to buy one U.S. dollar.

Illo was supposed to follow me very soon, but this would be our first separation. Our war experiences had made us fearful, and although Nanjing was not far from Shanghai, parting was not easy for us. Ever since I had said *Auf Wiedersehen* to my father and my sister that fateful day in March 1939, never to see them again, I had abhorred partings. But this was different; we were both optimistic and looking forward to the eventual new beginning, life in America. Working for the American armed forces became more than a job; it brought us in living contact with Americans. We both knew that working in Nanjing would provide us with new opportunities to learn more about what was to be our new country.

And so, sad and upset to leave Illo, yet very excited at the prospect of leaving Shanghai and starting a new phase of our lives, I got on the shuttle bus to Kiangwan Airport. I looked forward to my first airplane ride. I boarded the C-47, a two-engine propeller-driven aircraft, chose a bucket seat right behind the cockpit, and strapped myself into the parachute harness. As soon as everyone was accounted for, the door was closed. The plane lumbered down the runway and gradually gained altitude. What a sight! Down there I could see the Whangpoo and the Yangtze delta. I watched excitedly as Shanghai disappeared below me.

NANJING

With the Americans

15

The Joint U.S. Military Advisory Group

I tried to look at the countryside below, but as usual, it was too hazy to see much besides flat farmland. After about fifty-five minutes, however, I saw hills, real hills, and lakes and rice paddies. Soon the plane swooped low over the Yangtze River, and I could see clearly the Purple Mountain and the enormous mausoleum and memorial to Sun Yat-sen, father of the Chinese Republic.

After spending all these years in Shanghai, I had not had the chance to visit any other city in China. Now I eagerly took in the sights of Nanjing as I looked out of the window of the shuttle bus that took me to the U.S. Army compound. Nanjing was the seat of the national government and one of the most interesting cities in the country. Though not a very attractive city at first sight—being muddy and dusty, lacking adequate paving—it was rich in historic sights. It had been the capital in ancient times and now had again become the headquarters of the Kuomintang government. Purple Mountain was a series of rolling hills, about 1,600 feet high and easily climbed. With a Jeep one could drive up to the top, where an ancient observatory was located.

After I reported to the personnel department, the billeting officer assigned me to the "married couples Quonset huts" but told me that because the huts were sitting in a mud field, Illo would not be allowed to move in until the concrete walkways were completed. Why men but not women were permitted to walk to the huts through the mud was not explained, but by then I had learned that "there was a way and then there was the Army way."

Although the accommodations were rather spartan, I could not wish for anything better. Our Quonset hut was partitioned to accommodate six couples. Each room had two beds, a dresser, and a chair. Toilet facilities and a shower were at one end of the hut. The couples who eventually moved in were looked after by an amah who was at their beck and call and who cleaned their rooms and washed and ironed their laundry. In the center of each room a single electric light bulb hung suspended from the ceiling. As a rule, the portable electric generator was so overloaded at night that one had to look hard at the bulb to determine whether indeed the light had been switched on.

After I had unpacked my suitcase, I hitched a ride to the General Headquarters compound. The organizational structure of the headquarters command was highly unusual. Since this command served in an advisory capacity to the Generalissimo, the personnel consisted of selected uniformed army professionals, including attorneys, engineers, economists, and political scientists. There were many generals, presided over by the ambassador to China, former army general George C. Marshall, who directed the military advisory activities from the U.S. Embassy. It seemed there were more full colonels than lieutenant colonels, as many lieutenant colonels as majors, more majors than captains, and there was rumored to be a lone second lieutenant in the whole Air Division.

With trepidation, I entered the modern Air Division headquarters building. A guard directed me to the second floor, where I located the offices of A-4, Air Corps Supply, and reported to the chief clerk, Master Sergeant Francis W. Hugunin. Hugunin was regular army, a man who rarely smiled but was always polite and always correct. "Major Dodge's papers got lost in transit and his departure has been delayed," he declared, pointing to a corner of the room. "You will have to use this desk for the time being." He took me into the adjoining offices and introduced me to my immediate superior. In front of the window of a large office sat Lieutenant Colonel Harry W. Atkinson, Assistant A-4, his head cocked slightly, holding a pencil to the corner of his mouth. He wore a quizzical but warm smile as he looked me over and began to outline my duties: supervising coolies, loading and unloading airplanes, maintaining the inventory of the group's warehouses and supply depots, and typing reports on all activities. It was a responsible position, he informed me, and if the duties were performed well, there might be a promotion. It was a cordial group of officers and enlisted men with whom I was working, and I felt very comfortable and well treated by everyone.

I soon discovered that a person responsible for supplies was very popular, since there was always someone who needed something special and was anxious to avoid the red tape connected with going through channels. If a request was legitimate, I obliged, but until I was sure of my actions, I carefully checked with Colonel Atkinson. Slowly I became acquainted with my job. I worked hard, and one day the colonel called me to his office to tell me that Major Dodge was leaving the next day, and I would be able to move into his office and take over his duties. I was overawed to learn that I would be responsible for all materiel for the Air Division advisory teams throughout China, including expendable supplies such as pencils and high octane aviation fuel, as well as individually registered items such as airplanes. In addition, since this operation had not yet received sufficient funds from Washington to be fully operative, I was asked to maintain complete records of every transaction and report on my activities to expedite the funding request. Sergeant Hugunin showed me how to operate the "squawk box," as the shortwave radio was called, so that I could communicate at any time with the advisory teams in the field. A weapons carrier, ¾-ton truck number 13, was assigned to me, and when I was given my own private office I was in seventh heaven.

The advisory teams were distributed widely in China with army teams in some locations, army air corps teams in others, and navy teams in still others. In general, however, in accordance with decisions made in the United States, the teams were kept out of the Communist areas north of Beijing (formerly Peiping or Peking) and provided "advice" or training only to the Chinese Nationalist forces.

I was content except for my separation from Illo. I had access to a "squawk box," but Illo didn't; telephone communications were extremely poor, and telegrams expensive. Almost daily, I received a letter from Illo, but I was a very poor letter writer and used every possible excuse to find alternative methods of communication. I had buttonholed every officer in the command for help in getting Illo to Nanjing, but although they all sympathized with me, they could do nothing to override the decision of the billeting officer—without whose permission Illo could not get her orders cut, allowing her travel on a military airplane. Yet ironically, it was Illo who had gotten the job in the first place, and she was badly needed in A-3, the Air Corps Operations and Training. "Just stick it out," I was told, but I could not sit by idly and do nothing.

With the influx of military personnel, the only hotel suitable for foreigners was booked solid, and not a single room was available in Nanjing. I talked to some of the other men, exploring the possibility of smuggling Illo into the Quonset hut—but there was the amah. I went to see another civilian couple for advice. José Ozorio was Portuguese, and his wife, Wynn, was Australian. They lived in a rented room with a Chinese family, waiting for permission to move into the Quonsets. They were a charming couple, and Wynn, who was tough as nails, was the one and only female air control operator in China. José, an accountant shuffling papers in the PX, was always helpful, announcing the arrivals of goodies from the States.

"There is a small hotel in Footze-miaoh," José volunteered with a twinkle in his eye which momentarily puzzled me. "But Footze-miaoh is off limits. The red light district is in it," I replied, once I realized what had been suggested. "Just park your weapons carrier outside the district and walk half a block," suggested José. "They always have rooms available, and they are not expensive; we stayed there one night until we found this furnished room." Enthusiastically, I drove to the telegraph office and wired Illo: "Private billeting secured, come at once."

Illo was ready and eager. Since many of her co-workers had been sent home during the year that she had worked at the Port Command, she did not regret leaving Shanghai. And since she worked in the adjutant general's office, her orders to transfer were cut within hours after she produced my telegram. The next morning she locked the doors of the room on North Szechuan Road where we had lived since the end of the war and took a ricksha to the Broadway Mansions Hotel to check in for the ride to the Kiangwan airfield.

When she walked into the transportation office the major in charge looked at her: "I can't let you fly like this, Illo; you know that, don't you?"

"What do you mean, Richard?" she asked, puzzled.

"Someone woke up to the fact that it's difficult to strap on a 'chute over a skirt. Didn't you read yesterday's orders?" And he quoted: "Female personnel traveling on military aircraft are required to wear slacks."

"But I don't own any slacks," Illo retorted.

"I'm sorry, but there is nothing I can do about it. Just a few minutes ago I even turned the general's wife away."

Illo left her suitcase with the major and dashed home by ricksha, telling the coolie to wait for her. She raced up the four flights of stairs, unlocked the door, and in desperation took a pair of light green lounging pajamas out of the storage box and put them on. The major grinned when she returned to the transportation office. "Good, you made it back just in time. The wives are waiting for you in the truck, and it's ready to leave." When Illo went to the truck, she found a group of women, well dressed in pant suits. It dawned on her that this was October 10—or Double Tenth as it was called in China—a major holiday commemorating the founding of the Chinese Republic in 1911; that night there was to be a party in Chiang Kai-shek's residence in Nanjing, and the wives of the officers stationed there were flying to Nanjing for the command performance.

At Kiangwan Airport, when they assembled near the C-47, Illo, who did not know any of the women, noticed an older lady standing by herself beside the staff car that apparently had brought her to the airport. She was dressed in well-worn corduroy pants that were much too tight, and Illo felt better about her own outfit. Having never flown before, it was with some trepidation that she climbed up the few steps of the plane. The older lady in the corduroy pants, who did not seem to belong to the rest of the group, noticed Illo's hesitation and motioned her to the bucket seat next to her. The lady had no problem strapping herself into the parachute harness and, seeing Illo's confusion, helped her get into hers. She offered chewing gum and a *Reader's Digest*. Illo, unsure of herself, apologized for her lounging pajamas, wondering what her husband would say about her outfit. "I have been wondering, too," the lady said, "how my husband will react to these borrowed slacks."

I had arrived at Nanjing Airport early. I could not wait to show Illo the GI uniform I was permitted to wear and "my own" weapons carrier. Next to one of the staff cars stood General George C. Marshall. A lady in dark green corduroy pants was the first to emerge from the plane, followed by the other ladies and Illo. As we hugged each other, Illo was ready for my expected comment about her pajamas. "They don't look as funny as the ones that lady is wearing," Illo said defensively, pointing in the direction of the staff car. "You mean Mrs. Marshall?" I asked, and it suddenly dawned on her why the other women had kept their distance: Mrs. Marshall far outranked them. Later I learned that there was even more subtle distancing between the advisory group people and the Marshalls. Internal U.S. Army and U.S. State Department conflicts, jealousies, and policy differences kept many Americans apart.

General Marshall, appointed by President Truman as the U.S. ambassador to China, was to forge a coalition Nationalist and Communist government. Marshall had arrived in Shanghai in December 1945, but immediately found himself at odds with General Albert C. Wedemeyer, U.S. commander in chief of the China theater, and a confidant of the Generalissimo. Ambassador Marshall established field teams of generally high-ranking American army officers who were to monitor the amalgamation of Nationalist and Communist troops in North China. They were never put to work, however, but lingered in Beijing at Executive Headquarters, which the U.S. Army Advisory Group members in Shanghai and Nanjing referred to as the "Temple of the Ten Thousand Sleeping Colonels."

In contrast, after some delays in the United States the Joint U.S. Military Advisory Group was established in Nanjing (with teams in other cities) under the command of the Pentagon but actually operating under the control of

Ambassador Marshall and the U.S. Embassy in Nanjing. The advisory team members were in daily direct contact with the Nationalist military officers and officials but not with the Communists. By the fall of 1946 the army people were not sure that they and the U.S. State Department were on the same team. This conflict was even reflected in the separation between army wives and State Department wives.

After Illo made a quick stop in the ladies' room to exchange the pajamas for her skirt, I took my pretty wife to headquarters and proudly introduced her. Her office was located on the same floor as mine, on the opposite side of the building, but there would be little, if any, interaction between Illo's job and mine. Having learned about rivalries between the services and even within units of the armed forces, Illo suggested that we would never discuss any Air Corps business between us. It was a good thing that we adhered to this rule, because some time later questions were raised about a leak within Air Corps departments. It was only natural that suspicion would fall on Illo and me, and we found out later that specific questions had been posed to each of us to test us, but our answers proved that we were totally unaware of the problem.

That first day we both worked for a few hours before I took Illo on an inspection tour of the facilities. We stopped at the Quonset huts to drop off her suitcase and collect a few overnight items. Since meals were included in our pay, I usually ate in the mess hall. We also had the privilege of eating dinner in the Chinese officers' mess of OMEA, the Officers' Moral Endeavor Association, which was a sort of special services and recreation unit for Chinese government employees. That's where we went for some good northern Chinese cuisine, choosing two main dishes, carp and pressed duck. Both were well prepared, and the service was impeccable.

Illo and I had been separated almost a month, we had a lot to tell each other, and it had been a long, exciting day. We decided to go to the hotel early. We drove through Footze-miaoh's streets with their many curio and brocade stores. I had received explicit instructions from José about where I should park my weapons carrier, and I had no problem finding the Hotel of a Thousand Dreams. A slight communication problem arose as I was trying to register, because the hotel clerk spoke Mandarin, while I spoke only Shanghai dialect. When the receptionist wanted to rent me a room for only one hour, I finally realized to what kind of hotel I had taken my wife. Now I remembered the mischievous twinkle in José's eyes when he recommended this place!

I finally persuaded the reluctant clerk to give me a room for a whole night. And what a night it was! The rooms were more like stalls, each containing a bed, a chair, a small table, and a spittoon. They were separated only by card-board and newspaper sheets glued to wooden frames. Every whisper from adjoining rooms could be heard. All night, vendors roamed the corridors, going from room to room and touting their wares to the changing occupants. I jammed the chair against the shaky door to keep the traffic out, and despite the noises, the loud, annoying five-tone music, and the single red bulb hang-ing from the ceiling which could not be switched off, we were able to sleep fitfully for a few hours.

We rose before dawn, dressed, and stopped for showers at the Quonset huts, then drove to the mess hall for breakfast. For Illo this was a new ex-perience, a real, full American breakfast. We ate the cereal and the fruits and the eggs, and we ate and ate. I had told her about it, and now she too could experience this feast each morning before going to work.

Even after several cups of coffee we were still groggy from lack of sleep, and I was furious that I had been forced to take my wife to that place. All that ridiculous fuss because sidewalks were not yet ready. I told my boss about this dilemma. "Why don't you go to the billeting office one more time? If they still give you trouble, file a complaint with the inspector general," Colonel Atkin-son suggested. Illo, in the meantime, was trying to learn new procedures but could hardly keep her eyes open. When she noticed the questioning glances of Colonel Rector (chief of A-3), she decided to tell him about her sleepless night and my problem with the captain in charge of billeting. He took action immediately, and the timing could not have been better. As I entered the billeting office, the captain was on the phone, and I could hear him being chewed out, obviously by a higher-ranking officer. He was embarrassed when he turned and saw me standing in the doorway. "We have found a way to in-terpret the regulations differently," he proclaimed cheerily. "I see no reason why you can't both move in immediately." That set the precedent, and within days several other couples were also established in the Quonset hut.

Illo and I made many new civilian friends and also enjoyed a very harmo-nious working relationship with Air Corps personnel. One morning a strange rumor swept the second-floor offices. The previous day a new civilian secre-tary had started working in the adjutant general's section. She was brought to work in the morning and picked up in the afternoon in a chauffeur-driven Cadillac. Cadillacs were a rarity in Nanjing; even the generals' staff cars were usually Plymouths. What kind of secretary could this be? Sometime before lunch Illo went to the ladies' room, where she saw a young woman putting on her makeup in front of the mirror. As their glances met in the mirror, both of them let go with a shriek: "Illo!" "Marion!" They could not believe their eyes, and yet there they were, friends meeting in a ladies' room in China years after having attended the same school in Berlin. Neither one could eat much for lunch; they had too much to talk about, telling each other their experiences during the war years.

By special arrangement in 1938, England had permitted approximately 1,000 Jewish children to immigrate. Many parents, unable to find a way to get out of Germany, accepted this painful separation in order to save their children. Later, between December 2, 1938, and September 1, 1939, an additional 8,540 children were rescued. With few exceptions, most of these children never saw their parents again. Marion survived the war in England where, in Cambridge, she met and later married Ling-Chou Loh, a graduate student at the university. They subsequently went to live at his parents' home in Nanjing.

Ling's father was well educated and familiar with Western customs; his mother, however, was still bound by Chinese tradition. The family lived in a large comfortable house, and Mrs. Loh ruled over a staff of servants with an iron hand. The Lohs were members of the upper class, and old Mr. Loh was a member of Chiang Kai-shek's government. Ling kept busy in his office, but Marion was bored at home with nothing to do except occasional shopping with her mother-in-law for jewelry or brocade; Marion was spoiled to a degree unknown in Western households. Servants were at her beck and call at all times; she felt like a bird in a jeweled cage and finally could not bear it any longer. Ling understood the problem and discussed it with his father, who persuaded his wife to give her blessing for Marion to leave the house and take on a job. Of course, she had to meet certain conditions to get her in-laws' permission for this totally unorthodox endeavor. So, at a request from the office of the president of China, a position was made available for her in the adjutant general's office of the advisory group to the Chinese armed forces.

Illo and I were invited for dinner at the home of Marion's in-laws, where we spent a delightful evening getting to know each other. Little did we suspect that a couple of years later, Ling's family would be forced to flee China a step ahead of the Communist forces. Marion and Ling emigrated to the United States, and we remained good friends and have kept in contact during the past forty-five years.

Apparently my boss was satisfied with my job performance, for at the end of January 1947 Colonel Atkinson called me into his office and told me that I was being promoted, reclassified from clerk-typist to clerk-specialist with a salary of CNC$1,073,000. As a matter of fact, I discovered that with the exception of a physician and an engineer, I had become one of the highest-paid civilians in the command.

My promotion gave me additional incentive to complete my assignments on schedule. I was always in a rush; rounding a corner I more than once inadvertently bumped into an officer and was reprimanded for walking too fast in the hallways. Illo and I both worked hard, and for the first time since we had left Germany we led a carefree life with sufficient time to relax and enjoy ourselves. Special Services had a small library, which we used extensively. There was a choice of movies every night, and whenever we got tired of mess hall food, we went to OMEA's dining room for a good Chinese dinner.

One of our friends who worked at the American Embassy had heard of an outstanding restaurant, and we decided to try it one evening. The restaurant, which was located on an unpaved dirt road, served Muslim-style food, and we were amazed to see limousines with diplomatic license plates parked in front. Like most Chinese shops, during the day it had neither a door nor a wall; only at night would the shutters be replaced. Plain wooden tables and chairs stood on the earthen floor facing the hearth in the rear of the room. The dinner was superb, proving that ambience definitely is not a necessary ingredient for excellent food.

By January 15, 1947, the Air Division was almost completely manned. It had 296 officers and enlisted men assigned to its several units, and nearly 100 civilian employees.[1] More than half—175—of the officers and men were stationed in Nanjing, where the Chinese Air Force headquarters and the Air Staff College were located. There, three teams operated from the airfield with Chinese Air Force units. Another fifty-four officers and enlisted men were in Shanghai with four Chinese Air Force units, fifteen at Hangzhou (formerly Hangchow), twenty-three at Wuhan (Hankow), and twenty-four at Chengdu (Chengtu). Another three were to advise a Chinese Air Force fighter group stationed at Beijing, but the advisers themselves were held back at Nanjing. Beijing was already full of American military personnel attached to Marshall's peace effort headquarters.

Each Air Division team had its own cargo aircraft, a C-47 or the larger four-propeller C-54. They made weekly trips to Nanjing and called me on the squawk box whenever they needed to update their list of needed supplies. I had mixed feelings when I supervised the loading of high octane aviation fuel into the belly of C-47s flying to Chengdu; the plane was forced to use a hazardous riverbed as a runway, and a crash with a full load of gasoline would spell instant disaster. The Chengdu team was very popular, however. Chengdu, the "city of brocade," located about 860 miles inland, was famous for its beautiful arts and crafts, especially the lacquerware and silver that were handcrafted and sold there. The team members were nice enough to take orders and buy finely filigreed candlesticks, plates, ashtrays, and miscellaneous solid silver curios, which they brought back for their friends.

In the spring of 1947 the Protestant chaplain of the Air Corps, Captain Kenneth Fristoe, obtained matzoth for Passover from Special Services Supply in Japan, and he arranged for a complete Seder meal to be prepared for the Jews then living in Nanjing. On the evening of Passover, Captain Fristoe conducted the Seder service. For many participants, this was the first Seder in many years, and it was a very emotional and memorable event. In return, I assisted the chaplain in wiring and setting up the public address system for the Easter sunrise service. It was held in a very scenic setting, a new amphitheater built by the Chinese government in anticipation of the Olympic Games being held in Nanjing (a plan that never materialized). You did not have to be a Christian to be profoundly moved when the sun rose majestically behind the amphitheater. It was a very beautiful service, and despite the religious difference I felt a strong kinship with the worshipers.

For years Illo and I had been cooped up in Hongkew, and now we and the other refugees who worked in Nanjing used every opportunity to see the surrounding countryside. Lotus Lake, a very scenic spot, was a popular excursion site. We rented a small gondola and, propelled by a coolie, leaned back in the boat and enjoyed the scenery. Once, as we drove along a deserted road, it occurred to me that this was a good time to give Illo driving lessons. She had fun and did exceptionally well driving through the countryside until she apparently tired of handling the heavy weapons carrier and, while I gently pulled back on the handbrake, slowly let the truck veer into a ditch. Aside from the versatile Jeep, the weapons carrier was one of the best vehicles in the U.S. Army's arsenal. It was just as easy getting it out of the ditch as driving it in.

One evening after dinner, together with friends, we drove out of the city gates to the "street of the animals," an avenue lined with oversized stone animal sculptures dating back to the Ming dynasty. In a good mood after having had a few drinks, we decided to check whether the animals normally standing up changed positions at midnight with those normally lying or sitting down. We piled out of the car and, to music from the car's radio, started to dance. By the time we decided to leave, the battery was too weak to start the car. Only a concerted effort by the whole group to push the car enabled us to get back to the city. But when we arrived at the city wall, we found the gates closed. It had been a very happy group, but now we fell silent. How could we get back into the city? We could not possibly spend the night in the country. Depending on the local topography, the wall was maybe fifty feet high and about twenty-two miles long. Of its thirteen gates, nine were usually open during the day but were closed at nightfall. Fortunately, old-fashioned as the city gates were, a peephole provided communication with the soldiers on the inside. Although they were obviously impressed that American Embassy people were trying to enter, it took lengthy negotiations and a few thousand dollars of cumshaw to persuade the soldiers to open the gate and let us back in.[2]

It was early spring when I received a cable from my mother, who was still living in her room on Ward Road in Shanghai. A letter from the American consulate had informed her that our quota numbers had finally been called. I was to appear for an interview and a health examination. I was given time off (TDY—temporary duty) and was able to fly to Shanghai and back on a military plane. I was very excited at the prospect of getting my visa and finally going to America. All went well at the consulate except that when the doctor checked my pulse rate, it was too fast. "I cannot give you a clean bill of health," the doctor proclaimed. "You will have to come back, and I'll have to recheck your pulse." My explanation that I was excited did not help, nor did my protestations that I was needed in Nanjing.

On the return flight, the plane unexpectedly ran into a rare snowstorm, and to complicate matters, the pilot announced that both radios and the navigational gear had somehow been knocked out; he was unable to communicate with either the Shanghai or the Nanjing tower. In the meantime, back in Nanjing, Illo happened to phone Wynn Ozorio, who was on duty in the tower, to arrange for a dinner date. Wynn did not know that I had flown to Shanghai and promptly upset Illo with the latest: "Have you heard that we lost the Shanghai shuttle?" Well, like a cat with nine lives, I was lucky again. The Air Corps had a bunch of good pilots who could read their maps. After ours got out of the snow squalls, he found his way back to Nanjing and the airport before the plane ran out of fuel.

When Colonel Atkinson heard the story about my fast pulse rate, he went to see John P. McConnell, the commanding general (later to become chief of staff of the Air Corps), who arranged for a checkup by the Air Corps surgeon general, Colonel Harris. My pulse rate was found to be normal, and the Army Air Corps sent an official health certificate to the consulate officials. Nothing doing, they replied; the applicant has to come back to the consulate in Shanghai to have his pulse rate checked. Exasperated, the Air Corps arranged for the physician of the American Embassy in Nanjing to check my temperature and pulse rate over the course of a whole day, and again everything was found to be normal. Both the consulate and the embassy were part of the State Department, yet the consulate would not accept the embassy's health certificate either. Finally, I had to fly again to Shanghai just to have my pulse checked. Dr. Kurt Wolff, our good friend and private physician, gave me something to make sure that I would not be so excited this time, and I finally received a certificate stating that there were no medical objections to my entry into the United States of America.

This convoluted procedure gave me the impression that some person or persons at the State Department intended to make it difficult for Jews to emigrate to the United States. Fortunately, however, Illo encountered no such problems and passed all examinations.

16

Going "Home"

Word spread around headquarters: "Illo and Ernst are going 'home'!" It sounded wonderful! Our friends were not saying that we were "leaving" for the United States. Our co-workers, officers and enlisted men and women as well as civilians, congratulated us: "When will you go 'home'?" they asked. General McConnell himself told me that he was going home at about the same time and graciously offered Illo and me a ride in his own plane. I regretfully had to decline, explaining that my mother and Illo's father were going with us.

Once again I had to fly to Shanghai, this time with Illo, to get our visas, and all went well. When Consul Elizabeth Engdahl asked us to swear that all statements we had made were the truth, the whole truth, and nothing but the truth, instead of saying "I do" I excitedly replied, "Yes, Ma'am."

With our departure imminent, I was preoccupied with being able to turn over the huge inventory of war materiel in good shape. Driving past one of the warehouses I accidentally discovered a fenced-in lot with hundreds of drums of high octane aviation fuel. No one was able to tell me who owned this small fortune. It seemed that no one knew anything about the existence of this fuel dump. Fleetingly, I thought about how easy it would be to sell the whole lot. I would be a rich man! My conscience won out, however, even though adding the "non-existing" dump to my inventory resulted in no end of problems and paperwork. At least the dump made up for a missing C-54 whose whereabouts I was unable to ascertain. The last stage to completing my work included arrangements to fly with the team's shuttle planes to Beijing, Hangzhou, Wuhan, and Chengdu, and I was overjoyed at this chance to see something more of China. These plans were dashed, however, when the long-awaited cable arrived that my mother, Illo and her father, and I were booked to leave immediately on a former troop transport ship, the American President Line's SS *General Gordon*.

We did not have much to pack. We wanted to avoid the hassle of paying cumshaw to the customs people and the dock stewards, so we let the storage company deal with it. Our pride and joy, the crated Beijing chest, and our stored suitcases were delivered to the dock on time. Chinese regulations prohibited us from taking out more than U.S.$100 per person. Since we did not have that kind of money, we carried $100 for our good friend Kurt Wolff. My mother, who had continued to live in her attic room on Ward Road until the day of our departure, had her few suitcases packed, and so did Illo's father. As we prepared to leave, we could not help thinking of all the good friends— Chinese, British, Americans, and refugees alike—we were leaving behind. Because few of them had telephones and people's plans were so unpredictable, we were not sure which of our friends had already left Shanghai or where they had gone. We had no way of saying goodbye. Perhaps it was just as well; parting would have been very painful. But how and when would we ever be able to find again these close friends with whom we had shared many experiences and some very hard times? What would happen to those still in China if the Communists some day advanced south and occupied Shanghai? We feared for our friends' well-being and safety.

After seemingly endless red tape with Chinese officials, with mixed emotions we boarded the *General Gordon* for the journey "home." During the war the *Gordon* had been used as a troop carrier, and in 1947 it was chartered to carry Jewish refugees from Shanghai to the west coast of the United States. Men were quartered in the stern, and women in the bow. The ship had not even left the Yangtze River when already some of the women became seasick. It took a strong stomach to stay in the pitching bow. Men were not permitted to enter the women's quarters, but as soon as I heard about the squalid conditions, I went forward to look for Illo. To the screams of the women that there was a man in the "room," I took her by the hand and pulled her out of that mess. The weather was exceptionally nice, and I had seen a stack of blankets in one of the supply rooms. I "liberated" a few and moved them to one of the lifeboats, and we spent the nights of the two-week Pacific crossing hidden in this boat. The blankets kept us warm, and the tarpaulin covering the boat kept the moisture out. We were far more comfortable than the passengers down below, and the sailors, with whom we soon become friendly, looked the other way. We spent most of our days on deck. Food was served in a cafeteria, where I was introduced to my first bottle of root beer. I passed it on to Illo, who did not like the medicinal taste any more than I did. We wondered who would choose to drink such a beverage.

When the ship entered the bay of Tokyo, a mine was spotted almost dead center ahead, and for a few brief moments panic broke out. The *Gordon* was too near to that ominous-looking sphere to stop, but the captain somehow managed to swing hard to starboard and avoid hitting the mine, which passed within a few feet of the side.

Accommodations aboard the *Gordon* certainly were different from the luxurious amenities of the *Potsdam*, the liner that had brought my mother and me to China from Italy. But after Shanghai, nothing could ever be bad. Nothing mattered any more, nothing, because now I was no longer alone, and Illo and I were on our way to the Promised Land, America. We got our foretaste of what America would be like when we arrived at Honolulu. Although as "stateless displaced persons" we had no passports, we had valid papers issued by the American consulate, and we were permitted to go ashore. We did not encounter the difficulties I had faced on my voyage to China.

The *Gordon* stayed in Honolulu for only a day, perhaps to load and unload cargo. The Jewish community had been alerted that a shipload of emigrants from Shanghai would arrive, and scores of volunteers were at the wharf to meet us. An elderly gentleman asked Illo and me if we would like to see the city. Would we! He took us to his car, a convertible, and drove first to a Jewish club or community center for refreshments. We were offered coffee and cake and ice cream, after which our host took us on a tour of Honolulu, even up to an old crater that is now called the Punch Bowl. We went to the rim of the crater to admire the spectacular scenery. Below us was beautiful, unspoiled Waikiki Beach with just a couple of hotels at the edge.

Illo and I marveled at the city's beautiful homes and were incredulous when told that none of the people locked their doors. Our host assured us that anyone who worked hard and saved his money should be able to buy a home. This indeed was the essence of the American dream we had heard about, and now we were observing it in reality. We had escaped the Holocaust, survived the ghetto and the bombardment, and lived through the misery of the Shanghai period. A new life lay before us.

Much too slowly, the *Gordon* steamed toward the Golden Gate. I stood with my wife, my mother, and my father-in-law on the forward deck and silently watched the approaching coastline. Relieved that the crossing of the Pacific was over, Illo and I eagerly looked forward to this moment, to seeing the

Golden Gate Bridge, the symbol of hope for countless immigrants arriving on the west coast. Many of us lining the railings had tears in our eyes.

We had been briefed by our American buddies in Nanjing; "Don't forget to make a wish and throw a penny into the water as you pass under the bridge; all your dreams will come true." Illo looked at me and protested, "We have only eleven dollars. We can't afford to waste any money." Although I readily agreed, and it was true that we were poor and not superstitious, we looked at each other and threw a penny into the waters.

Members of the HIAS met us at the Embarcadero to assist with immigration and customs formalities. Our jubilant spirits contrasted sharply with the despair I had felt when I arrived penniless in Shanghai. A bus took us to a hotel on Fillmore Street. We settled in our room and went down to the street again. When we arrived at the hotel, we had noticed a bakery next door with the window full of pastries we had not seen for years. We went in and settled for a large strawberry whipped cream pie. We took it back to our room, sat on the bed, and ate it all in one session. A letter from Illo's aunt and uncle arrived at the hotel. They were expecting us and would send us rail tickets to New York.

San Francisco is a beautiful city. Our GI friends in Nanjing had told us to "go up to the Top of the Mark and have a drink and look at the skyline." They had given us detailed instructions about how to enjoy our new surroundings. The next morning, Illo and I set out to explore. We went up to the top of the Mark Hopkins Hotel, did not have a drink, marveled at the breathtaking scenery, and left. We walked, only occasionally taking a streetcar, carefully counting our change. When we came to the seal rocks I was tempted to look at the seals through the powerful coin-operated binoculars mounted at the shore, but who could waste a dime looking at seals? Illo and I had always tried to be independent and had only reluctantly accepted a loan from the HIAS to pay for our passage on the *Gordon*. Soon we would earn money and repay the committee, as I had done in Shanghai.

As soon as the railroad tickets arrived from Illo's aunt and uncle, we left for New York.

AMERICA

A Home at Last

17

Greenhorn in New York

Illo and I acted like children when we boarded the train that would take us all the way to Chicago, where we would change trains and go directly to midtown Manhattan! All day we were glued to the window, spending as much time as possible in the observation car. At night I climbed down from my windowless upper berth to Illo's bunk, and we both watched in fascination as the train crossed the Continental Divide. We were overwhelmed by the size of the country, the spectacular sights, especially the Royal Gorge in the Rocky Mountains and the horseshoe curve in Pennsylvania.

What an opportunity to see this big country before we had to settle down and start our lives! We had been living in limbo, in an alien world. No matter how many friends I had made among the Chinese, ours had been an artificial existence. We had struggled to survive the murderous climate, hoping not to succumb to some tropical disease as Illo's mother and thousands of others had done. After our liberation, all Illo and I could think of was getting out of China to the United States. After all, Shanghai was supposed to have been a temporary stopover until our quota number was called. Yet the closer we came to New York, the more apprehensive I grew. I would not share my worries with Illo, my gnawing fears of the uncertainties of earning a livelihood. How would I find a job and what kind of a job? Would I be a laborer for the rest of my life?

I recognized Eric and Alice Goss, Illo's uncle and aunt, from their pictures as they stood on the platform of Grand Central Station waiting for us. It was a very emotional reunion; so much had happened, so many had died since they had left Germany with their young son, Bernie, in the mid-1930s.

Eric Goss was a physician. They lived in a comfortable two-story townhouse in Woodside, Long Island. Their son Bernie was away at summer camp, so Illo

and I could have stayed in his room. But I wanted to establish my independence and insisted on trying to find a place of our own. Within a few blocks, I
found and, using part of our friend's $100, rented a bedroom in a one-family
house. The room had a double bed, dresser, straight chair, and small table,
but best of all it came with kitchen privileges. The kitchen had a real refrig-
erator with a freezer compartment. And there was hot water for baths and
showers; that the bathroom had to be shared did not bother us. After years
of deprivation it was heaven.

Illo's uncle lent us some money and told me to buy a suit. We took the
subway to Times Square and entered Bonds, a large men's wear store. "Can I
help you folks?" was the salesman's greeting. Illo and I looked at one another.
Folks? Flabbergasted by this familiar greeting, we turned and, without saying
a word, left to find a suit in another store. Even though we had both worked
with Americans, having just left China and the polite formality of Chinese and
Europeans, we were not prepared for such casual manners.

Within two days of our arrival, Illo found a job and started earning money.
She had gone to the "United Service for New Americans" which offered
employment counseling, and impressed the interviewers with her trilingual
secretarial and shorthand abilities. They referred her to an import/export
company looking for someone with her skills. She was to start work the next
morning. Illo, an extremely resourceful person, felt good about herself and
confidently worked her first day in the modern, well-equipped office in lower
Manhattan. The only snag occurred late in the afternoon after she sealed the
last letter she had typed. What was the postage for a letter within the United
States? She had to go to an adjoining office to ask that question of a rather
disbelieving secretary.

While Illo was at work, I sat at home and brooded. How would I find a job
and make a living? This was the moment I had dreaded since we had left Nanjing. I had held many different jobs in China but had no profession. I knew a
little about many things, but I did not even have a high school diploma. I realized that I had been able to bluff my way through interviews, and I recalled
how I had joined the Transport Company of the Shanghai Volunteer Corps as
a driver. Without lessons, I had passed the tough police tests and driven the
British lorries through the narrow streets of Shanghai during the rice riots.

I went to the library and scanned the Help Wanted ads in the newspapers.
I found one that intrigued me: "Typewriter mechanic wanted, immediately,
apply in person." The next morning, at eight o'clock, I presented myself to the
owner of a small typewriter shop in Harlem. In Shanghai, I had watched Chi-

nese typewriter repairmen at work, and I did not think this work would be too difficult. The shop owner asked me to overhaul an Underwood typewriter. I set to work removing all rubber and chromed parts, first disassembling the carriage and then tearing the machine down to its base. I was almost ready to lower the machine base into the chemical bath when the owner stuck his head in the door. He saw the bare machine base, a sight he most likely had never seen before. "What are you doing to the machine? What are you doing to me? Why did you break the machine? Who is going to reassemble this machine? Who is going to pay for this?" If he had had any hair, he surely would have pulled it out. He wrung his hands and came after me, but by that time I had taken off my shop apron, grabbed my coat, and dashed out the back door.

I felt puzzled and confused; I could not figure out what I had done wrong. Why was the owner so angry? I had done what the man had told me to do; I had started to overhaul the machine the way my Chinese mechanics had done it. I was devastated. With no place else to go, I went home and waited for Illo. I was totally dejected, and in the evening Illo persuaded me to visit Eric and Alice. "It's no shame to get fired. That can happen to anyone, especially newcomers who may be trained to do things differently than we do them here in New York. Now you already have some experience," Eric told me. "Go and find another job as a typewriter mechanic. Besides, you get ahead faster when you change jobs a few times."

"Typewriter mechanic for outside inspections wanted," the ad said. Addressing Machine and Equipment Corporation was supposed to be one of the world's largest dealers in used office machines, and I would have great opportunity for advancement, I was told. I mustered all my courage and applied. "Yes," I responded during the interview, I had experience inspecting typewriters. After all, I had taken my Chinese crew on board American battle cruisers anchored in the Whangpoo and had brushed out, cleaned, and lubricated equipment throughout the huge ships. Next morning I was given a tool kit and some twenty ledger cards. Each card represented one machine belonging to a customer located on either the sixty-seventh or sixty-eighth floor of the Chrysler Building. I began on the top floor, cleaning, lubricating, and checking each machine and getting the operator's signature to certify that the work had been completed satisfactorily. After I finished on the top floor, I made a mistake only a greenhorn would make. Not wanting to waste time waiting for the elevator, I walked out the door. What I did not know was that this was a rarely used emergency exit, and the door on the sixty-seventh floor did not open from the stairwell. Neither did those on any of the lower floors.

I kept walking down the stairs, banging on every door until finally, on the thirty-second floor, someone heard me calling and opened the door. At that point I swore never to walk the stairs again.

Every morning, after receiving the cards and before going to their customers, the inspectors would meet in a neighborhood cafeteria for breakfast and a leisurely cup of coffee. I thought this a strange habit, and I was even more surprised to learn that about 3:30 P.M. they would meet again before reporting back to the office. I did not join my fellow workers; I had no spare money. I ate breakfast at home, and Illo usually packed a sandwich for my lunch. As a result, I finished my assigned work earlier, and the foreman gave me more cards the following days. Without any special effort, my production increased by more than 50 percent, and my customers continued to be pleased with my service. Without being told, I instinctively smiled and always treated them politely.

After working for A & E Corporation for about two months, I was puzzled when one morning the foreman did not have my assignment for the day. Instead, he told me to go to the top floor; the big boss wanted to see me. I wondered what I had done wrong this time, and my heart pounded as I was ushered into the big office. Behind the large desk a well-dressed man, perhaps in his late fifties, looked at me quizzically and finally spoke: "This has never happened to me before, and I do not like to do this." He relit his big black cigar and continued: "I am sorry, but I have to let you go. You have been a good worker and you will get two weeks' severance pay, and I will give you a good reference. It's either you or the rest of the guys, and I cannot afford to lose those bastards." I was stunned. I could barely thank the boss for the envelope he handed me as I stumbled out of the room. I had produced more than any of the others. I had put in an honest day's work, and the others did not like this one bit. They had threatened to walk out unless the greenhorn got fired. Aimlessly, I walked around midtown Manhattan, not wanting to go home. Just when I had started to make money and learn a trade, I had been fired again. As a matter of fact, a week earlier the foreman had been complimentary and had hinted of a quick promotion to a bench job. This time I was not quite as depressed when I came home and told Illo that I had been fired again. As always, she was supportive and quickly understood that this time it was not my fault.

Remembering what Illo's uncle had told me, I scanned the Help Wanted ads the next morning and landed a job as a bench mechanic. Tytell Typewriter Company was located near Wall Street and specialized in converting typewriters to foreign alphabets. This was a new field for me, and it was only a few days before I again ran into trouble. I had asked the foreman a question. "What I know is my property and I am not about to tell you," he told me in a hostile voice.

This time I was determined to fight it out. I went straight to Mr. Tytell and complained. I was willing to work hard, I told the owner, but the attitude of the foreman was not in the best interest of the company. Tytell nodded and agreed to help as much as he could. He had a warehouse loft full of broken army surplus machines that needed to be rebuilt. Would I be interested in doing piecework at night?

So far, America had turned out to be different from what I had anticipated. I had learned that in America time was money, and quality products and service took second place. I could not agree with the prevailing attitude that shortcuts should be taken and that it was permissible to steal time from the company or the customers as long as nobody found out about it. Still, I quickly learned the ropes. When Tytell hired another mechanic, an immigrant from Scotland, I discovered that others encountered problems too. The newcomer, used to European methods, was given a Smith Corona to overhaul and promptly proceeded to tear it down as I had done on my first job with the Underwood. I stopped the lad and explained that here in the States a so-called "overhaul" merely required replacement of the rubber parts, a chemical wash, adjustments, and lubrication.

I started the piecework that Tytell had offered. Alone at night in the big loft, I faced what seemed an impossible task. The pile of typewriters reached almost to the ceiling. They were not just out of order; they were broken as if a tank had rolled over them. Tytell had warned me that it would take a master technician to rebuild the junk heap, but I needed the experience and the money. I felt very confident anyway. Most of the machines were Remingtons, and I liked to work on them. I admired their design, compared with Royals and Underwoods. Remingtons were the only ones using a modular concept affording relatively easy access to the interior of the machine, making it easier to assemble and to adjust. The carriage and rail assembly were one unit, the type bars in their segment another, leaving the base easily accessible for needed adjustments. I had never attended a trade school, and what I knew of mechanical engineering I had learned in my informal lessons with Captain Groddeck. Frequently, when I had problems, I remembered Groddeck's admonition to sit back and "illuminate the problem" from all angles. I wondered what had happened to the kind old captain and recalled with fondness the tropical starlit nights when we sat in front of the Japanese house, discussing mechanical principles.

I felt that assembling typewriters from junk was good experience for me, and no one was looking over my shoulder. The time came when I completed the job converting the pile of junk to usable typewriters. When I heard of another job with more money, I gave notice. I had become quite good at my work, and I was proud that the completed machines performed and looked almost like new ones.

It was about that time that Illo told me she might be pregnant. In my travels around Manhattan I had passed the large building of the Metropolitan Life Insurance Company, and it occurred to me that with a baby on the way, life insurance was an absolute necessity. And what company was bigger or better than the Metropolitan? This was its home office, so I entered the lobby and made inquiries. "You want to buy life insurance?" was the incredulous response. Apparently no one had ever before walked in off the street to buy insurance. I was sent to one of the upper floors and was met by two gentlemen. "How long have you been in the States?" they wanted to know. "Not even five months! Very sorry, but we do not sell life insurance to immigrants until after the first year." I figured I could do without the Metropolitan and took out life insurance by mail.

I found a well-paying job with All Languages Typewriter Company in midtown Manhattan, specializing in converting typewriters to foreign alphabets and exporting them to foreign countries. I had to install new types in Arabic and Hebrew and convert these machines so that the carriages would move from right to left rather than left to right. One day a few months later, I had forgotten to bring my sandwich and returned from lunch early—to discover the shop foreman stashing office machine parts in his lunch box. I had noticed discrepancies in the parts inventory before, and now I knew the reason. I had no choice but to report the incident to the owners of the company. And in the best American tradition the foreman got sacked, and I became his replacement.

After my earlier experiences I had made up my mind to become as independent as possible. I had learned a trade; I had found a marketable skill that was in demand! I had always enjoyed working with my hands and now felt confident that I was ready to tackle more complex jobs. Soon word spread in the trade that I was the man to see when some of the new imported equipment arrived damaged and no one else seemed to be able to repair it. I instinctively did what thousands of immigrants before me had done: freelancing. I repaired odd office equipment late at night at home on the kitchen table, still keeping my other job at All Languages.

By now, I considered myself a better than average technician with managerial skills in the office equipment industry. Starting out had not been easy, I thought to myself, but I had made it in a very short time. The only problem was that I had now reached the top of my new profession: service manager of a large company. Is that what I wanted to be for the rest of my life?

In June 1948 I fell ill and was taken to City Hospital on Welfare Island. Spots covered my aching body, and I had a high fever that lasted for weeks. Twenty-seven physicians and interns visited me, trying to diagnose my mysterious illness. It could be a strain of poliomyelitis, they guessed, but the spots indicated the possibility of typhoid fever. I was placed in an isolation ward, and Illo was not permitted to visit me. I remembered that Dr. Friedrichs, the father of my good friend Gert, was living in New York; he had been a highly respected internist in Shanghai, well versed in tropical diseases. When contacted, however, Dr. Friedrichs sent his regrets. He was studying for his New York State medical examination, and if he were seen at the bedside of a patient before he had his license, he would never be permitted to practice. Regrettably, medical associations in many states did not recognize the foreign licenses of qualified physicians and made it extremely difficult for them to open a practice.

The high fever continued, and during the night of July 6, 1948, the doctors feared I would die. But I was told that Illo had been brought to the maternity ward in the same hospital and that our baby was due any time. In the morning hours of July 7 my fever went down, and I got word that I had become a father. Anita Irene was three weeks old before I was able to go home and see our new baby. I had finally recovered from what I thought was either typhoid fever or a strain of infantile paralysis. I was gratified that the owners of All Languages had been satisfied enough with my work to keep my job open for me.

Life began to settle down to a routine. We moved into a one-bedroom apartment in a multistory apartment building where, although all our windows faced brick walls, we enjoyed the spaciousness and privacy. Then it was time to buy one of America's necessities—a car. We had saved a little money, and I began to scan the ads for a used car. One ad caught my eye: "Buick, mechanic's special," it said. I went to have a look at it and was surprised at the shiny blue finish. "Mechanic's special," I assumed, meant that it was a car in good mechanical condition. After I bought it, I found out differently. It needed work, lots of it. For one thing, it had no shock absorbers.

Shortly after making this purchase, we were invited to visit Rabbi Sober, who had been one of our closest friends in Shanghai and had officiated at our wedding. Like many newcomers, he was encountering hard times. He was a very forthright person who usually said what was on his mind, and his refusal to kowtow to a congregational board had forced him to change pulpits several times. Now he invited Illo and the baby and me to visit him and his wife in their new home in a town in the Adirondacks.

We loaded our luggage into the trunk of the car and started out. No one had warned me not to drive a car without shocks, as one could lose control. Fortunately, neither Illo nor I had a tendency to motion sickness. The Buick bobbed up and down even on smooth roads; on bumpy stretches it swayed dangerously, forcing me to drive more slowly than I liked. We arrived late, but the Sobers greeted us warmly. We had not seen each other for a long time, and there was much to talk about. They had insisted on putting us up, and after we had a bite to eat we started talking. Later we put Anita to sleep and continued talking far into the night.

The Sobers were depressed, and they had reason to be. This was their third congregation since their arrival in the States. They both liked the picturesque town and the people, but the future there did not look good for them. Before coming to town for the interview, Rabbi Sober had even shaved off the beard he had worn in the past to present a warmer, friendlier appearance, but to no avail. He could not effectively represent the congregation, he was told by the president; he had a foreign accent, and the members wanted an "American" rabbi as their spokesman in the community. Sober felt sorry for the timidity of the membership of his congregation and in his Saturday sermon spoke about the need for maintaining a strong Jewish identity within a pluralistic society.

I became agitated and extremely disturbed by what I heard. I was puzzled by the obvious insecurity of this rich and doubtlessly powerful Jewish community. They had never experienced any real danger. What was the cause of their insecurity? Instead of presenting an image of positive pride in their Jewishness, their leadership apparently was satisfied with having built a synagogue. Outwardly, they would rather blend in with the community at large than give the appearance of being different.

The next day we all went to a lake and had a typical American picnic with cold cuts and cold chicken. The Sobers had brought Cokes along in a cooler, and we all commented how long it had taken us to get used to the taste, yet now we would not be without it. The few days that I was able to take off from work passed much too quickly, and soon we had to get back to New York.

Driving through the Catskills along the scenic Hudson River, we made up our minds. There was more to America than New York. We remembered the unlocked homes in Honolulu and decided not to stay in New York. There was nothing to keep us here. Now that we had a baby, it occurred to us that a child needed fresh air, sunshine, a back yard to play in. We decided that I would accelerate my search for another job, no matter where as long as it would get us out of the big city.

During this time Illo's father had settled in Chicago where until his death he worked as an accountant. My mother had become a companion to an elderly lady and lived in Brooklyn until 1964. She then moved to a retirement home in Basel, Switzerland, where she passed away at the age of ninety-seven.

Four years after our arrival in the United States I had reached the top in my profession. In 1951 Illo, our young daughter Anita, and I packed our bags and left the stone canyons to move to a midwestern city, where we worked hard, eventually bought a house, and settled down to the American way of life.

18

"The Wretched Refuse . . ."

W hile Illo and I faced the realities of a young family trying to get established and make a living, we could not forget the friends we had left behind.

Tragically, my worst fears were realized when Chiang Kai-shek's government fell and was replaced by a dictatorship. In 1949 Mao Tze-tung's Communist forces advanced south and occupied Shanghai along with the rest of China. We feared for our friends' well-being and safety. In retrospect, we know that we had reason to be fearful. Accused of spying, Heinz Egon Heinemann, Illo's former boss and our good friend, languished in a Communist jail in Shanghai for several years before he was able to emigrate to Canada in 1952.

By 1949, many refugees had settled on the west coast of the United States, in Australia, and in the newly created state of Israel. The Russian Jews who in 1917 had fled the Bolshevik revolution became refugees for a second time. A few of them returned to the Soviet Union, never to be heard from again. The rest, who had no affidavit from relatives in America or one of the Jewish organizations, or were unable to pass the rigid health examination, were moved to Israel. In the fall of 1949, however, about 2,000 refugees were still stranded in Shanghai.[1] The Chinese Communist authorities requested that all Jewish refugees who were not productive members of the Chinese economy leave China. But the U.S. consulate had been closed, and no agency was processing American visa applications. The Yangtze River was said to be mined, and American ships were no longer permitted to enter the Yangtze delta area. Those refugees who had been waiting for their quota number became desperate.

The International Refugee Organization (IRO), which had assumed responsibility for the resettlement of displaced persons all over the globe, attempted to assist them several times. In 1949 a contingent of refugees was transported on sampans and junks from the Shanghai harbor down the Whangpoo River to the Yangtze delta and out to the open sea, to be picked up in international waters by an American troop carrier. Another pickup was planned for the spring of 1950, but the Communist government made any evacuation extremely difficult. Finally, after several attempts, about 260 refugees were permitted to travel overland to Tianjin (Tientsin), where the *General Gordon* picked them up. On May 23, 1950, they arrived in San Francisco.

One hundred six of these passengers had relatives in the United States and had been waiting for their quota numbers or their visas when the Communists took over. Now they learned to their dismay that without valid visas they would not be permitted entry into the United States. The bureaucrats would not do what even the Japanese did, who in 1941 gave temporary shelter to more than 2,000 Polish Jews. In 1951 the Philippine government provided temporary asylum for up to two years to approximately 5,500 White Russian refugees; one must wonder why it was impossible for the United States to offer asylum or at least issue temporary visas for these 106 Jews, the majority of whom were aged and not well. Among them were sixty-one-year-old George Lissner and his wife Kate, fifty-five, uncle and aunt of my sister-in-law, Alice Heppner, who were not permitted to join their children Steffi and Klaus in San Francisco.

In Oakland, the group was loaded on a "bonded" train to be transported across the United States to Staten Island, New York, and sent back to Germany to obtain entry visas. This was the third overland movement by train, and in charge was a highly competent officer of the IRO, Susan Pettiss, assisted by Herbert McGushin. In contrast to their long and unpleasant trans-Pacific crossing, the trip across the country was pleasant. The armed guards who accompanied the train were very kind and thoughtful. There was no real evidence of any confinement; the guards even called themselves "escorts," and the dining car served excellent meals and generous portions.

While on board the *Gordon* the group had cabled a petition to President Truman asking for asylum in the United States. Now, on board the sealed train, what was uppermost on the minds of the immigrants was their status as DPs, displaced persons. A bill had been submitted to the U.S. Congress to establish a DP quota, and this bill was still being debated. Would their group be covered by the new DP legislation, or would they be sent back to Germany?

During the time it took the train to cross the United States, many organizations—including the JDC and the United Service for New Americans—petitioned Congress to delay the departure of the refugees. They offered to pay all expenses for their stay at Ellis Island until the amended DP legislation was signed or until every opportunity had been given to ascertain their DP status.

The train proceeded straight to the pier on Staten Island, and the refugees went directly to their assigned cabins aboard a navy ship, the *General Ballou*. Finally, 500 relatives were permitted to meet them in the ship's mess hall for two hours. It was a highly emotional scene for the group to see their children, parents, husbands, wives, and other relatives for the first time in many years. There were many tears, gift exchanges, and photographers' flash bulbs.

It was only at the last moment, Sunday, May 28, shortly before the *Ballou* was to cast off from the pier, that confirmation of an order by the attorney general's office arrived: the refugees had been given a reprieve and were to be allowed to stay on Ellis Island until June 21. It was a very dramatic scene when the refugees assembled in the mess hall and were given the news. They did not look forward to returning to Germany and were grateful for the additional time their relatives could visit. Among the shouts of joy and tears one man in a quivering voice started to sing "God Bless America," and the whole group joined in.

Representatives of the group, very appreciative of the care and good treatment they had received on board the sealed train, sent a letter of thanks to Dr. Pettiss for her sensitivity and efficient management of the transport. They hoped that their visas would be processed at the consulate in Germany and that they would ultimately be reunited with their relatives in the United States, but the thought of being forced to leave their loved ones and return to postwar Germany was heart-breaking to all. George and Kate Lissner were optimistic; they were looking forward to completing their eleven years' odyssey. They did not know that they did not fit the DP law as it was written by Senator Patrick McCarran, the guardian of America's shores. They did not know that they would have to spend three years in a Displaced Persons camp in Germany before they could finally get their visa and be reunited with their son and daughter.

The mood was somber when a replacement ship, the *General Sturgis*, finally left for Bremerhaven on June 21. Almost all had tears in their eyes as they lined the decks to look out at the Statue of Liberty. They, like other refugees, were familiar with the famous inscription on the statue that had welcomed millions of immigrants. But perhaps it was just as well that they were too far away to be able to read Emma Lazarus's poem. As they sailed away from Liberty Island to continue their 10,000-mile journey to the Promised Land, America, the irony of the lines did not escape them.[2]

In Retrospect

n recent years, when travel into China was again possible, a few of the former refugees traveled back to Shanghai. This time they went as tourists, taking their video cameras to record the street scenes in the lanes of Hongkew. They wanted a permanent record of the ghetto where they had lived to show to their children and friends. They were disappointed to find that some of the Jewish buildings had been razed, while others were occupied for other purposes. All four Jewish cemeteries had been demolished, and no remains could be found. They searched for the *Heime* and remnants of Jewish life, but except for a stone menorah over the entrance to the former Museum Road synagogue, they found little to record.[1]

Within a short time span of ten years European Jews had introduced to Shanghai a hitherto unknown degree of Western culture and European crafts, skills, and talents. At the end of 1952 about 570 so-called "hard core" cases were still in Shanghai; they were the very ill and handicapped who had no one to care for them. Their care and final evacuation were made possible by the continued financial aid of the American Joint Distribution Committee. According to a report in a news bulletin published by the Jewish Telegraph Agency, the last member of the European Jewish community of Shanghai, Max Leibovich, passed away there on January 15, 1982, at seventy-five years of age.

The Shanghai refugee community, short lived as it was, had existed under an extraordinarily difficult set of circumstances and had much to be proud of. It represented a test case for the nation-building capacity of the Jewish people. Many refugees who had been estranged from Judaism rediscovered it and became conscious Jews again, so conscious that in spite of the often strong temptation for an easier life, only a small percentage returned to their former homelands. For many Jews, living in the Hongkew ghetto with all its hardships and misery was satisfactory in another respect: it was living in a real Jewish community with a foretaste of life in a Jewish state.[2] It is a reason to be proud that in spite of the poverty, which anywhere breeds crime, the incidence of crime was amazingly low, almost nonexistent. In a period of ten years, out of a population of approximately 18,000, a total of only forty-one cases were turned over to the police by the arbitration court and tried in the Chinese courts: twenty-three cases of embezzlement, fifteen cases of theft, two burglaries, and one homicide caused by jealousy.[3] Petty thefts of food are not included in these statistics; the human instinct for survival is powerful. Is it theft when a hungry person takes food from another camp inmate? One respected Viennese lawyer who was caught in this situation, apparently unable to survive the shame, committed suicide.

Despite all the trials and tribulations, Shanghai provided us with a haven from the Holocaust. Years ago, life in the East European *shtetls* was full of hardship and danger; still, there existed an atmosphere of warmth and community. In the twentieth century, in the Far East, West Europeans—modern, assimilated Jews—were once again confined to a ghetto. Again this environment, or set of circumstances, produced a closely knit community and a microcosm of Jewish life that flourished in an alien and hostile environment. The bonds of friendship among many who shared this experience did not end when the refugees left Shanghai; they have lasted to this day, across oceans and continents.

I am very proud to have been a part of this unique community, which existed for just about one decade. It developed and it disappeared before our eyes, but it taught my wife and me the priorities for an ethical and moral way, a Jewish way of life.

Notes

Preface

1   The author received this allegory from playwright Dore Schary.

1   Under the Nazi Boot

1   Several laws defined a Jew: decrees of April 7 and 11, 1933 (a section stated that a non-Aryan was inferior to an Aryan); Nuremberg laws of September 1935; Reich citizenship law of November 14, 1935.
2   For a biography of Leo Baeck, see Leonard Baker, *Days of Sorrow and Pain: Leo Baeck and the Berlin Jews* (New York: Oxford University Press, 1978).
3   On Jewish youth under the Nazis, see Werner T. Angress, "Jüdische Jugend zwischen nationalsozialistischer Verfolgung und jüdischer Wiedergeburt," in *Die Juden im Nationalsozialistischen Deutschland*, ed. Arnold Paucker (Tübingen: J. C. B. Mohr, 1986), pp. 211–21.
4   See Jeremy Noakes and Geoffrey Pridham, eds., *Documents on Nazism, 1919–1945* (New York, 1974), pp. 473–74.
5   See Leni Yahel, *The Holocaust: The Fate of European Jewry* (New York: Oxford University Press, 1990), p. 108; Joachim Remak, *The Nazi Years: A Documentary History* (Englewood Cliffs, N.J.: Prentice-Hall, 1969), p. 150.

2   The November Pogrom

1   A partial explanation of Hitler's hate for the Jews can be found in the foreword to the English edition of *Mein Kampf* (Boston: Houghton Mifflin, 1943), p. xvi.
2   For further details, see Raul Hilberg, *The Destruction of European Jews* (New York: Harper & Row, 1961), pp. 90–97.
3   Michael Mashberg, "American Diplomacy and the Jewish Refugee, 1938–1939," *YIVO Annual of Jewish Social Science* 15 (1944): 339–54; see also *Manchester Guardian*, July 16, 1938.

4   See Wolfgang Benz, "Der November Pogrom 1938," in *Die Juden in Deutschland, 1933–1945*, ed. Wolfgang Benz (Munich: C. H. Beck, 1989), pp. 499–505.

5   See William L. Shirer, *The Rise and Fall of The Third Reich* (New York: Simon & Schuster, 1960), p. 431.

6   See Rabbi Haskel Lookstein, "Kristallnacht and American Jewry," *Congress Monthly*, November–December 1988, pp. 7–10. Also see Rafael Medoff, *The Deafening Silence: American Jewish Leaders and the Holocaust* (New York: Shapolsky, 1987).

7   See Hugo Burkhard: *Tanz mal Jude!* 2d ed. (Nuremberg: Richard Reichenbach KG, 1967), pp. 115–16.

8   Ibid., pp. 116–17.

9   See Shirer, *Rise and Fall*, p. 434.

3   "Get Rid of the Jews"

1   This document has been donated to the U.S. Holocaust Memorial Museum in Washington, D.C., one of a collection of documents pertaining to Shanghai and Nanjing; copies are in author's collection.

2   For verification on the corruption of German officials, see Benz, *Die Juden in Deutschland*, p. 427.

4   A Strange and Alien World

1   For a historical perspective of Shanghai, see C. A. Montalto de Jesus, *Historic Shanghai* (Shanghai: Shanghai Mercury, 1909). Also see the map in the front of this book.

2   For details, see *The Chinese Inflation 1937–40*, by Shun-Shin Chun (New York: Columbia University Press, 1963). My thanks to Harry W. Atkinson.

3   *Shanghai Evening Post & Mercury*, September 9, 1939.

4   Quoted in David H. Kranzler, "Restrictions against German-Jewish Refugee Immigration to Shanghai in 1939," *Jewish Social Studies* 36 (January 1974).

5   For a detailed analysis of this chapter of Jewish history, see David H. Kranzler, "The History of the Jewish Refugee Community of Shanghai, 1938–1945" (Ph.D. diss., Yeshiva University, 1971), esp. chaps. 5–6 and app., pp. 474–76. Also see Kranzler, *Japanese, Nazis, and Jews: The Jewish Refugee Community of Shanghai, 1938–1945* (New York: Yeshiva University Press, 1976), pp. 151–52, 159–60, and 166–67nn.

6   Laura L. Margolis, "Report of Activities in Shanghai, China, from December 8, 1941 to September 1943" (JDC archives, New York), p. 1. Also see Hans Jacoby, "*Tagebuch*" (Leo Baeck Institute archives, New York). Both cite the total number of refugees as high as 21,000.

7   Margolis, "Report."

8   *Shanghai Evening Post & Mercury*, June 21, 1939; *Gelbe Post*, nos. 1, 3, and 5, 1939; *China Weekly Review*, July 22, 1939.

9   JDC files, no. 458, p. 176, July–December 1939.

5   Now What?

1   See *Shanghai Evening Post & Mercury,* November 11, 1939.
2   Rena Krasno, *Strangers Always* (Berkeley, Calif.: Pacific View Press, 1992), p. 110.
3   See Ernest O. Hauser, *Shanghai, City for Sale* (New York: Harcourt, Brace, 1940).
4   For details of Shanghai climate see E. A. Pearce and C. G. Smith, *World Weather Guide,* (New York: Times Books, Random House, 1990), p. 221; and *Almanac: Shanghai 1946/47.*

6   Of Toys, Books, and Angels

1   From "Zutfense Krant," an account by a Dutch government agency, dated December 24, 1963, translated by Jan Zwartendyk, Jr.; copy in author's collection.
2   Copy of letter from Nathan Gutwirth to Rabbi Tokayer, dated September 24, 1974, is in author's collection. According to Jan Zwartendyk, Jr., Gutwirth lived in Antwerp, about an hour's drive from his father's residence, but never contacted him after the war.
3   See Marvin Tokayer and Mary Swartz, *The Fugu Plan* (New York: Paddington Press, 1979), p. 275.
4   Correspondence relating to this incident is in author's collection.

8   Of Scouts, Soldiers, and Deadly Games

1   This information was furnished by Benis M. Frank, head of the Oral History Section, History and Museum Division, U.S. Marine Corps.
2   A copy of Peter Witting, "Brief History of the 13th Shanghai Boys Scout Troop on the Scouts' Activities," is in author's collection.
3   Benis M. Frank, "The Shanghai Volunteer Corps: A Socio-Military History." Archives of the U.S. Marine Corps.

9   Survival

1   Laura L. Margolis, "Race against Time in Shanghai," *Survey Graphic* 33 (March 1944): 11–16; and Margolis, interview.
2   For a detailed description of "lane" houses and rooms, see H. Eisfelder's memoir, "Chinese Exile: My Years in Shanghai and Nanking, 1938 to 1947" (July 1972).
3   "Die Geschichte des Hongkewer Ghettos" (The story of the Hongkew ghetto), *Shanghai Herald* (special ed.), April 4, 1946, p. 2.
4   An example of this Chinese wedding certificate has been donated to the U.S. Holocaust Memorial Museum.
5   See Kranzler, *Japanese, Nazis, and Jews,* p. 415; and Kurt Redlich's voluminous correspondence with Kranzler (supplied by Redlich).

6   Margolis, "Report"; Manuel Siegel, "Report of Activities in Shanghai," dated August 26, 1945.
7   See Kranzler, *Japanese, Nazis, and Jews*, pp. 461–62.
8   Author's translation. A copy of the German original has been deposited with the U.S. Holocaust Memorial Museum.
9   A copy of this letter, addressed to a Mr. Peter and signed by H. Wasmer, Manager of the Relief Division, is in the author's collection. Only pertinent portions are quoted there.
10 See Margolis, "Report"; and Kranzler, *Japanese, Nazis, and Jews*, chap. 19.

10 War in the Pacific

1   The SVC insignia have been donated to the U.S. Holocaust Memorial Museum.
2   See Albert Parry (member of the research staff of the University of Chicago), "The Jews in East Asia," *Shanghai Evening Post & Mercury*, September 19, 1939.
3   For a detailed report on this subject, see Kranzler, *Japanese, Nazis, and Jews*, chaps. 7, 11. Also see David Kranzler, "Japanese Policy toward the Jews, 1938–1941," *Forum* 34 (Winter 1979).
4   Parry, "Jews in East Asia."
5   See Margolis, "Report," p. 3.
6   See Alfred Dreifuss, "Schanghai—Eine Emigration am Rande," in *Exil in den USA*, vol. 3 (Leipzig: Philip Reclam, 1983), p. 579.
7   See Herman Dicker, *Wanderers and Settlers in the Far East* (New York: Twayne, 1962), pp. 114–117.
8   See "Geschichte des Hongkewer Ghettos," p. 25.
9   See Dreifuss, "Schanghai," p. 580; and Krasno, *Strangers Always*, p. 55.
10 The most detailed description of this meeting is to be found in Tokayer and Swartz, *Fugu Plan*, chap. 16.
11 Ibid., p. 233.
12 Fritz Kaufmann, "Die Erlebnisse der Juden in Shanghai unter der Japanischen Besetzung im 2. Weltkrieg" (talk at the Shanghai Tiffin Club of New York, December 2, 1963), transcript, pp. 5–6; and Kaufmann, "Die Juden in Shanghai im 2. Weltkrieg," *Bulletin of the Leo Baeck Institute* 73 (1986): 13–23.
13 The reports about the circumstances of the meeting at the Japanese consulate differ somewhat, but Kaufmann's account was corroborated by Kurt Redlich.
14 See Tokayer and Swartz, *Fugu Plan*, p. 232.

11 The Ghetto

1   During the research for this book an examination of the map of Hongkew revealed a discrepancy in this published description. Chaoufong Road formed most of the ghetto's western boundary; the "line" connecting it with Muir-

head and Dent Roads (running almost parallel with Chaoufong) was East Seward Road, part of the southern boundary.

2 A copy of the proclamation has been donated to the U.S. Holocaust Memorial Museum.

3 See Dicker, *Wanderers and Settlers*, p. 114.

4 Quoted in ibid., p. 115.

12 "Let's Get Married!"

1 Correspondence with National Archives, Military Reference Branch, Washington, D.C., in author's collection; attachments include Hans Mosberg's case record and "Order on Review."

13 B-29s Overhead

1 This incident was recounted to my wife and me by a close friend, a physician himself, and is confirmed in Jacoby's "*Tagebuch*," p. 395.

2 See Kranzler, "History of the Jewish Refugee Community," p. 360.

3 This testimonial letter has been donated to the U.S. Holocaust Memorial Museum.

4 See Jacoby's "*Tagebuch*," September 6, 1945, pp. 421–23.

14 Peace and Gold Dollars

1 See Dicker, *Wanderers and Settlers*, p. 136. One of the two army blankets has been donated to the U.S. Holocaust Memorial Museum.

2 See Dreifuss, "Schanghai," pp. 567–68. Dreifuss attended that trial as a reporter.

15 Joint U.S. Military Advisory Group

1 The background information and statistics on JUSMAG-China were furnished by Harry W. Atkinson, Colonel (Ret.) U.S. Army Air Corps.

2 Some details about the city of Nanjing were made available to the author by H. P. Eisfelder, "Chinese Exile."

18 "The Wretched Refuse . . ."

1 See Dicker, *Wanderers and Settlers*, pp. 140–51.

2 Much of this material was gleaned from the reports and notes of Susan Pettiss, former resettlement officer of the U.S. office of the IRO (copies in author's collection). Other sources include Clint Mosher, "Refugees Arrive from Red China, Tell Ordeals," in unidentified San Francisco newspaper (May 1950); Phil Pearce, "Long Flight to Freedom, Refugees Here from Shanghai", *San Francisco*

Chronicle, May 24, 1950; Michael L. Hoffman, "U.S. Aid Plan Irks U.N. Refugee Chief," New York Times, May 26, 1950; "108 D.P.'s from Shanghai win a 12-day respite on deportation," New York Times, May 29, 1950; Max Lerner, "The 106," New York Post, June 20, 1950; Manfred Jackson, "Hier wollen sie nicht bleiben" (They don't want to stay here), in unidentified Bremen, Germany, newspaper; and miscellaneous news clippings from San Francisco and New York papers dated February 14, March 12, and June 19, 1952, and October 19, 1953.

In Retrospect

1   For a listing of Jewish sites in Shanghai, see Professor Gao Wang-zhi, "Jewish Sites in Shanghai," Points East (a publication of the Sino-Judaic Institute), February 1987, p. 3.
2   These are Kurt Redlich's sentiments as told to the author.
3   See Felix Grünberger, "The Jewish Refugees in Shanghai," Jewish Social Studies, February 1948, p. 335.

Bibliography

Books and Articles

Almanac: Shanghai 1946/47. Shanghai: Shanghai Echo, 1946.

Angress, Werner T. "Jüdische Jugend zwischen nationalsozialistischer Verfolgung und jüdischer Wiedergeburt." In *Die Juden im Nationalsozialistischen Deutschland, 1933–1945,* ed. Arnold Paucker. Tübingen: J. C. B. Mohr, 1986.

Baker, Leonard. *Days of Sorrow and Pain: Leo Baeck and the Berlin Jews.* New York: Oxford University Press, 1978.

Bauer, Jehuda. *My Brother's Keeper: A History of the American Jewish Joint Distribution Committee, 1929–1939.* Philadelphia: Jewish Publications Society of America, 1974.

Benz, Wolfgang, ed. *Die Juden in Deutschland, 1933–1945.* Munich: C. H. Beck, 1989.

Burkhard, Hugo. *Tanz mal Jude! Von Dachau bis Shanghai: Meine Erlebnisse in den Konzentrationslagern Dachau, Buchenwald, Ghetto Shanghai.* 2d ed. Nuremberg: Richard Reichenbach KG, 1967.

Chinese Ministry of Information. *China Handbook, 1937–1945.* New York: Macmillan, 1947.

Crow, Carl. *Foreign Devils in the Flowery Kingdom.* Pirated ed. Shanghai, c. 1930.

Dicker, Herman. *Wanderers and Settlers in the Far East: A Century of Jewish Life in China and Japan.* New York: Twayne, 1962.

Dreifuss, Alfred. "Schanghai—Eine Emigration am Rande." In *Exil in den USA: Kunst und Literatur im antifaschistischen Exil 1933–1945.* Vol. 3. Leipzig: Philip Reclam, 1983.

Eisfelder, H. P. "Chinese Exile: My Years in Shanghai and Nanking, 1938 to 1947." Manuscript memoir, July 1972.

Frank, Benis M. "Shanghai's 4th Marines: The Glory Days of the Old Corps." *Shipmate* (publication of the U.S. Naval Academy Alumni Association), November 1979.

———. "The Shanghai Volunteer Corps: A Socio-Military History." Oral History Section, History and Museum Division, Headquarters U.S. Marine Corps.

Gao Wang-zhi. "Jewish Sites in Shanghai." *Points East* (publication of the Sino-Judaic Institute), February 1987, p. 3.

"Die Geschichte des Hongkewer Ghettos." *Shanghai Herald, Sondernummer* (special edition), April 4, 1946, p. 25.

Grünberger, Felix, M.D. "The Jewish Refugees in Shanghai." *Jewish Social Studies,* February 1948.

Hauser, Ernest O. *Shanghai, City for Sale.* New York: Harcourt, Brace, 1940.

Hilberg, Raul. *The Destruction of European Jews.* New York: Harper & Row, 1961.

Hitler, Adolf. *Mein Kampf.* English ed. Boston: Houghton Mifflin, 1943.

Hoffman, Michael L. "U.S. Aid Plan Irks U.N. Refugee Chief." *New York Times,* May 26, 1950.

Jackson, Manfred. "Hier wollen sie nicht bleiben" (They don't want to stay here). Unidentified Bremen, Germany, newspaper.

Jacoby, Hans. *"Tagebuch."* Archives of the Leo Baeck Institute, New York.

Katz, L. G. "Shanghai Story." *Congress Weekly,* March 21, 1949.

Kaufmann, Fritz. "Die Erlebnisse der Juden in Shanghai unter der Japanischen Besetzung im 2. Weltkrieg." Talk given at the Shanghai Tiffin Club of New York, December 2, 1963. Transcript. Archives of the Leo Baeck Institute, New York.

——— . "Die Juden in Shanghai im 2. Weltkrieg: Erinnerungen eines Vorstands-mitglieds der Judischen Gemeinde." *Bulletin of the Leo Baeck Institute* 73 (1986): 13–23.

Kranzler, David H. "The History of the Jewish Refugee Community of Shanghai, 1938–1945." Ph.D. diss., Yeshiva University, 1971.

——— . *Japanese, Nazis, and Jews: The Jewish Refugee Community of Shanghai, 1938–1945.* New York: Yeshiva University Press, 1976.

——— . "Japanese Policy toward the Jews, 1938–1941." *Forum* 34 (Winter 1979).

——— . "Restrictions against German-Jewish Refugee Immigration to Shanghai in 1939." *Jewish Social Studies* 36 (January 1974).

Krasno, Rena. *Strangers Always.* Berkeley, Calif.: Pacific View Press, 1992.

Kreissler, Françoise. *Exil in Shanghai.* Paris: University of Paris, n.d.

Langer, William. *An Encyclopedia of World History.* Boston: Houghton Mifflin, 1972.

Lerner, Max. "The 106." *New York Post,* June 20, 1950.

Lookstein, Haskel. "Kristallnacht and American Jewry." *Congress Monthly,* November–December 1988.

McCormick, Elsie. *Audacious Angles on China.* Pirated ed. Shanghai, c. 1930.

Magic Welcome to China. Compendium of articles prepared from lectures given at China Orientation School by Headquarters, American Armed Forces. Shanghai, 1946.

Margolis, Laura L. "Race against Time in Shanghai." *Survey Graphic* 33 (March 1944).

——— . "Report of Activities in Shanghai, China, from December 8, 1941, to September 1943." Archives of the American Joint Distribution Committee, New York.

Mashberg, Michael. "American Diplomacy and the Jewish Refugee, 1938–1939." *YIVO Annual of Jewish Social Science* 15 (1944): 339–54.

Medoff, Rafael. *The Deafening Silence: American Jewish Leaders and the Holocaust.* New York: Shapolsky, 1987.

Montalto de Jesus, C. A. *Historic Shanghai.* Shanghai: Shanghai Mercury, 1909.

Mosher, Clint. "Refugees Arrive from Red China, Tell Ordeals." Unidentified San Francisco newspaper, May 1950.

Noakes, Jeremy, and Geoffrey Pridham, eds. *Documents on Nazism, 1919–1945.* New York, 1974.

"108 D.P.'s from Shanghai Win 12-Day Respite on Deportation." *New York Times,* May 29, 1950.

Parry, Albert. "The Jews in East Asia." *Shanghai Evening Post & Mercury,* September 19, 1939.

Pearce, E. A., and C. G. Smith. *World Weather Guide.* New York: Times Books, Random House, 1990.

Pearce, Phil. "Long Flight to Freedom, Refugees Here from Shanghai." *San Francisco Chronicle,* May 24, 1950.

Questions on German History. English ed. Bonn: German Bundestag, Press and Information Centre, 1984.

Redlich, Kurt. "Report by Kurt Redlich to World Jewish Congress on the Activities of the *Jüdische Gemeinde.* June 24, 1946.

Remak, Joachim. *The Nazi Years: A Documentary History.* Englewood Cliffs, N.J.: Prentice-Hall, 1969.

Robonson, Nehemiah. "Jewish Communities of China in Dissolution." Paper presented to Institute for Jewish Affairs, World Jewish Congress.

Schulhof, Joseph. *From Prague to the Far East.* New York: Society for the History of Czechoslovak Jews, 1990.

Shirer, William L. *The Rise and Fall of the Third Reich.* New York: Simon & Schuster, 1960.

Siegel, Manuel. "Report of Activities in Shanghai." August 26, 1945. Archives of the American Joint Distribution Committee, New York.

Silbert, Layle. "Report from Overseas: Shanghai." *Congress Weekly,* January 16, 1948.

Tokayer, Marvin, and Mary Swartz. *The Fugu Plan.* New York: Paddington Press, 1979.

Witting, Peter. "Brief History of the 13th Shanghai Boys Scout Troop on the Scouts' Activities." Manuscript.

——— . "Report: Visit to China, 10/1–10/25, 1974." Manuscript.

Yahel, Leni. *The Holocaust: The Fate of European Jewry.* New York: Oxford University Press, 1990.

Zeitin, Josef. "The Shanghai Jewish Community (An Historical Sketch)." *Jewish Life,* October 1973.

Correspondence, Interviews, and Archival Materials

American Joint Distribution Committee, New York. Correspondence with Shanghai office; Shanghai miscellaneous reports and correspondence with HIAS,

New York; miscellaneous files and correspondence. Copies in author's collection.

Atkinson, Colonel Harry W. Personal documents, memos, and miscellaneous material pertaining to Air Division, Joint U.S. Military Advisory Group, Nanjing, China. Copies in author's collection.

Hanin, Leo. Correspondence with author, May 5, 1976.

Margolis, Laura L. Interview with author, August 1968.

National Archives, Military Reference Branch, Washington, D.C. Correspondence with author re Hans Mosberg case.

Pettiss, Susan. Miscellaneous reports and notes re International Refugee Organization. Copies in author's collection.

Redlich, Kurt. Correspondence with Charles Jordan, JDC representative; correspondence with David H. Kranzler. Copies in author's collection.

Shanghai refugees. Author's correspondence and interviews with H. P. Eisfelder, Carnegie, Australia; Curt Maiman, Tel Aviv, Israel; Esther Marcus, San Francisco, Calif.; Les Salter, Bremerton, Wash.; Peter Witting, Hughes, Australia; and others.

Zwartendyk, Jan, Jr. Correspondence with author; correspondence and documents re "Curaçao visas." Copies in author's collection.

Index